an IISS *strategic dossier*

ASIA-PACIFIC REGIONAL SECURITY ASSESSMENT 2025

Key developments and trends

published by

The International Institute for Strategic Studies
ARUNDEL HOUSE | 6 TEMPLE PLACE | LONDON | WC2R 2PG | UK

an IISS *strategic dossier*

ASIA-PACIFIC REGIONAL SECURITY ASSESSMENT 2025

Key developments and trends

The International Institute for Strategic Studies
ARUNDEL HOUSE | 6 TEMPLE PLACE | LONDON | WC2R 2PG | UK

DIRECTOR-GENERAL AND CHIEF EXECUTIVE **Dr Bastian Giegerich**
EDITOR **Dr Evan A. Laksmana**
ASSISTANT EDITOR **Gregory Brooks**
RESEARCH SUPPORT **Hasan AlHasan, Douglas Barrie, Jonathan Bentham, Nick Childs, Johannes Fischbach, Paul Fraioli, Erik Green, Jumpei Ishimaru, Evan Laksmana, Antoine Levesques, Fenella McGerty, Morgan Michaels, Dzaky Naradichiantama, Meia Nouwens, Veerle Nouwens, Marine Ourahli, Rahul Roy-Chaudhury, Ben Schreer, Virpratap Vikram Singh, Albert Vidal, Tom Waldwyn, Robert Ward**
EDITORIAL **Nicholas Fargher, Christopher Harder, Jill Lally, Michael Marsden, Ng Jun Jie, Nicholas Woodroof, Adam Walters**
GRAPHICS COORDINATOR **Nicholas Fargher**
DESIGN AND PRODUCTION **Alessandra Beluffi, Ravi Gopar, Jade Panganiban, James Parker, Kelly Verity-Cailes**

This publication has been prepared by the Director-General and Chief Executive of the Institute and his staff. It incorporates commissioned contributions from recognised subject experts, which were reviewed by a range of experts in the field. The IISS would like to thank the various individuals who contributed their expertise to the compilation of this dossier. The responsibility for the contents is ours alone. The views expressed herein do not, and indeed cannot, represent a consensus of views among the worldwide membership of the Institute as a whole.

First published May 2025 by the International Institute for Strategic Studies.

© 2025 The International Institute for Strategic Studies

COVER IMAGES: (BACKGROUND) the *Virginia*-class fast-attack submarine USS *Minnesota* (SSN-783) docked at a port visit at HMAS Stirling in Rockingham, Australia, 26 February 2025 (Colin Murty/Pool/Getty Images); (CENTRE) India's Defence Research and Development Organisation *BrahMos* missile at the DefExpo 2018, Chennai, 11 April 2018 (Arun Sankar/AFP via Getty Images); (CENTRE R) Japanese Minister of Defense Minoru Kihara inspects a guard of honour ahead of a meeting during the Global Combat Air Programme at the Japanese Ministry of Defense in Tokyo, Japan, 14 December 2023 (David Mareuil/Anadolu via Getty Images); (TOP R) a Japan Ground Self-Defense Force member engages in simulated contact during bilateral convoy-simulator training in support of *Iron Fist 25* at Camp Hansen Camp Hansen, Okinawa, Japan, 20 February 2025 (Lance Cpl. Raul Sotovilla/DVIDS); (BOTTOM R) a Vietnamese military official tries out a pistol during the Vietnam International Defense Expo 2022, in Hanoi, Vietnam, 10 December 2022 (Linh Pham/Bloomberg via Getty Images); (BOTTOM L) He Xiaoli participates in the celebrations marking the 50th anniversary of the establishment of China–Thailand diplomatic relations at Don Mueang International Airport in Bangkok, Thailand, 8 March 2025 (VCG/VCG via Getty Images).

Printed and bound in the UK by Taylor & Francis Group.

All rights reserved. No part of this book may be reprinted or reproduced or utilised in any form or by any electronic, mechanical, or other means, now known or hereafter invented, including photocopying and recording, or in any information storage or retrieval system, without permission in writing from the publishers.

British Library Cataloguing in Publication Data
A catalogue record for this book is available from the British Library

Library of Congress Cataloging in Publication Data
A catalog record for this book has been requested

ISBN 978-1-041-10439-1 (Print) / ISBN 978-1-003-65504-6 (eBook)

About The International Institute for Strategic Studies

The International Institute for Strategic Studies is an independent centre for research, information and debate on the problems of conflict, however caused, that have, or potentially have, an important military content. The Council and Staff of the Institute are international and its membership is drawn from over 100 countries. The Institute is independent and it alone decides what activities to conduct. It owes no allegiance to any government, any group of governments or any political or other organisation. The IISS stresses rigorous research with a forward-looking policy orientation that can improve wider public understanding of international security problems and influence the development of sounder public policy.

CONTENTS

INTRODUCTION 6
Dr Evan A. Laksmana

CHAPTER 1: SPECIAL TOPIC
Concerted Autonomy: Defence-industrial Partnerships in the Asia-Pacific 14
Dr Evan A. Laksmana, Fenella McGerty, Tom Waldwyn, Albert Vidal,
Antoine Levesques and Douglas Barrie

CHAPTER 2
Six Questions: Trump and International Security 46
Paul Fraioli, Robert Ward, Ben Schreer, Hasan Alhasan,
Rahul Roy-Chaudhury and Veerle Nouwens

CHAPTER 3
Tokyo's Threefold Test: Triangular Ties Between China, North Korea and Russia 62
Meia Nouwens, Erik Green and Jumpei Ishimaru

CHAPTER 4
Deep Dive: Subsea Warfare Trends in the Asia-Pacific 84
Nick Childs and Jonathan Bentham

CHAPTER 5
Growing Pains: Military Cyber Maturity and Risks in the Asia-Pacific 106
Virpratap Vikram Singh and Marine Ourahli

CHAPTER 6
Arrested Development: Southeast Asia's Rudimentary UAV Capabilities 124
Dzaky Naradichiantama and Morgan Michaels

INDEX 154

COMMON ABBREVIATIONS

APRSA	Asia-Pacific Regional Security Assessment
ASW	anti-submarine warfare
AUV	autonomous undersea vehicle
C-UAV	counter-uninhabited aerial vehicles
CUI	critical undersea infrastructure
FPV	first-person view
GCAP	Global Combat Aircraft Programme
GNSS	global navigation satellite system
INDOPACOM	United States Indo-Pacific Command
ISR	intelligence, surveillance and reconnaissance
MALE	medium-altitude long-endurance
MRO	maintenance, repair and overhaul
OWA	one-way attack
PAF	Philippine Air Force
PDFs	People's Defence Forces
PLAN	People's Liberation Army Navy
RAN	Royal Australian Navy

SLBM	submarine-launched ballistic missile
SLCM-N	nuclear-tipped sea-launched cruise missile
SSBN	nuclear-powered ballistic missile
SSGN	submarine nuclear-powered guided-missile submarine
SSK	conventionally powered attack submarine
SSN	nuclear-powered attack submarine
ToT	transfer of technology
UAE	United Arab Emirates
UAV	uninhabited aerial vehicle
UMV	uninhabited maritime vehicle
USV	uninhabited surface vessel
UUV	uninhabited underwater vehicle
VLS	vertical launch system
VTOL	vertical take-off and landing
XLUUV	extra-large uninhabited underwater vehicle

INTRODUCTION

Security trends and policies are not driven by security developments alone. While this is certainly not a novel insight, it is one often overlooked, if not forgotten altogether, when assessing the Asia-Pacific security landscape. Over the past decade, as the regional-security environment has gradually deteriorated – from the South China Sea to the Taiwan Strait, the Korean Peninsula and beyond – it feels intuitive to view security policies, from military-capability development to alliance management, as being driven by geopolitical security concerns. Regional countries are responding to perceived threats and challenges, as the argument goes, by building defence capabilities and alliances.

Regional policymakers are certainly aware of the deteriorating security environment in the Asia-Pacific. But their resulting policy responses to that environment are rarely a straightforward or direct process from the identification of the problem to finding the solution. Instead, 'in between' security problems and policy responses or behaviours, there are many 'filtering layers' shaping the processes through which Asia-Pacific countries seek security. Put differently, there are often non-security factors and considerations shaping regional policymakers' assessment and planning. The resulting accumulative security policies and trends across the Asia-Pacific over the past decade therefore rarely represent the 'ideal' response to regional security challenges.

These many non-security filtering factors range from domestic partisan politics, bureaucratic contestations between security agencies, civil–military relations, and economic and market drivers of capability development to the entrenched doctrinal domination of a certain armed service across the defence establishment (see Figure 0.1). These variables commonly get 'in between' the geopolitical and security realities and the ensuing responses by the individual Asia-Pacific states, making the 'end product' – a security policy or behaviour – often less than ideal.

There are three ways in which such filtering factors can shape security policies, behaviours and trends across the Asia-Pacific. Firstly, they could exacerbate or downplay threat perceptions and assessments when mixed with security and geopolitical dynamics. The rise of China as a naval power in the Asia-Pacific, for instance, has not been uniformly or coherently perceived by different regional states. Some countries, such as Australia, Japan and the Philippines, may double down on their military alliance with the United States and boost their defence capabilities, while other countries, such as Indonesia, Malaysia or Vietnam, may assume less competitive postures and double down on strategic engagement with China instead. Domestic politics in Australia and Japan could also elevate their threat assessment of China on the one hand, but they could also downplay the threat on the other, like in Indonesia and Malaysia.

Secondly, non-geopolitical security filters can influence the defence-capability development plans and operational readiness of regional armed forces in different ways. That some defence companies are selected over others to provide arms and equipment may be shaped less by hard cost–benefit analysis and more by domestic and bureaucratic politics, and possibly even corruption. A thorough assessment of the acquisition of some sophisticated assets in Southeast Asian states, such as Thailand's aircraft carrier HTMS *Chakri Naruebet* or Indonesia's 42 *Rafale* fighter jets, would have to account for those non-strategic factors, given the plethora of operational-demand mismatches and inter-operability problems associated with them. In any case, analysts and policymakers simply cannot assume that all capability-development plans and acquisitions are driven by hard-security-risk assessment alone.

Finally, non-security filtering factors can shape and influence the broader foreign-policy and strategic outlook of many regional states,

Figure 0.1: **Analytical filtering of regional security trends**

Geopolitical security realities
- US–China competition
- Transnational organised crime
- China's assertive behaviour
- US coercive statecraft

Non-geopolitical security filtering factors
- Political leadership
- Army domestic domination
- Bureaucratic politics
- Globalisation

Security policies and behaviours
- Alliances and partnerships
- Defence capability development
- Regional security policy trends

©IISS

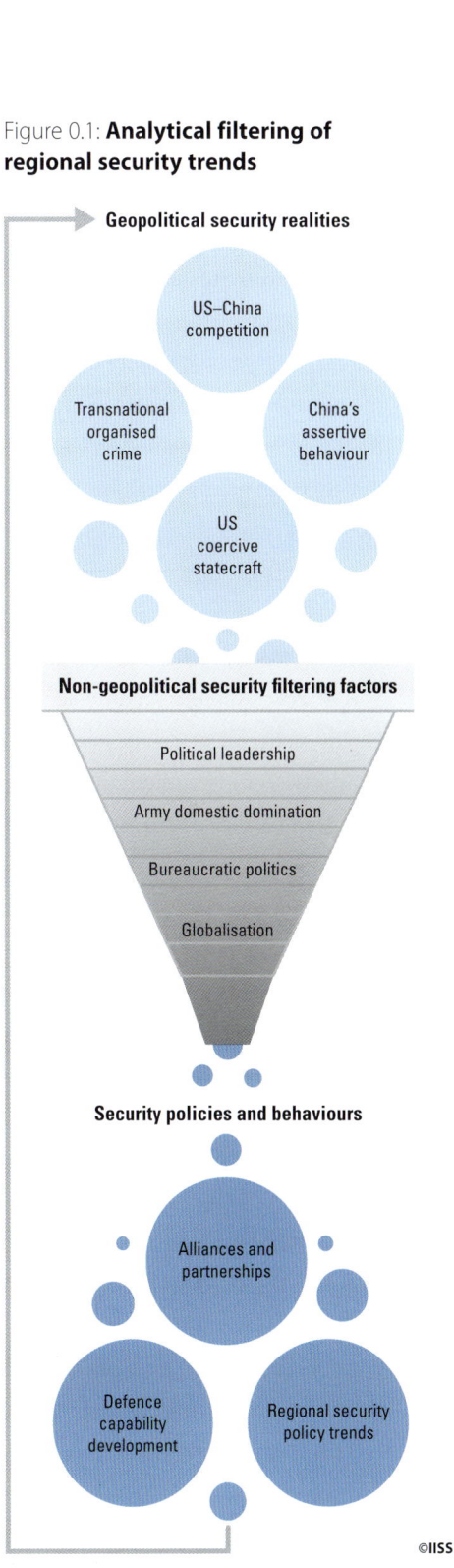

Note: Examples of security realities, filtering factors and policies and behaviours are illustrative only. They are neither exhaustive nor definitive.

Source: IISS

which in turn leads to the narrowing of some strategic choices, such as defence partnerships. The domestic balance of power, for example, can shape a government's choice of allies and partners, driven by the political platform and preference of the ruling elites, rather than the defence establishment's fact-based cost–benefit security analysis. Political familiarity and institutionalised defence partnerships can also lead to path-dependent security policies – meaning that states need to buy more costly arms because they need to keep their allies. The arrival of a new political leader with an entirely different strategic outlook can also upend established foreign-policy orthodoxy.

In short, a deeper understanding of Asia-Pacific security dynamics requires an examination of when and how non-geopolitical filtering factors matter in shaping the security policies and trends across the region. This year's *Asia-Pacific Regional Security Assessment 2025* (APRSA 2025) examines three such factors: (1) global market and economic forces, (2) military operational history and (3) domestic political leadership. These three drivers are, of course, not independent of the unfolding security realities across the Asia-Pacific; they do not in and of themselves constitute nor fully explain the broader security dynamics. But they better contextualise the trends witnessed for more than a decade. These three factors as overarching themes run through the six chapters of the APRSA, written by 21 IISS experts across its offices in London, Washington, Berlin, Manama and Singapore.

MARKET MACHINERY

For all their different security considerations and challenges, it is safe to argue that Asia-Pacific states all value their strategic autonomy – the ability to define and defend their strategic interests without the interference of external actors. Many regional defence policymakers further define one of the key benchmarks of strategic autonomy as the ability to independently produce their own necessary arms and equipment. In other words, defence industrialisation is a pursuit that is part and parcel of pushing for strategic autonomy.

The problem, of course, is the reality that a state independently producing all of its own arms and equipment (also known as 'defence autarky'), from sophisticated platforms and systems to low-tech ammunitions, remains an illusory aspiration across the Asia-Pacific. The APRSA 2025 special-topic chapter, 'Concerted Autonomy: Defence-industrial Partnerships in the Asia-Pacific', examines why and how Asia-Pacific states develop and engage in defence-industrial partnerships among themselves and with extra-regional states. The chapter locates the growth in defence-industrial partnerships across the region within the broader trends of the globalisation of the defence industry for more than three decades. The rise and fall of defence-industrial partnerships has led some regional states to certain forms of partnerships, such as joint ventures or offset programmes, even as security flashpoints and great-power competitive dynamics provide the broader rationale for military modernisation efforts.

The chapter evaluates how Southeast Asian states work with European defence companies on various offset programmes, how Gulf Arab states perceive their defence-industrial partnerships with major Asia-Pacific countries, and how co-development programmes like the Indian–Russian *BrahMos* supersonic-missile system and the Global Combat Aircraft Programme were formulated and implemented. The authors further assess the promised benefits and emergent challenges in developing and implementing defence-industrial partnerships involving regional and extra-regional actors in the Asia-Pacific. Overall, despite the worsening of the regional-security environment over the past decade, market forces and considerations, especially the globalisation of defence-industrial production, continue to exercise significant influence over defence-capability development.

Visitors try a demo rifle at the DSA and NATSEC defence expo in Kuala Lumpur, Malaysia, 6 May 2024

(Supian Ahmad/NurPhoto via Getty Images)

Meanwhile, global economic forces, underpinned by the free flow of goods, services and information criss-crossing the Asia-Pacific, highlight the importance of maritime security. While many policymakers and analysts focus on the security challenges on the surface, from armed robbery to territorial disputes to gunboat diplomacy, what happens underwater should not be overlooked. Chapter 4 of APRSA 2025, 'Deep Dive: Subsea Warfare Trends in the Asia-Pacific', examines the ongoing transformation of the underwater domain driven by the development and deployment of new technologies, the concerns over 'seabed warfare' and the vulnerabilities of critical underwater infrastructure (CUI).

While the improvement to and growth of submarine capabilities across the region over the past decade – especially China's attempt to counter American ones – may have jump-started the focus on underwater security, the geo-economic significance of the subsea data-cable and pipeline networks and their potential vulnerabilities have driven the growing importance of private industries operating and maintaining CUI. The suspected sabotage of underwater CUI, from oil and gas pipelines to data cables, in both Europe and Asia, highlights this concern. The additional focus on deep-sea mining for resources like nickel, cobalt and manganese further underscores the concerns over seabed warfare. Taken together, underwater-security concerns are no longer driven by submarine proliferation alone.

PRESENT PAST

While global economic forces often accentuate security concerns – and shape the available options to address them – the operational histories of individual Asia-Pacific armed forces significantly influence how they assess their defence-capability requirements. Militaries with a long history of internal-security challenges will find it difficult, for example, to quickly focus their energy and resources on confronting major geopolitical challenges. APRSA 2025's Chapter 6, 'Arrested Development: Southeast Asia's Rudimentary UAV Capabilities', discusses how the operational history and recent experience of counter-insurgency operations continue to shape how Indonesia, Myanmar, the Philippines and Thailand develop and deploy uninhabited aerial vehicle (UAV) capabilities. The chapter also examines the extent to which the operational lessons of contemporary conflicts in Ukraine and the Middle East may be less salient than the UAV warfare unfolding in Myanmar since the February 2021 coup.

Given the dominant role of the armies in Indonesia, the Philippines and Thailand, the operational necessity to prepare the defence establishment to fight domestic insurgents continues to exercise a significant influence over how doctrinal approaches to UAV warfare are developed. More broadly, domestic politics and foreign-policy orientation also shape the conditions under which UAV-development partnerships were forged by these Southeast Asian states. Geopolitical contingencies like the South China Sea have provided some degree of 'pull factor' when it comes to UAV mission planning, but they have not fundamentally transformed the strategic outlook and doctrinal approaches of these defence establishments.

An Indonesian soldier checks a UAV displayed at a military parade held as part of celebrations marking the 79th anniversary of the Indonesian National Armed Forces in Jakarta, 5 October 2024

(Yasuyoshi Chiba/AFP via Getty Images)

In Northeast Asia, however, the strategic challenges that confront Japan have grown significantly as the relationship between China, North Korea and Russia has strengthened since the invasion of Ukraine. As examined in Chapter 3, 'Tokyo's Threefold Test: Triangular Ties Between China, North Korea and Russia', Japan's defence-capability development has largely been driven by its military-alliance requirements with the US, as well as its concerns over the three competitive, if not hostile, nuclear-armed powers in its immediate neighbourhood. The acrimonious bilateral-security history between Japan and, respectively, China, North Korea and Russia also continues to shape Tokyo's threat assessment.

Chapter 3 shows further that the triangular ties between China, North Korea and Russia, while converging in new circumstances following the war against Ukraine, are not yet a full alliance or even an aligned, collective 'trilateral' partnership. But the complexity and unpredictability of the triangular relationship presents heightened risks to Japan's regional security environment. Tokyo thus seeks to double down on its alliance with the US, boost its defence capabilities and grow its partnerships with like-minded regional states. It is in Northeast Asia therefore that geopolitical security risks, unlike in Southeast Asia, seem to be the primary driver of security policies and behaviours, although other non-geopolitical trends, such as domestic politics, can still shape and drive those risks.

POWERS THAT BE

Despite the proliferation of geopolitical security risks and the powerful influence of non-geopolitical filtering factors, such as defence-industrial globalisation, on Asia-Pacific countries, it is ultimately political leaders that will determine the path taken. Chapter 5 of APRSA 2025, 'Growing Pains: Military Cyber Maturity Across the Asia-Pacific', discusses how, despite the growing centrality of the cyber domain, the political leadership determines how and to what extent regional defence establishments could 'mature' their military cyber capabilities. It examines how more Asia-Pacific leaders have paid political attention to developing new or restructuring existing military cyber forces to support economic security, accelerate military modernisation plans and respond to geopolitical concerns.

Despite these political commitments and policy directions, the chapter describes how such 'strategic maturity' remains inconsistent while these cyber forces' institutional and operational maturity remains underdeveloped. The restructuring and development of effective military cyber forces has to account for non-geopolitical and even non-security factors. After all, since many Asia-Pacific countries rely on cyberspace for their economic, military and policy governance, their cyber-security capabilities need to be robust. And yet, the patchy strategic, institutional and operational maturity of regional cyber forces show the significant influence of domestic political forces and the centrality of (in)consistent leadership from the top.

President of Ukraine Volodymyr Zelenskyy gathers with European leaders during a summit in London, 2 March 2025

(Justin Tallis/Pool/AFP via Getty Images)

On the other hand, perhaps no other political leader has more regional and global impact than the president of the US, with Donald Trump's second term having profound implications for international security. The APRSA 2025's second chapter, 'Six Questions: Trump and International Security', examines how Trump could redefine major questions, from the wars in Ukraine and the Middle East to the role of the Quad and any possible Taiwan Strait contingencies, shaping the international security landscape.

At the final time of writing in March 2025, the Trump administration is roughly two months old. And yet, the manner in which he and his team have upended, perhaps permanently, the European security order through their management of Russia's war against Ukraine suggests that a short time does not equal a marginal impact. That Trump focused immediately on major foreign-policy questions after his inauguration, as opposed to zooming in only on inward-looking domestic political questions, suggests the areas in which he thinks he can quickly leave a notable legacy. But whether a 'speedy resolution' of the war against Ukraine, no matter how possibly unsustainable or unjust it might turn out to be, means that Trump could soon 'prioritise' the Asia-Pacific theatre and the United States' strategic competition with China, remains to be seen.

FEELING THE CURRENTS

APRSA 2025 focuses on how non-geopolitical filtering factors, from economic globalisation to domestic politics, continue to shape major security trends and policies across the Asia-Pacific and beyond. This overarching theme allows a deeper look at and a better understanding of the underlying strategic currents across the Asia-Pacific, as they flow through a series of deeply rooted structural barriers, from defence-capability development, emerging contested domains and technology to alliance and partnership management amid strategic competition. The path to understanding Asia-Pacific security dynamics does not begin and end with security realities and developments alone.

As a final note, the 'Six Questions' chapter is the APRSA's new feature starting this year. It is similar to the special-topic chapter in the sense that it is collectively written by several IISS experts. But unlike the special-topic chapter, which focuses on deeper, structural security trends and challenges in the Asia-Pacific, 'Six Questions' focuses on profound developments with global, not just regional, implications. The arrival of Trump's second term during a heightened period of geopolitical uncertainty fits that bill. It seems likely the international security landscape will look and feel fundamentally different by the end of his term in 2029. Whether 'Six Questions' will be a permanent feature of every APRSA edition, however, remains to be seen. As 'Six Questions' only emerged during tectonic shifts in the global order, it is in that sense a 'special' occurrence essay for the APRSA.

DR. EVAN A. LAKSMANA

Shangri-La Dialogue Senior Fellow for Southeast Asian Security and Defence;
Editor, *Asia-Pacific Regional Security Assessment*, IISS–Asia

CHAPTER 1

CONCERTED AUTONOMY: DEFENCE-INDUSTRIAL PARTNERSHIPS IN THE ASIA-PACIFIC

This chapter examines why and how Asia-Pacific countries engage in defence-industrial partnerships with regional and extra-regional counterparts, as well as their benefits and challenges.

ARGUMENTS AND FINDINGS:

- The growth of defence-industrial partnerships in the Asia-Pacific over the past decade stems from the nexus of regional-security flashpoint proliferation and defence-industrial globalisation, as well as the search for strategic autonomy by regional countries.

- European defence-industrial partnerships across Southeast Asia have grown over the past decade, from transfer of technology (ToT) to local licensed production, anchored by offset programmes and joint ventures to boost defence-industrial-base development.

- New defence-industrial actors from the Gulf Arab states, primarily Saudi Arabia and the United Arab Emirates (UAE), have recently grown their partnerships with major Asia-Pacific countries.

- The Indian–Russian *BrahMos* supersonic-missile programme, as well as the Global Combat Aircraft Programme (GCAP), anchored by Italy, Japan and the United Kingdom, offer important lessons in developing, managing and marketing co-development and production partnerships involving regional and extra-regional countries.

IMPLICATIONS FOR REGIONAL SECURITY:

- Defence-industrial partnerships have significant implications for how regional countries respond to contingencies and whether their military modernisation plans are sustainable.

- Defence-industrial partnerships need to balance military modernisation needs, defence-partnership and alliance management as well as domestic technological capacity and policy infrastructure.

The Asia-Pacific remains the growth area for defence-industrial partnerships between regional countries as well as with extra-regional ones. How these countries develop and implement their defence-industrial partnerships significantly shapes their ability to respond to contingencies and whether their military capability-development plans are sustainable. The regional growth of defence-industrial partnerships comes on the heels of several key trends.

Firstly, the Asia-Pacific continues to deal with major security flashpoints, including the South and East China seas, the Taiwan Strait and the Korean Peninsula. The security situation in those three areas has gradually worsened since the 1990s. But the competitive dynamics between regional powers such as India and China or Japan and China and North Korea (see Chapter 3 of this dossier), as well as between the United States and China, over the past decade have introduced further uncertainty and driven regional countries to boost their defence capabilities. Competitive security dynamics over simmering flashpoints, in other words, feed into the need to develop modern military capabilities to address them.

Secondly, as seeking strategic autonomy remains an important part of any effort to modernise military establishments, defence-industrial-base development remains the top priority for many Asia-Pacific countries. Regional countries are concerned with both the ability to sustain prolonged military operations and the potential of external parties 'vetoing' their capability and future operations if they have no substantial domestic defence-industrial base. There are times, however, when domestic politics and prestige-seeking override hard cost–benefit analysis in those defence-industrialisation efforts. Regardless, defence industrialisation has been part and parcel of, and even legally codified as part of, major long-term military-modernisation efforts across the region.

Thirdly, the globalisation of the defence industry which picked up steam from the late 1980s onwards – despite waxing and waning over time – has provided a wide range of partnership opportunities for established and emerging defence-industrial states in the Asia-Pacific. These partnerships range from licensed production and joint ventures to co-development programmes and offset arrangements involving regional and extra-regional countries (see Table 1.1). Indeed, the defence industries have formed 'complex global networks' over the past few decades, enabling defence firms to access 'foreign markets, technologies, and capital'.[1] These networks have also grown increasingly 'formal, integrative, and permanent' while seeking to cooperate further by starting earlier in the product cycle via multinational co-development programmes.[2]

The economic growth across the Asia-Pacific over the past two decades has further provided the initial fiscal space necessary for regional countries to import large numbers of expensive and sophisticated arms and equipment. Indeed, the Asia-Pacific has been the 'leading consumer of arms' in recent years, constituting the second-largest, and sometimes even the largest, market for defence imports in the world.[3] The prosecution, and the subsequent reduction, of major American and European military operations in the Middle East and Central Asia in the 2000s to 2010s also led to the rise and decline of major defence-industrial globalisation waves across the Asia-Pacific. But recent conflicts in Ukraine and the Middle East, coupled with worsening US–China strategic competition and deterioration of the Asia-Pacific security landscape, may lead to another rising tide of defence-industrial partnerships.

Nevertheless, many of the most critical pieces of military equipment that Asia-Pacific countries rely upon are still imported, including advanced combat aircraft, submarines, uninhabited aerial vehicles (UAVs) (see Chapter 6 of this dossier), most missile systems (air-to-air, anti-ship and air-defence), jet engines and highly advanced electronics critical for intelligence-gathering, surveillance, communications and cyber security.[4] Such reliance suggests that while the region has been part of the globalisation of the defence industry, regional defence firms have not truly globalised their operations and production.

If anything, a high degree of protectionism continues to dominate Asia-Pacific defence-industrial policies. Many of them, therefore, often prefer partnerships that provide significant offset benefits to help them move up the ladder of defence production. Indeed, European defence-industrial partnerships across Southeast Asia over the past decade have been anchored by such offset programmes, including ToT with local licensed production or assembly, even if they rarely encompass joint designs. While Southeast Asian countries predominantly lack the requisite experience or the necessary suite of development and design capacities, many have codified defence-industrial offset policies as part of their long-term military modernisation plans.

In some cases, such offset policies could also provide these European companies with a qualitative 'edge' against their rival American ones in some defence markets like Southeast Asia. New defence-industrial actors from the Gulf Arab states, primarily Saudi Arabia and the UAE, have also recently started to make inroads in the region, even if they are relatively new at the game compared to established European companies. These Gulf states have nevertheless grown their defence-industrial partnerships with major Asia-Pacific countries as they continue to seek technological and strategic alignments across the region.

India can be added to the list of emerging defence-industrial states seeking to export their arms and equipment. While India may still lag behind established Chinese, Japanese

Table 1.1: **Selected defence-industrial partnership models**

Partnership models	Features
Joint venture	The setting up of a new firm or entity (with ownership share to be negotiated based on contributions and other deliverables) to manage and market collaborative military products.
Licensed production	Transnational sale or transfer of the rights to manufacture a weapon system originally developed in the supplier's country.
Co-production	The joint manufacture of a weapon system originally developed in one country.
Co-development	The joint development and production of a weapon system entailing cooperation from concept evaluation through to production, involving cost- and benefit-sharing throughout a weapon system's life cycle. A state-level commitment to procure the jointly produced weapon system is often needed.
Consortium	Ad hoc arrangements for joint project management: pooling resources together for a certain project, or perhaps for a one-off contract bid, without constructing a new organisational form.
Offset	Arrangements whereby, as a condition of the sale, the buyer is allowed to directly manufacture components or subsystems of the weapon system, or be part of the seller's supply chain. Offsets may also cover other 'indirect' in-lieu-of arrangements such as skills-development projects paid by the seller or the use of 'counter-trade' to cover parts of the cost using non-cash commodities (e.g., oil).
Collaboration	A workshare agreement between partners for a project where no entity is formed, and costs are not necessarily shared equally.
Strategic alliance	Generally loose agreements between two or more defence firms to explore future collaboration or technology sharing.

Sources: Richard Bitzinger, 'The Globalization of the Arms Industry' (1994); Colin Butler, Brian Kenny and John Anchor, 'Strategic Alliances in the European Defence Industry' (2000)

and South Korean companies, it hopes to make inroads in marketing its *BrahMos* long-range supersonic cruise missile to regional countries. The missile itself, however, is one of the rare co-development programmes between India and Russia (via a joint venture established in 1998). Despite its slow progression – the Philippines became the first non-Indian importer when it signed a USD375 million deal in 2022 – the *BrahMos* missile could offer important lessons on the challenges of co-development projects.[5]

A CASA C-212 aircraft sits at a Dirgantara Indonesia (DI) plant in Bandung, West Java, Indonesia, 13 May 2019

(Dimas Ardian/Bloomberg via Getty Images)

Similarly, the GCAP, consisting of Italy, Japan and the UK, is an important test case for co-development projects involving both regional and extra-regional countries. There are of course major differences between Indian–Russian missile-technology cooperation and the decades of defence-industrial cooperation between the UK and Italy, as well as Japan's experience of working with the US on developing its combat aircraft. Nevertheless, examining the process under which the GCAP came about is helpful in understanding how the three partners think about their future domestic defence aerospace industry and the extent to which partnerships are critical factors in sustaining it.

PARTNERSHIP PARAMETERS

While there are various policy trends shaping the growth of defence-industrial partnerships across the Asia-Pacific, the globalisation of the defence-industrial ecosystem since the 1990s still significantly shapes the ways in which those cooperative activities have taken place recently and the promised benefits and potential challenges they bring. The rising costs of military research and development (R&D) for major defence companies and states, their inadequate base markets, the limited technological and industrial sources and the rapid advances in production technologies still facilitate the growing integration of defence production lines.[6]

Defence-industrial partnerships, however, remain in general a 'second-best solution' to defence procurement, as they enable states to boost their own defence-industrial base while incorporating capital and technology from abroad.[7] But as the globalisation of the defence industry over the past three decades shows, this 'second-best' solution is perhaps closer to an ideal long-term goal, especially given the costs of seeking autarky. Defence-industrial partnerships nevertheless can still help states (1) share the costs and reduce the risks of researching, developing and manufacturing new weapons systems; (2) gain access to innovative foreign technologies; and (3) achieve economies of scale in the production of increasingly expensive weapons systems.[8]

Defence-industrial partnership also promises inter-operability advantages, as different weapons systems deployed across different countries would originate from the same source.[9] The decreasing transportation costs and advances in automated supply-chain management further renders it even more advantageous to import weapon components from an

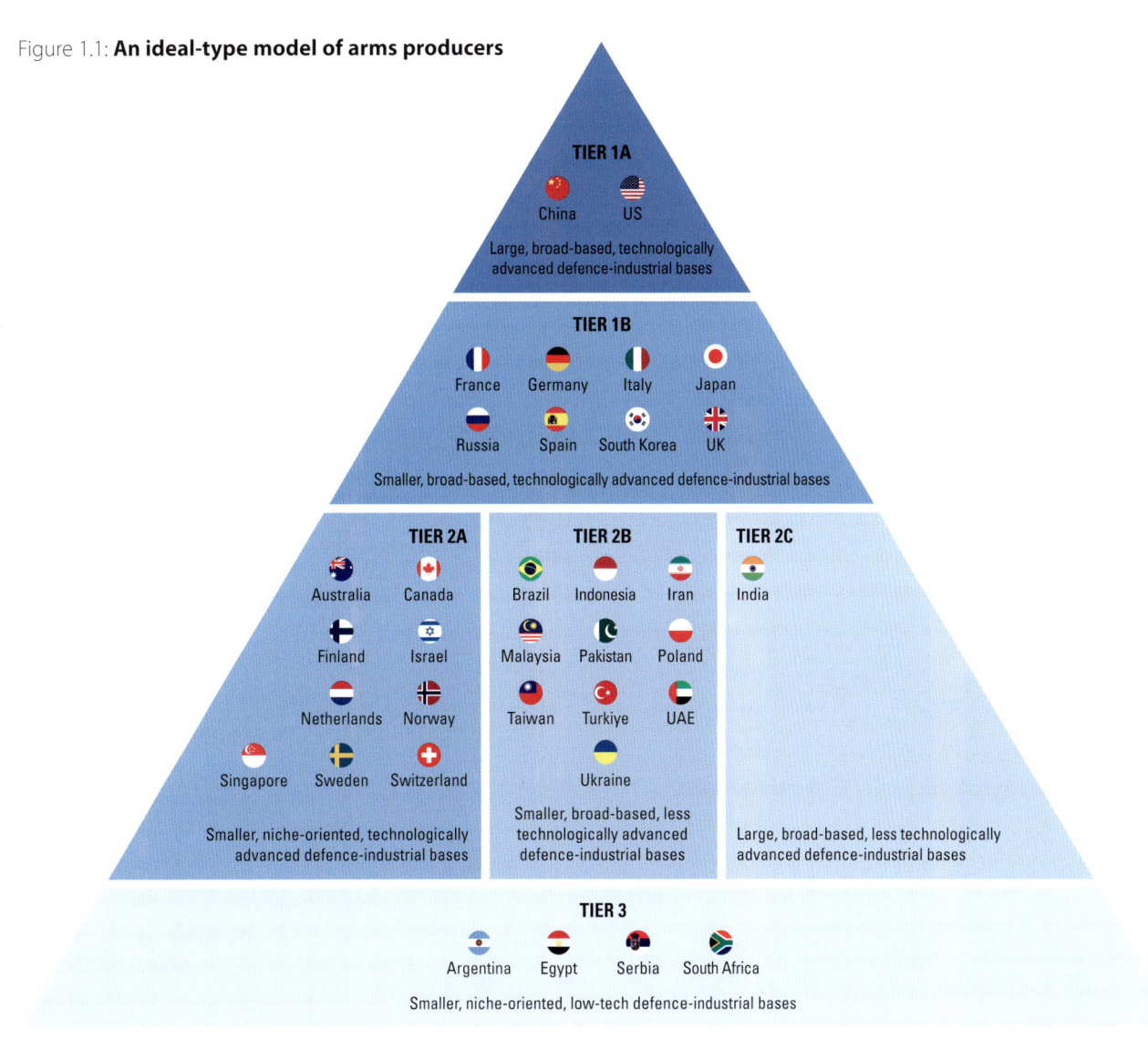

Figure 1.1: **An ideal-type model of arms producers**

TIER 1A
China · US
Large, broad-based, technologically advanced defence-industrial bases

TIER 1B
France · Germany · Italy · Japan
Russia · Spain · South Korea · UK
Smaller, broad-based, technologically advanced defence-industrial bases

TIER 2A
Australia · Canada
Finland · Israel
Netherlands · Norway
Singapore · Sweden · Switzerland
Smaller, niche-oriented, technologically advanced defence-industrial bases

TIER 2B
Brazil · Indonesia · Iran
Malaysia · Pakistan · Poland
Taiwan · Turkiye · UAE
Ukraine
Smaller, broad-based, less technologically advanced defence-industrial bases

TIER 2C
India
Large, broad-based, less technologically advanced defence-industrial bases

TIER 3
Argentina · Egypt · Serbia · South Africa
Smaller, niche-oriented, low-tech defence-industrial bases

©IISS

Note: The tiers are illustrative and based on analytical ideal-type models. They are neither empirically exclusive or static. Producers have moved across tiers (for various reasons) over the past decade since the model was developed.

Sources: IISS; Richard Bitzinger, 'New Ways of Thinking About the Global Arms Industry'(ASPI, 2015)

expanding range of foreign suppliers built around a wider range of partnerships.[10] This trend offers opportunities for states seeking to jump-start or expand their defence-industrialisation efforts. After all, the growing number of arms suppliers increases access to the technology transfers needed to boost domestic defence industries.[11]

But for such partnerships to work well, the companies and the states that back them should ideally enjoy 'complementary capabilities', including technological and industrial synergies.[12] Across the Asia-Pacific, this benchmark could be challenging, given that the majority of the established partners come from outside the region with (North America and Europe) and have different strategic priorities, operational requirements and defence-industrial bases and policies. Furthermore, both regional and extra-regional defence-industrial companies and states fall into different theoretical ideal-type tiers (see Figure 1.1) of production capabilities, limiting the availability and effectiveness of certain types of partnerships.

At the top of the pyramid (see Figure 1.1) are the first-tier states with high levels of indigenous capabilities for independent defence-related R&D and manufacturing of advanced conventional weaponry.[13] This tier consists of the US and the four largest European arms producers (Britain, France, Germany and Italy). The four European producers increasingly only remain at this tier through collaborative arrangements with each other (as we shall see below), or through pan-European defence enterprises and joint ventures. The United States' preponderant defence-industrial capabilities – especially its defence R&D – place it above others as a Tier 1a country, and the others as Tier 1b producer-states. Russia falls into this Tier 1b category, based on its inheritance of the Soviet military-industrial complex and its domestic investment and military modernisation reforms following its war with Georgia in 2008.[14]

The Tier 2 producers include those seeking to create large, sophisticated defence industries commensurate with their great-power aspirations as well as those developing countries possessing modest (but growing) defence-industrial bases, such as Indonesia, Singapore, South Korea, Taiwan and Turkiye. This tier also includes those producers with highly developed defence-industrial bases but with limited production, such as Australia, Israel, Japan and Sweden. At the bottom are the various Tier 3 states, which possess only very limited and generally low-tech arms-production capabilities, such as the manufacture of small arms or the licensed assembly of foreign-designed systems.[15]

Many among these Tier 2 and Tier 3 (and increasingly Tier 1B) states consider defence-industrial partnerships as potential pathways to maintain or boost their own domestic defence-industrial base and production. Established defence companies in those states prioritise access to defence-industrial bases which could deliver high-quality products and services when they consider partnership arrangements.[16] Since the 1990s onwards, Western defence companies increased their outreach to and partnerships with Asia-Pacific countries to ensure their commercial viability under pressure from shrinking defence budgets in their traditional home markets. Since then, geopolitical and foreign-policy considerations, such as the proliferating security flashpoints and great-power competition, have also come to shape those overtures and partnership assessments.[17]

On the other hand, other emerging Tier 2 and Tier 3 countries perceive defence-industrial partnerships as a means of reducing complete dependencies on foreign sources to produce sophisticated weapons and technologies. This could start with partnerships allowing for the assembly of weapons systems from imported parts and components, moving up to licensed production with the domestic production of some components or subsystems, to limited co-development and joint production of relatively simple, low-tech arms and equipment, to the co-development of sophisticated ones.[18] We can see this last step in the Indian–Russian *BrahMos* supersonic-missile platform discussed below.

For many of these Tier 2 and Tier 3 countries, however, domestic factors often take precedence in the decision-making calculus of defence industrialisation. These include a concern with building or protecting domestic companies, the search for political prestige, or even bureaucratic and patronage politics preferring certain foreign partners. In Southeast Asia, for example, 'a mix of desires for international prestige and the aspiration for an independent, strong, and rich country' continue to drive the pursuit for defence-industrialisation.[19] Despite the cost, many Tier 2 and Tier 3 countries consider the need to decrease their dependency on foreign suppliers – and to reduce their ability to shape and drive the recipient's military capability and foreign policy – as an important measure of strategic autonomy.[20] Many of them, in other words, consider a national defence industry as a 'tool to create an image of a weighty state'.[21]

Defence-industrial partnerships therefore often include offset arrangements such as ToT, as seen with European companies in Southeast Asia (discussed below), as well as other efforts to 'build up' the defence 'production capacities' of the recipient state.[22] On the other hand, for many Tier 2 and Tier 3 countries, access to high-quality, cutting-edge equipment and through-life support services means they need to develop partnerships with each other and ideally with those from a higher tier. Partnering with Tier 1 countries could also bring broader non-defence-industry benefits from a foreign-policy or bilateral-relations standpoint. In any case, despite the different motives for defence-industrial partnerships, where they are located within the pyramid often suggests which options are available or better suited for their specific capabilities and needs (see Table 1.1).

ANCHORING OFFSETS

European defence-industrial engagement in Southeast Asia has grown over the past decade as regional countries have enacted industrial policies and procurement programmes to foster greater investment in their domestic industry from foreign entities. European companies, including Airbus, Damen, Naval Group and Thales, have a long-standing presence in Southeast Asia, and other European actors have established themselves in the market in the last decade, including Italy's Fincantieri and Sweden's Saab.

The combined defence spending of Indonesia, Malaysia, the Philippines, Singapore, Thailand and Vietnam – the five largest markets in Southeast Asia – was around USD50.7 billion in 2024, just under Japan's defence budget for that year.[23] On average, these countries spent 1.5% of GDP on defence in 2024, which has been relatively constant for the past decade.[24] However, defence-investment (procurement and R&D) growth has accelerated over the last two years, from a combined total of USD7.8bn in 2022 to USD10.5bn in 2024 (see Figure 1.2).

Indonesia and Singapore have made significant spending increases. The former has pursued its Minimum Essential Forces plan since the late 2000s to modernise the military (with a new long-term plan on the way), while Singapore's budget was increased in 2023 to counter heightened inflationary pressures, to catch up on 'critical projects deferred or disrupted due to COVID-19' and to accelerate the 'digitalisation and non-kinetic capabilities build-up'.[25] The average allocation within the defence budget for defence procurement and R&D among these countries has risen from 15.7% in 2014 to 21.1% in 2024, with increases primarily focused on recapitalisation rather than R&D.[26]

Industrial or collaborative arrangements with foreign partners tend to include some ToT with local licensed production or assembly. Very few programmes encompass joint designs, largely because the region's nascent defence industries lack the requisite experience and/or the necessary suite of development and design capacities, although

Malaysian marines watch as the country's first *Scorpène*-class submarine KD *Tunku Abdul Rahman*, made by France's Naval Group, prepares to dock in Port Klang on the outskirts of Kuala Lumpur, 3 September 2009

(Saeed Khan/AFP via Getty Images)

Figure 1.2: **Selected Southeast Asian countries: defence-investment* budgets, 2014–24**

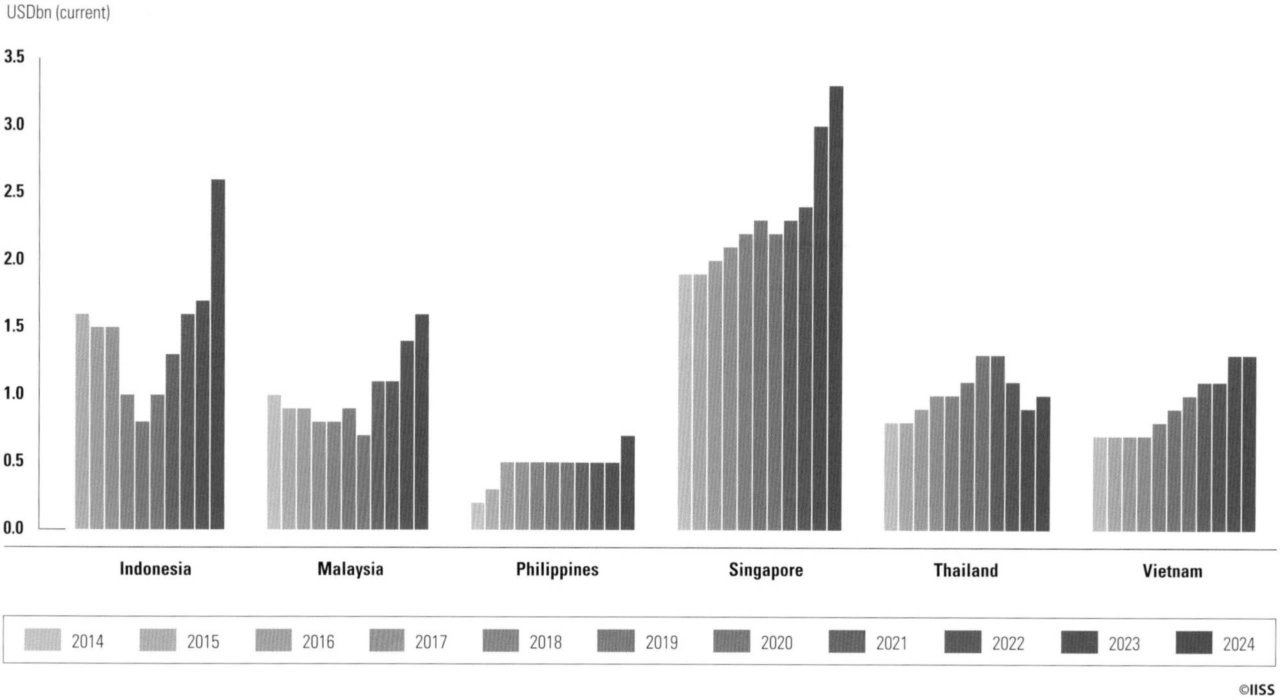

USDbn (current)

Legend: 2014, 2015, 2016, 2017, 2018, 2019, 2020, 2021, 2022, 2023, 2024

©IISS

*Procurement + R&D.

Source: IISS, Military Balance+, milbalplus.iiss.org

this will likely shift as offset policies develop those domestic capabilities to facilitate such agreements. Indeed, most countries in Southeast Asia have some form of offset or industrial policy intended to help their indigenous defence industries develop, improve their self-sufficiency and minimise their dependence on a single or small number of suppliers.

Such policy requirements in Indonesia are also driven by its experience of being subjected to arms embargoes and trade restrictions in the past. Indonesia's recent extensive offset policy requires foreign contractors to provide an offset of at least 85% of the total contract value.[27] Around 50% of the total contract value must be spent on purchasing Indonesian components, while the remaining 35% needs to satisfy offset arrangements within Indonesia. This has usually been implemented through licensed production, co-production, training, investment and ToT. The Indonesian preference for local procurement means that most foreign partners do not have an in-country production presence, as technology transfer and licensed production with a domestic partner has been the usual form of industrial engagement in Indonesia in line with offset requirements.

Malaysia also has formal offset requirements.[28] Contracts with a foreign-based contractor that are valued at over RM50m (USD10.6m) require some form of local content, investment, market access, ToT, training or R&D.[29] The Philippines introduced the Self-Reliant Defense Posture (SRDP) Revitalization Act in October 2024, which seeks to bolster the previous SRDP policy first formalised in 1974.[30] The Act aims to reduce dependence on foreign suppliers and their supply chains, instead prioritising investment in domestic R&D. Bangkok also wants to be self-reliant, reduce imports, facilitate technology transfer and export military equipment which it has produced domestically.[31] As such, it is seeking to establish a defence-industrial estate in Kanchanaburi province, northwest of Bangkok, in a public–private partnership collaboration with local and foreign companies.[32]

Singapore has no formal offset policy, but major acquisitions are subject to an extensive case-by-case evaluation system that includes an assessment of the domestic-growth potential and local industrial involvement when determining whether to offer the award.[33] Vietnam's system is more opaque, but the 2019 National Defence White Paper promoted the development of its defence industry, in keeping with the country's doctrine of self-reliance. It has also recently passed the 2024 Law on the National Defense and Security Industry and Industrial Mobilization seeking to boost the country's defence-industrial base.

European companies have nonetheless been able to adapt their proposals and offerings to accommodate Southeast Asia's greater offset or local industrial-participation requirements. The long-standing regional engagement by key European prime contractors strengthens their position. However, Southeast Asia's preference to avoid dependence on a small number of suppliers means the market is increasingly contested (see Table 1.2).

Airbus in Indonesia

The partnership between Airbus and the Indonesian state-owned aerospace company DI consists of several programmes and covers both licensed production and co-development. The engagement dates to 1976 when DI, the Indonesian prime contractor, was contracted to manufacture under licence NC212-200 light transport aircraft from the Spanish CASA (now Airbus Defense and Space). According to DI, it has produced as many as 103 NC212-200s (both civil and military versions) and it has been the single source producer of the NC212 family since 2014. It ceased production of the NC212-200 and NC212-400 and instead is focused on the updated NC212i variant, including the Maritime Surveillance Aircraft version.[34] Indonesia has since exported these to Vietnam and the Philippines.[35]

In 1979, the two companies went on to establish a joint-venture company, Aircraft Technology (Airtech), to design the CN235 medium-range twin-engine transport aircraft.[36] According to DI, the two companies now market different variants of the platform, with a collaboration agreement in place for exports.[37] More recently, following the 2012 agreement with Airbus for the supply of Indonesia's nine C295M medium-lift transport aircrafts, DI produces horizontal and vertical stabilisers and the rear fuselage for the aircraft and operates a final assembly line in Bandung, Indonesia, for the type.[38] Indonesia therefore eventually became part of the global supply chain for these platforms, rather than just engaging in licensed production for domestic demand.

The partnership also extends to rotary-wing aircraft. This dates back to 1976 when IPTN (now DI) first obtained a licence to produce the NBO-105 helicopter from Messerschmitt-Bölkow-Blohm, which is now part of Airbus Helicopters.[39] In 1982 the company began licensed production of Airbus N-SA330 *Puma*s and N-AS332 *Super Puma*s for the Indonesian Air Force.[40] Since 2008, DI has had an industrial-framework agreement in place with Airbus Helicopters to manufacture the main tail boom and fuselage for the *Super Puma* MkII family, that is, for both civil and military variants of Airbus's H225s, with full production in place in Indonesia since 2011.[41]

When Indonesia ordered eight further H225Ms in 2019, to add to their six in inventory, the agreement between the Indonesian Ministry of Defence and DI stated that the helicopters will be delivered to the Indonesian Air Force with reassembly and completion of the mission equipment outfitting and any further customisation made by DI at its facility in Bandung.[42] Such arrangements are in line with the 2014 agreement for 11 AS565MBe *Panther* anti-submarine warfare (ASW) helicopters, under which Airbus Helicopters would supply the platforms to DI to then reassemble and outfit them in-country, acting as the design authority. This covered the installation of the ASW suite, which included a dipping sonar and torpedo launch systems.[43] Again, similar arrangements were put in place in September 2024 when the Indonesian Air Force ordered four Airbus H145 helicopters.[44]

Over the past decade, the two companies have repeatedly expanded cooperative memorandum of understanding (MoU) agreements. In February 2014, DI and Airbus signed an MoU covering maintenance, repair and overhaul (MRO) for the various Airbus Helicopters products operated within Indonesia – in particular, the AS365 *Dauphin*, EC725 *Cougar* and AS350/AS555 *Fennec* rotorcraft acquired by the country's government.[45] This was further expanded in 2017 to cover support and services, and both signed an MoU to explore the expansion of MRO capabilities for rotary- and fixed-wing aircraft delivered from DI in 2022.[46] These programmes with differing extents of local participation from Indonesia suggest that future engagements will continue.

The partnership with Airbus, as well as with Bell Textron, has enabled DI to develop domestic capabilities in the production, systems integration and MRO of aircraft, with deliveries of more than 460 units of aircraft to 50 customers.[47] Despite the long-term partnership, however, there are challenges to future engagement, not least the number of recent agreements between Indonesia and other foreign aerospace prime contractors to avoid over-reliance on sole suppliers. DI itself signed MoUs with Boeing, Sikorsky and Turkish Aerospace Industries in November 2022.[48]

Indonesia's aim to reduce dependence on single suppliers has increased the long-term costs of MRO, training, education and exercises, all of which are required to operate its multitude of weapons systems. The impact on future funding potentially threatens the sustainability of Indonesia's long-term plan to modernise its armed forces.[49]

FNSS in Malaysia and Indonesia

As Turkish defence exports began to grow in the mid-1990s, Southeast Asia quickly became one of the most important markets for Turkish companies. With technical capability developed through joint ventures and ToT with US and European firms, Turkish companies have been able to offer increasingly high-quality equipment at competitive prices. Successive Islamist governments in Ankara have further cultivated ties with other predominantly Muslim nations, such as Indonesia and Malaysia.[50]

As a result, Turkish companies have seen significant success in the region, none more so than armoured-vehicle manufacturer FNSS. In 2000 FNSS became the first Turkish company to secure a defence export to Malaysia, when it was awarded a USD278m subcontract to supply 211 of its ACV300 tracked armoured vehicles, locally called *Adnan*.[51] Prime contractor DRB-HICOM Defence Technologies (DEFTECH) was designated by the Malaysian government as the ToT recipient for the programme and went on to assemble some of the vehicles at a new facility in Pekan and subsequently, with its subsidiary

Table 1.2: **Selected Southeast Asian procurement which includes collaboration between local and European industry since 2010**

Country	System	Type	Qty	Value	Contract year	Local contractor	Lead foreign contractor	Nature of collaboration
Malaysia	AV8 *Gempita*	Wheeled-armoured-vehicle family	257	USD2.47bn	2011	DRB-HICOM Defence Technologies (DEFTECH)	FNSS	Local production of Turkish-design vehicle
Malaysia	*Maharaja Lela* (FRA *Gowind* 2500)	Frigate	5	USD2.46bn	2011	Lumut Naval Shipyard	Naval Group	Local construction of vessels and assembly of some subsystems
Indonesia	C295M	Light transport aircraft	9	USD325m	2012	DI	(M) Airbus	Final assembly of seven of the nine aircraft as well as additional aircraft in follow-on orders; production of rear fuselage and empennage for this and global orders
Vietnam	DN2000 (Damen 9014)	Offshore-patrol ship	4	n.k.	2012	Song Thu Corporation	Damen Shipyards Group	Local construction of Damen design with ToT
Thailand	AW139	Multi-role helicopter	10	USD88.8m	2012–15*	SFS Aviation	Leonardo	Local assembly and ToT
Thailand	H225M	Heavy transport helicopter	12	n.k.	2012–18*	Thai Aviation Industries (TAI)	(M) Airbus	Safran and TAI team to provide engine maintenance
Singapore	*Invincible* (GER Type-218SG)	Attack submarine	4	USD1.83bn	2013 & 2017	ST Engineering	ThyssenKrupp Marine Systems (TKMS)	CMS jointly developed with TKMS subsidiary Atlas Elektronik; ST Engineering providing in-service support with TKMS
Indonesia	*Harimau*	Light tank	18	USD135m	2019	Pindad	FNSS	Co-development and sharing of IP, final assembly in Indonesia with ToT
Indonesia	*Bergamini* (ITA FREMM) *Maestrale***	Frigate	6 / 2	n.k.	2021	Penataran Angkatan Laut (PAL) Indonesia	Fincantieri	To be determined
Indonesia	*Red White* (UK *Arrowhead* 140)	Frigate	2	USD720m	2021	PAL Indonesia	Babcock International	Local construction with a design licence provided by Babcock International
Indonesia	*Rafale*	FGA aircraft	42	USD8.1bn	2022	DI	Dassault Aviation	ToT to local industry
Singapore	Multi-role Combat Vessel	Frigate	6	n.k.	2023	ST Engineering	Saab Kockums	Saab providing design assistance and producing composite superstructures

*Several contracts. **Second-hand vessels. (M) = multinational; CMS = combat-management system; FGA = fighter ground-attack; IP = intellectual property; ToT = transfer of technology

Sources: IISS, Military Balance+, milbalplus.iiss.org

Defence Services (DSSB), carry out complex maintenance of the *Adnan*.[52]

The success of the *Adnan* programme, which included follow-up orders for an additional 56 vehicles, led to a more ambitious project: the Malaysian Army's Armoured Wheeled Vehicle 8x8. Again, DEFTECH was contracted in 2011 to work with FNSS in a deal worth MYR7.55bn (USD2.47bn) to supply 257 vehicles based on FNSS's *Pars*.[53] On this project, however, DEFTECH took on a greater role in design, system integration and production, with FNSS engineers working on the production line in Pekan following a MYR100m (USD32.37m) upgrade of the facility.[54] DSSB would also integrate turrets provided by South African defence contractor Denel. Project completion was delayed until 2022, however, due to financing issues on Malaysia's side, supply-chain disruption caused by the COVID-19 pandemic and Malaysian investigations of corruption at DEFTECH.[55]

A *Harimau* tank, designed and developed by Indonesian company PT Pindad and Turkish company FNSS, performs during the Indo Defence Expo in Jakarta, 5 November 2022

(Eko Siswono Toyudho/Anadolu Agency via Getty Images)

In Indonesia, government-to-government agreements kick-started FNSS's presence, partnering with Pindad from 2014 to co-develop a light tank based on the former's *Kaplan* medium tank. A 2019 production contract for 18 vehicles saw FNSS manufacture the first ten in Turkiye and then ship them to Pindad for integration with the 105mm turret supplied by Belgium's John Cockerill.[56] The final eight vehicles were then manufactured by Pindad in Bandung. Pindad delivered all vehicles, called *Harimau* locally, in 2024.[57] The Indonesian Army has a requirement for several hundred *Harimau*s to replace the legacy AMX-13 and both companies are now developing an armoured personnel carrier variant of the *Kaplan* for an Indonesian requirement, which may also number several hundred vehicles.[58] Funding these ambitions, however, may prove challenging, with Indonesia already committed to several multibillion-dollar navy and air-force programmes over the next decade. That the current Prabowo administration seeks to expand the army's territorial-command structure and establish 100 new 'food resilience' battalions further strains future resources.

Naval Group in Malaysia

French naval exports to Malaysia date back to the 1970s when Constructions Mécaniques de Normandie delivered four *Perdana*-class (*La Combattante* II) fast patrol craft to the Royal Malaysian Navy (RMN). Although French industry armed other RMN naval vessels acquired in the 1980s and 1990s, it was not until 2002 that French shipbuilders secured their next export to the RMN. In June of that year, Malaysia awarded a consortium, which included French companies DCN International (now part of Naval Group), Thomson-CSF (now Thales) and Spain's IZAR (now Navantia), a EUR1.08bn (USD1.02bn) contract for two *Scorpène*-class diesel-electric attack submarines.[59] Although both submarines were built in France and Spain, MRO was to be provided locally through Boustead DCNS Naval Corporation, a joint-venture company between Naval Group (60%) and Boustead Heavy Industries Corporation (BHIC).[60]

The construction of the submarines was relatively straightforward, but the programme was dogged by corruption investigations in both France and Malaysia, with Naval Group's offices raided by French authorities in 2010 and the Malaysian Anti-Corruption Commission announcing in 2024 that it was reopening its investigation into the affair.[61] And yet, Boustead and Naval Group combined forces again a decade later for the RMN's Second Generation Patrol Vessel – Littoral Combat Ship (LCS) programme. In December 2011, Malaysia awarded Boustead Naval Shipyard (BNS) a MYR9bn (USD2.94bn) Letter of Award for the construction of six frigates based on DCNS's *Gowind* 2500 design, the *Maharaja Lela*-class.[62] The production contract was then signed in July 2014, following a significant upgrade of BNS's facilities in Lumut.

As Malaysia decided to build all six vessels locally, rather than have the original equipment manufacturer-shipyard build the first batch followed by building the next locally, the LCS programme had been complicated from the start. Other planned local industrial involvement included the assembly of four of six Thales Nederland's SMART-S Mk2 radars by Malaysian company Contraves Advanced Devices (CAD), a joint venture between BHIC and Rheinmetall. However, this arrangement ended in the courts following BNS's cancellation of CAD's Letter of Award on the project.[63] Naval Group also transferred technology to establish a shore integration facility at BNS to test combat systems ashore before integration into the vessel. However, the programme has been plagued by delays due to financial issues at BNS, the COVID-19 pandemic and corruption investigations.[64]

A contract amendment in May 2023 increased the programme budget to MYR11.23bn (USD2.46bn), cancelled the sixth vessel and agreed on a new delivery schedule with programme completion now expected in 2029, seven years later than originally planned in 2011.[65] The RMN has an ambitious modernisation programme that includes a reduction from 15 classes of vessels to just five. One of these classes is the LCS, with plans for 12 of these vessels.[66] At present, it is unclear whether the RMN would procure further *Maharaja Lela*-class vessels or seek a different design that would also be classified as an LCS.

BRIDGING THE GULF

Saudi Arabia and the UAE are the top Arab Gulf defence-industrial partners for Asia-Pacific countries. There are four key drivers behind the UAE's defence-industrial collaboration with Asian counterparts. Firstly, the UAE's search for greater strategic autonomy has led it to diversify its network of political allies, economic partners and defence-equipment suppliers. Secondly, partnering with Asian countries creates opportunities to access different and complementary technologies and intellectual property, such as UAV technology from China's NORINCO and gas-turbine engines from India's Hindustan Aeronautics (HAL).

Thirdly, co-production ventures abroad enhance the UAE's defence-industrial capacity and strengthen its supply-chain resilience. Licensing agreements to produce the EDGE

Group's arms in Malaysia and India, as well as ammunitions in Indonesia (see Figure 1.3), exemplify this strategy. They also provide access to a larger and more cost-effective workforce, particularly for high-volume production of items like ammunition. Moreover, repackaging these products as 'locally produced' allows the UAE to export to clients like the Indian Army that would otherwise be more reluctant to purchase directly. Fourthly, the UAE hopes to gain a first-mover advantage in the Asia-Pacific by establishing defence-industrial partnerships before its Saudi counterpart Saudi Arabian Military Industries (SAMI).

A display of weaponry by NORINCO in the Chinese pavilion at the International Defence Exhibition in Abu Dhabi, UAE, 22 February 2011

(Gabriela Maj/Bloomberg via Getty Images)

Defence-industrial partnership selection depends partly on the alignment between what Emirati entities seek (e.g., a specific technology or a production licence) and what their Asian counterparts can offer (e.g., the desired technology and the ability and willingness to produce under licence), which tends to vary on a case-by-case basis. But political relationships and alignments between the UAE and its defence-industrial partners in Asia are also important considerations. For instance, India and Indonesia, whose ruling elites have very close ties to their Emirati counterparts, are two of the UAE's most prominent defence partners in Asia.

But determining the preferences of Saudi and UAE defence entities is often challenging, as they often face constraints regarding what they or their partners can offer or are willing to share. In general, the UAE maintains a more diverse range of partnerships than Saudi Arabia. Additionally, Saudi entities tend to be on the receiving end of defence-industrial cooperation with most – if not all – programmes located in Saudi Arabia, whereas Emirati companies have recently been able to provide defence-industrial technology and assistance.

For instance, Singapore's ST Engineering is helping the Saudi companies SAMI, ERAF and AEC (now SAMI Advanced Electronics) transform a basic patrol craft into a smart uninhabited surface vehicle (USV), with the goal of selling it to the Royal Saudi Navy and coastguard.[67] Another Saudi firm, Power for Defence Technologies, has signed an agreement with India's Bharat Electronics (BEL) to integrate critical technologies – for both defence and civil applications – into the Saudi ecosystem.[68] Saudi ACES, in partnership with China Electronics Technology Group Corporation (CETC), also seeks to localise know-how on drone payload design and manufacturing.[69]

Saudi entities have also signed agreements with companies and ministries across Asia, though not all have yielded results, and those that do can take time to materialise. For example, in early 2024, the Saudi Ministry of Defense signed an agreement with South Korea's Defense Acquisition Program Administration (DAPA) to cooperate on weapons R&D.[70] Additionally, SAMI has been in discussions with South Korea's Hanwha Corporation for a joint venture to produce munitions in the Kingdom, tentatively named SAMI–Hanwha Munitions Systems.[71] As of February 2025, this joint venture has yet to come to fruition.

CONCERTED AUTONOMY: DEFENCE-INDUSTRIAL PARTNERSHIPS IN THE ASIA-PACIFIC

Figure 1.3: **Saudi and Emirati defence-industrial partnerships with Asian countries**

- - Defence-industrial partnership announced, but status unclear.

Selected examples of defence-industrial partnership

UAE

2019

- International Golden Group and China North Industries Corporation (NORINCO) establish the China-Emirates Science and Technology Innovation Laboratory to transfer Chinese drone technology and initiate joint projects.

2021

- GAL and China's CATIC open the first regional distribution hub for aircraft logistics in Abu Dhabi.
- Nimr and Singapore's ST Engineering sign an MoU to build innovative hybrid electric drive systems for Nimr's armoured vehicles.

2022

- Calidus and Indonesia's Pindad sign an MoU to cooperate in the joint development and production, engineering design, technical assistance and supply of components for 8×8 combat vehicles.
- Lahab and Indonesia's Dahana sign an MoU to cooperate in the manufacturing and production of explosives and explore a joint investment in the construction of a TNT plant at the Dahana Energetic Material Center area in Subang, West Java.

2023

- EDGE Group and India's HAL sign an MoU to explore cooperation in the joint design and development of missiles and uninhabited aerial vehicles. They will also explore using HAL's small gas-turbine engines on EDGE's guided weapons and EDGE's GPS jamming and spoofing equipment on HAL's platforms.
- Caracal signs a licensing agreement with India's ICOMM to localise the production of Caracal's arms in India, marking the first technology transfer in small arms from the UAE to India.
- Abu Dhabi Ship Building (ADSB) and India's Sagar Defence Engineering sign an MoU to assess the viability of entering into definitive agreement for the provision of 12-metre platforms, as well as a technology-transfer programme for the Indian market.
- Al Tariq and India's Bharat Dynamics sign an MoU to jointly produce *Al Tariq* long-range precision-guided munition (LR-PGM) kits in India for the Indian Armed Forces. EDGE also announces the successful completion of feasibility studies for integrating the *Al Tariq* LR-PGM on the HAL *Tejas* combat aircraft.

- Caracal signs a technology-transfer agreement enabling Malaysia's Ketech Asia to assemble the Caracal CAR 816 tactical assault rifle at its new facilities in Pahang state. Ketech Asia will also become an official reseller of the rifle, and both companies will review the potential co-development of new firearms.

2024

- EDGE signs an agreement with India's Adani Defence & Aerospace to cooperate across multiple domains, including exploring the establishment of R&D, production and maintenance facilities in India and the UAE.
- EDGE signs a USD27 million (AED99m) agreement to supply an ammunition production line to Pindad, for 5.56×45 millimetre and 7.62×51mm calibre ammunition. Production is scheduled to start in 2026.
- Lahab and Pindad sign a Head of Agreement to collaborate in establishing defence manufacturing capabilities, and an MoU for Lahab to supply defence equipment for production purposes to Pindad.

Saudi Arabia

2022

- Advanced Communications and Electronics Systems Company (ACES) signs an agreement with state-owned China Electronics Technology Group Corporation (CETC) for knowledge transfer to locally manufacture drone payload systems.

2024

- GAL and China's CATIC open the first regional distribution hub for aircraft logistics in Abu Dhabi.
- At the World Defense Show in Riyadh, Singapore's ST Engineering showcases its partnership with Saudi Arabian Military Industries (SAMI) Sea, Advanced Electronics Company, and Eraf to develop an uninhabited surface vessel for the Saudi navy.
- SAMI and South Korea's Kia sign an MoU to strengthen the competencies of SAMI Land Systems to build light tactical vehicles through collaboration and R&D.
- Saudi Arabia's defence ministry signs two MoUs: one with South Korea's Defense Acquisition Program Administration to launch a bilateral committee to jointly conduct R&D of weapons systems, and one with Hanwha for defence-industrial cooperation.

©IISS

Source: IISS

The UAE's defence industry has prioritised R&D partnerships over the past decade to absorb technical expertise and technology from international partners, including through project co-developments and the establishment of R&D centres. For example, EDGE subsidiary Nimr, which manufactures armoured vehicles, partnered with ST Engineering to build hybrid electric drive systems. EDGE also signed an agreement with Adani Defence & Aerospace to explore the establishment of R&D facilities in India and with the UAE for defence and aerospace solutions.[72] EDGE hopes to jointly design and develop missile systems and UAVs with HAL.[73] They will explore, inter alia, the use of HAL's small gas-turbine engines on EDGE's guided weapons, and the use of EDGE's GPS jamming and spoofing equipment on HAL's platforms.

International Golden Group (IGG) also established a lab with NORINCO in 2019 to transfer Chinese drone technology and conduct joint R&D. The facility is based in IGG's industrial complex in the Tawazun Industrial Park. Tawazun Council, which in collaboration with the Ministry of Defence oversees governmental defence and security R&D programmes in the UAE, signed an MoU with South Korea's DAPA in January 2023 to strengthen defence-industry cooperation.[74] That same month, Tawazun signed another MoU with Korea Aerospace Industries to co-develop a multi-purpose transport aircraft.[75]

While the focus on absorbing ToT and know-how remains central, Emirati companies since 2022 have transitioned from being recipients to suppliers in their defence-industrial partnerships (see Figure 1.3). Companies like CARACAL, LAHAB Defense Systems and Al Tariq have started partnering with counterparts in India, Indonesia and Malaysia to produce assault rifles, ammunition, precision-guided munition kits and potentially other equipment under licence.[76] Emirati shipbuilder ADSB is even considering a technology transfer to India's Sagar Defence Engineering, which focuses on USVs, and Lahab is exploring a joint investment in Indonesia with PT Dahana to build a TNT-production facility.[77]

Despite such progress, legal and political challenges continue to hinder the UAE's and Saudi Arabia's defence-industrial collaboration in the Asia-Pacific. These include US sanctions and other restrictions on partnerships with Russian and Chinese companies. For example, RTX terminated a multibillion-dollar contract with Saudi company Scopa Defense in 2023, after discovering that at least two companies linked to Scopa had dealings with sanctioned Belarusian, Chinese and Russian entities.[78] Other European companies, like Fincantieri and Beretta, reportedly backed away from working with Scopa partly due to similar concerns. Other examples include deals for SAMI to manufacture Russian weaponry in the Kingdom and a partnership between the UAE and Russia's Rostec to co-develop a fifth-generation fighter that ultimately did not materialise.[79]

Both the UAE and Saudi Arabia maintain ongoing partnerships with Chinese defence companies, which could be harder to sustain if geopolitical tensions escalate. These include, for example, IGG's lab with NORINCO in the UAE mentioned above and Global Aerospace Logistics' regional distribution hub for aircraft logistics (established jointly with the China National Aero-Technology Import & Export Corporation in 2021). In Saudi, the King Abdulaziz City for Science and Technology and China Aerospace Science and Technology Corporation signed an MoU in 2017 to manufacture UAVs in Saudi Arabia, but it is unclear if the factory was ever built. In 2022, Saudi company ACES partnered with

CETC to design and manufacture drone payload systems locally; arrangements like these might be at risk if the US and other European partners leverage the two Arab Gulf states' access to their military technology to get them to reduce their partnerships with China.[80]

In addition to such political and legal challenges, some Asia-Pacific countries also appear reluctant or unable to transfer technology or engage in defence-industrial partnerships with Middle Eastern counterparts. For one thing, defence-export controls complicate any potential ToT or co-production agreements, as many Japanese and South Korean defence products contain US-made subcomponents. For another, some Asian countries are wary of being drawn into the geopolitical rivalries in the Middle East. In Japan, for instance, defence-equipment transfers, and presumably defence-industrial partnerships, are not permitted to countries involved in or likely to be involved in international conflicts.

But more broadly, there may be misalignments in the maturity levels of their defence industries. In some cases, Asian counterparts may find it hard to localise manufacturing in the Gulf region due to the challenges of transferring very high-tech automated processes to locations where the infrastructure and human capital may be lacking. In other instances, countries that would be more politically inclined to share technology tend to have less-developed defence-industrial capabilities and be unsuited to provide the advanced technologies that the UAE and Saudi Arabia seek, such as electronic warfare, missile or UAV technologies.

TWO IN ONE

India and Russia's long-standing defence cooperation is rooted in the Cold War, when defence-equipment sales by the West to India were hampered by cost considerations and, for exporter countries, insufficient political like-mindedness and strategic stability, as well as non-proliferation concerns. Russia supplied India with much of its foreign-origin equipment, sustaining an export market for its own industry while supporting India politically at the United Nations Security Council. In the 1990s, Indian and Russian leaders sought to diversify and future-proof their defence relationship, which still relied heavily on one-way trade of defence equipment from Russia to India. India also sought to capitalise on that strategic trust built during the Cold War, while Russia's defence-industry reliance on India as a defence market increased as investment in the Russian armed forces decreased.

India and Russia inaugurated the BrahMos Aerospace joint venture in 1998, focusing on a single item: a supersonic anti-ship missile programme based on Russia's NPO *Mashinostroyenia* 3M55 project, then in development. India's 50.5% ownership of this unique collaboration gave it an unprecedented symbolic weight. The supersonic missiles it would co-develop and produce would, from New Delhi's perspective, demonstrate India's attainment of its ambition to become a science and technology power, standing on its own alongside Russia. The capability would provide India with a versatile capability to adapt on existing platforms – beginning with Russian ones – in the air, surface-naval and land domains.

The *BrahMos* would be limited to a 290-kilometre range. This initially ensured compliance with Russia's membership from 1995 of the Missile Technology Control Regime (MTCR), an agreement intended to curtail the proliferation of ballistic and cruise missiles, and India's position outside of it but with an ambition to join it.[81] For Russia, the project

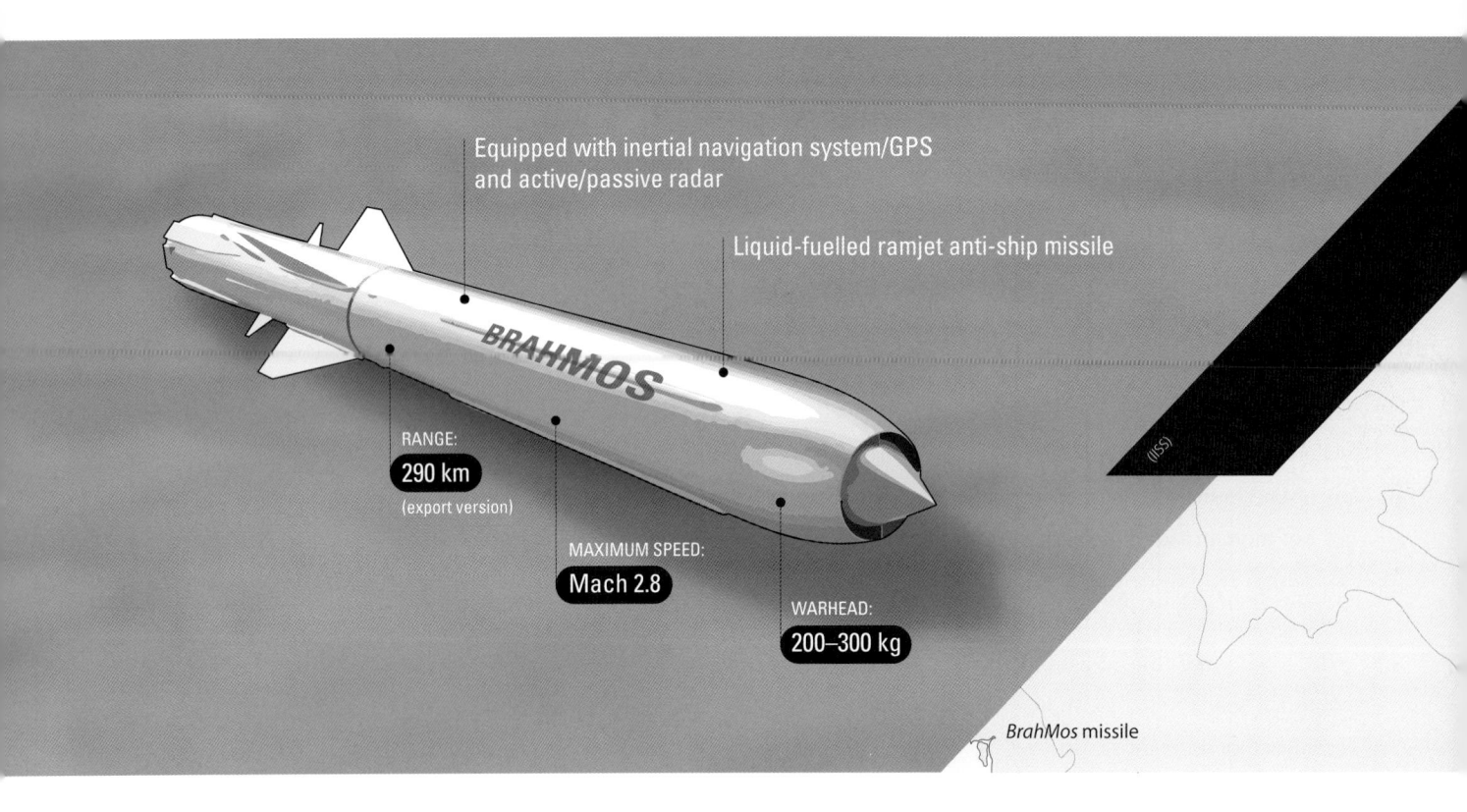

Equipped with inertial navigation system/GPS and active/passive radar

Liquid-fuelled ramjet anti-ship missile

RANGE:
290 km
(export version)

MAXIMUM SPEED:
Mach 2.8

WARHEAD:
200–300 kg

BrahMos missile

had the advantage of sharing existing technology with India without risking destabilising Moscow's relationship with China, Russia's other large defence-trade market and rising defence-industrial partner. For both countries, the co-development of a missile would be faster and provide a clearer demonstration of their common post-Cold War political ambitions, compared to work on a platform such as a tank.

The first successful test-firing of the *BrahMos* version of the 3M55 took place in India in June 2001, within two years of the two governments signing the first joint contract for USD250m.[82] Work was led by India's prime contractor, the public-sector Defence Research and Development Organisation, paired with Russia's NPO Mashinostroyeniya, a subsidiary of Tactical Missiles Corporation (Korporatsiya Takticheskoe Raketnoe Vooruzhenie, KTRV), a major missile designer and manufacturer.

Early on, BrahMos Aerospace benefitted from the support of India's and Russia's political leaderships, with prime ministers and defence ministers regularly and publicly pledging their backing. Russian President Vladimir Putin visited a key production facility in 2004 during a visit to India, as well as the BrahMos Aerospace stand at Russia's MAKS international air show in 2011. Besides its headquarters in New Delhi, there are two research and production sites for BrahMos Aerospace. The main site is located in Hyderabad, where India historically concentrated its ballistic-missile industry under engineer A.P.J Abdul Kalam, who later, as deputy defence minister, signed the inaugural BrahMos agreement.

Further defence-industrial partnership institutionalisation was greatly helped by the programme's focus on developing a missile which would also meet India Army and Indian Air Force requirements. This would ensure the product's industrial viability through economies of scale. As a result, early on the missile was developed with land-attack and surface-to-surface and coastal defence variants.

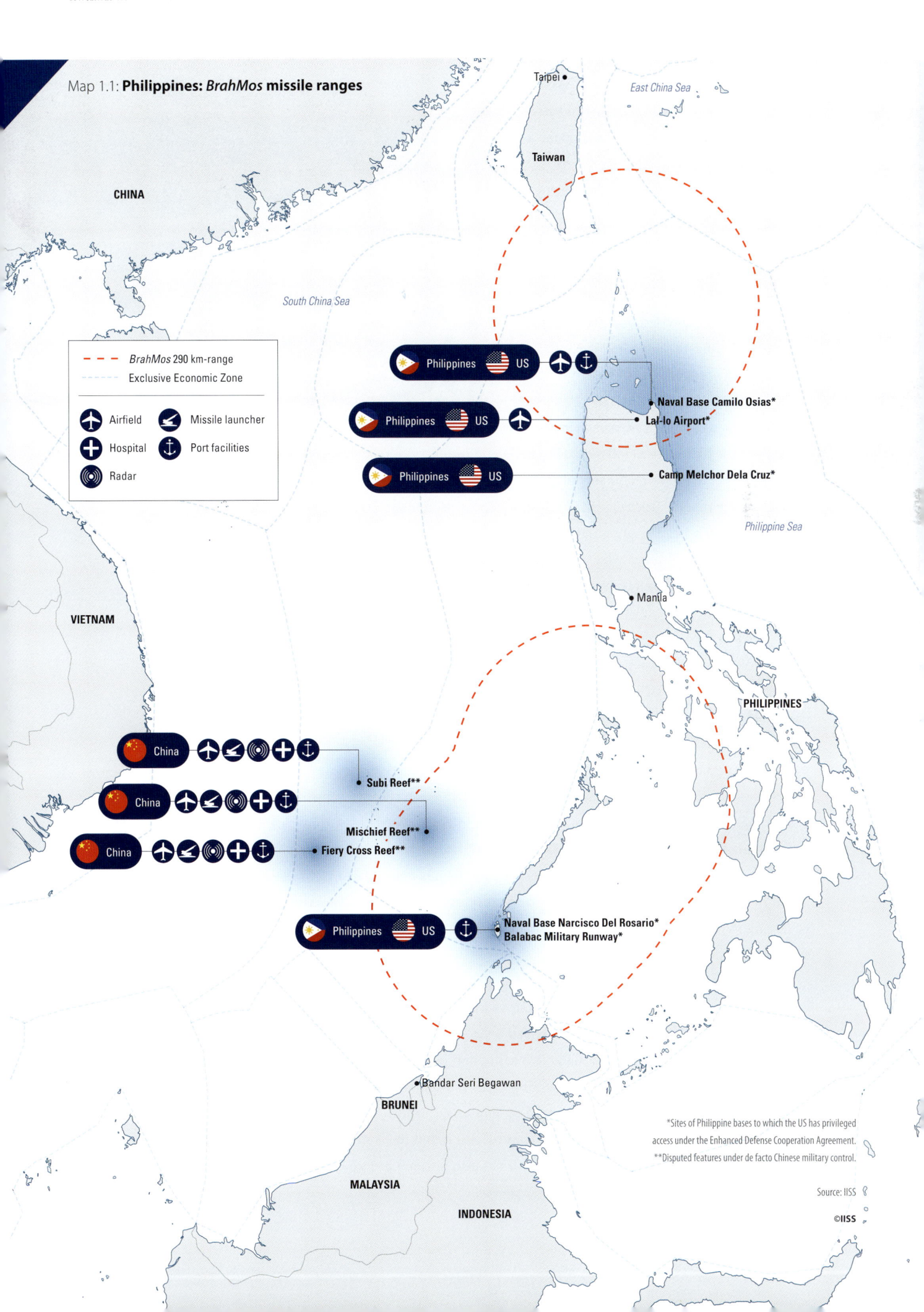

CONCERTED AUTONOMY: DEFENCE-INDUSTRIAL PARTNERSHIPS IN THE ASIA-PACIFIC

Map 1.1: Philippines: *BrahMos* missile ranges

*Sites of Philippine bases to which the US has privileged access under the Enhanced Defense Cooperation Agreement.
**Disputed features under de facto Chinese military control.

Source: IISS
©IISS

In 2007, the missile entered service with the Indian Army. In 2008, a sea-based land-attack version was test fired from a vertical launch system integrated onto the *Rajput*-class guided-missile destroyers.[83] This was followed by a test firing of missile from a submerged platform in 2013. Progress was slowest on the air-launched version: India's front-line Russian-designed Sukhoi Su-30MKI *Flanker* H tested *BrahMos* in-flight for the first time in 2017, but the missile entered service only in 2020.[84]

Nevertheless, the *BrahMos* has become a staple of India's Republic Day parade in New Delhi since 2003. Close civil–military, design and end-user service relations have been key to the success of the venture. Indian military service chiefs and doctrines also provided the underlying operational driver for the *BrahMos* since they seriously discussed the need for a fast missile early on. The organisational standing of Brahmos Aerospace within India's defence establishment grew when in 2024, Jaiteerth R. Joshi, the head of India's main missile-development complex, became CEO of BrahMos Aerospace.

By maximising technological relevance to India's defence forces, for which stand-off range was a key requirement, both India and Russia were able to work on extended-range versions of the missile, extending it to 450–500 km, at first, then to 800 km, after India's admittance into the MTCR in 2016.[85] Since 2011, the company has been working on a hypersonic missile known as *BrahMos* II. This work on a *BrahMos* II co-development was further formalised later that decade.

The prospect of export sales of *BrahMos* had always been touted by India and Russia as a likely outcome of their cooperation. India has marketed it as a cheaper anti-ship missile system than Western systems. It was, however, only in 2022, after at least three years of negotiations, that the Philippines and India signed a USD375m contract for the purchase of three batteries of *BrahMos* coastal defence systems for the navy (see Map 1.1).[86] Deliveries began in 2024, marking the missile's first third-party export sale. India was reported to be closing in on agreements to supply Vietnam and Indonesia as of late 2024, as well as systems for the Philippine Army.

However, its dependency on India's market – once a major advantage – has become an emerging and major challenge for BrahMos Aerospace. While the initial supersonic version of *BrahMos* is still being procured and stockpiled for existing and new Indian armed-forces platforms, it is possible this market will reach saturation point over the next decade. This prospect highlights the fact that, to date, Russia has not bought the missile for its own armed forces. Some analysts see the missile system as an export from Russia to India, rather than a co-owned development. This feature has limited the scale of its production and thus perhaps its market competitiveness. It has also resulted in India missing out on accessing the large market of a major military power.

BrahMos cruise missiles, built by India and Russia, are paraded in front of spectators during India's Republic Day celebrations in New Delhi, 26 January 2004

(Emmanuel Dunand/AFP via Getty Images)

Russia's 2022 full-scale invasion of Ukraine has not significantly impacted the procurement of *BrahMos* for the Indian armed forces, given that its production is located mainly in India. It is unclear but likely, however, that supplies of key subcomponents for *BrahMos* originating from Russia may have slowed due to its war effort in Ukraine, or the threat of related US sanctions. Likewise, the delay in India supplying *BrahMos* to the Philippines may also result from the need for it to prioritise its own stockpile of the missile, considering rising tensions with China since 2020.

Another growing challenge to the joint venture is Russia's closer political-strategic ties with China in the context of the Russia–Ukraine war. There is no evidence yet that this partnership has strained the *BrahMos* bilateral cooperation with India. Yet, with India and some of its Southeast Asian partners perceiving China as their main adversary, they consider the *BrahMos* as an important part of their defence. As such, the possibility of Russia prioritising ties to China, resulting in a lower momentum for the production of *BrahMos* in its third decade, cannot be overlooked. Such sensitivities could also affect the development pace of the hypersonic *BrahMos*.

THREE OF A KIND

Italy and the UK have cooperated in the realm of combat aircraft for over five decades, so collaborating for a future programme was unsurprising. Over the same period Japan had only worked with the US, and in the early 2010s the relationship looked likely to continue to meet Tokyo's next-generation combat-aircraft needs. What transpired, however, was a different model.

In the 2010s the three GCAP partners – Italy, Japan and the UK – faced fundamentally similar defence-industrial questions: whether and how to sustain domestic defence aerospace capacity, the implications of not doing so and, conversely, the challenges of pursuing a next-generation capability.[87] That the outcome would be a trilateral project between London, Rome and Tokyo, however, was anything but a foregone conclusion.

The international security environment has worsened over the past decade. Russia launched a proxy war against Ukraine in 2014, while China has grown more assertive in its regional ambitions. These were accompanied by increased defence investments: modest in the case of Moscow, not so with Beijing. In the air domain both countries were pursuing more advanced systems, although China's ambitions far outstripped those of Russia as it sought – and continues to seek – parity with the US.[88] The extent of Beijing's investment was reinforced at the end of 2024. Not content with showing the Shenyang J-35 combat-aircraft variant earmarked for the People's Liberation Army Air Force, two previously unseen Chinese combat-aircraft designs currently in development were also allowed to emerge by the end of 2024.[89]

This combat-aircraft triptych represents a clear picture of China's continuing defence aerospace ambitions, and of the challenge that Beijing presents in the air domain to other regional powers. As such, it also likely served to reinforce the next-generation combat-aircraft requirements of other Asia-Pacific countries, including Japan. Indeed, for Tokyo the GCAP aircraft is intended to begin to replace the Mitsubishi F-2 from around 2035, while the UK's first operational squadron is meant to be fielded by 2040 as a replacement for the Eurofighter *Typhoon*.[90]

The deteriorating security environment and the return of great-power competition over the course of the 2010s has led Italy, Japan and the UK to evaluate, or re-evaluate, their requirements for a next-generation crewed combat aircraft. The UK had in the early 2000s discounted the need for a crewed multi-role fighter beyond the Eurofighter *Typhoon* or the Lockheed Martin F-35B *Lightning* II, instead looking more to the uninhabited realm to address long-term requirements.[91]

Italian Minister of Defence Guido Crosetto, Japan's then-defence minister Kihara Minoru and the UK's then-defence secretary Grant Shapps meet to discuss the GCAP in Tokyo, 14 December 2023

(David Mareuil/Anadolu via Getty Images)

Japan, meanwhile, was initially seeking to replace its ageing McDonnell Douglas F-4EJ *Kai Phantom*, beginning by 2010. Its goal was to acquire the Lockheed Martin F-22 *Raptor*, but this ambition was initially thwarted by Washington's unwillingness to make the aircraft available, and finally by then-president Barack Obama's decision to end production of the type.[92] Japan would eventually opt for the F-35 to replace the F-4EJ *Kai*. Italy and the UK had already committed to acquiring the F-35 by then as well.

Indeed, all the GCAP partners envision the combat aircraft that emerges from the programme as being operated alongside the F-35, while providing greater capability in terms of combat radius and internal weapon carriage than the *Lighting* II (see Figure 1.4). Their respective experiences in participating in the F-35 programme, and the implications for their domestic defence aerospace industries – were this model to be their only path forward – almost certainly informed their respective decision-making on GCAP.

By the mid-2010s, London was reconsidering its earlier decision not to pursue a crewed combat aircraft beyond the *Typhoon* or *Lightning* II. In 2015 it established the Future Combat Air System Technology Initiative (FCAS TI) and in 2018 the Ministry of Defence released a Combat Air Strategy and unveiled what was dubbed the *Tempest*, a mock-up of a future crewed combat aircraft.[93] In the same period, Franco-British cooperation unravelled over what was also called the Future Combat Air System. The challenges of reconciling increasingly different requirements, industrial drivers and the sharing of very low observable technologies (or stealth), all contributed to the collapse of the cooperation.[94]

The UK also began to consider potential partners for any nascent crewed combat-aircraft programme alongside the FCAS TI. BAE Systems, Leonardo UK, MBDA UK and Rolls-Royce were the industry participants. As a core player in both the *Tornado* and *Typhoon* programmes, a European collaboration could have appeared an obvious path. The unsuccessful Franco-British FCAS work, however, cast against the backdrop of the UK's 2016 decision to leave the European Union, made this more problematic.

By early 2017, furthermore, Germany was in discussion with France, Spain and Sweden on what it called its Next Generation Weapon System to develop a new crewed combat aircraft.[95] Germany had previously partnered with the UK on both the *Tornado* and *Typhoon* projects. The increased political closeness between Berlin and Paris, and the vision of a Franco-German 'leadership' of Europe, however, drove industrial decision-making.

What is now the Franco-German-Spanish Future Combat Air System programme is led by France's Dassault in a sometimes difficult relationship with Airbus Defence and Space.[96]

But while London was looking for potential European partners, it had also set wider horizons from the outset. It had already looked to build closer defence relations with Japan, as prefigured by the decade-long Joint New Air-to-Air Missile programme begun in 2014 between MBDA UK and Mitsubishi.[97] While this project ultimately did not result in a joint acquisition, it did lay the groundwork for wider defence cooperation. This was followed in 2015 by the first foreign and defence ministerial meeting to be held between Japan and the UK.[98] The former country was from the outset a candidate partner, although the US initially looked a more likely option for Japan to meet its future crewed combat-aircraft needs.

Japan had begun to work on technology applicable to an F-2 replacement in the early 2000s with its Advanced Technology Demonstrator-X. A demonstrator was eventually flown in 2016, with flight trials concluding in 2018.[99] In parallel, Tokyo was also considering its options for what was initially titled its Future Fighter programme and later badged as F-X. An initial preference for a Japanese-led programme with external support resulted in the selection of Lockheed Martin at the end of 2020 as the candidate partner, in preference to BAE Systems or Boeing.[100]

Concluding an agreement with Boeing and the US government, however, proved difficult, in part due to the latter's restrictions on technology access. Contact with London had also continued during 2021 and by mid-2022, a UK – rather than a US – partnership increasingly looked like the more likely outcome. In December 2022, Japan joined Italy and the UK in formally launching GCAP as an equal partner, an outcome that would have been unlikely in any defence-industrial collaboration with the US.[101]

Rome had partnered with London in the *Tornado* and *Typhoon* programmes, and as such was a clear candidate to partner with the UK. The same had been true of Germany, and Berlin had chosen to commit to Paris. French President Emmanuel Macron and then German chancellor Angela Merkel raised the potential for a joint programme in July 2017, with a letter of intent signed in June 2018.[102]

As the two fighter camps began to come together, Italy risked being left out, or at least only able to pick up the leftovers. The Italian industry was keen to avoid such an outcome. Joining the FCAS programme would have arguably placed the Italian industry third in the queue behind their French and German counterparts. In September 2019, the Italian and UK governments signed a statement of intent, followed a day later by the Italian industry, led by Leonardo and including Avio Aero and Elettronica (now ELT Group).[103] Leonardo UK was already a core element of the industry's Team Tempest.

Figure 1.4: **GCAP partners: combat-aircraft fleets, 2025 and 2045**

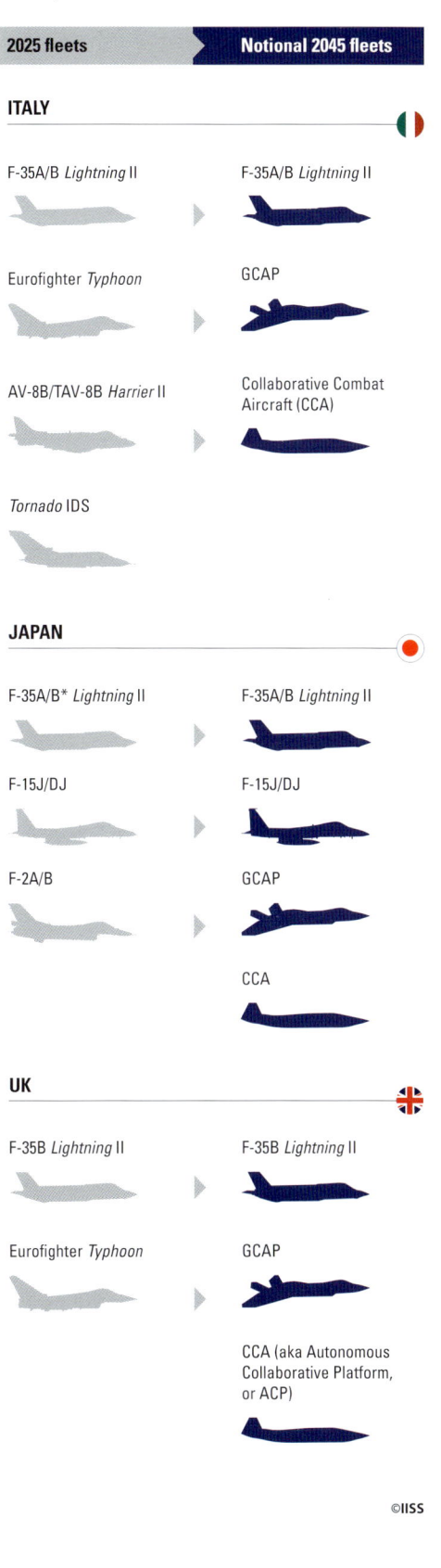

2025 fleets	Notional 2045 fleets
ITALY	🇮🇹
F-35A/B *Lightning* II	F-35A/B *Lightning* II
Eurofighter *Typhoon*	GCAP
AV-8B/TAV-8B *Harrier* II	Collaborative Combat Aircraft (CCA)
Tornado IDS	
JAPAN	🇯🇵
F-35A/B* *Lightning* II	F-35A/B *Lightning* II
F-15J/DJ	F-15J/DJ
F-2A/B	GCAP
	CCA
UK	🇬🇧
F-35B *Lightning* II	F-35B *Lightning* II
Eurofighter *Typhoon*	GCAP
	CCA (aka Autonomous Collaborative Platform, or ACP)

©IISS

*Delivery expected mid-2025.

Source: IISS, Military Balance+, milbalplus.iiss.org

AUTONOMY ALL THE WAY?

Across the Asia-Pacific, countries and firms from all defence-industrial tiers develop partnerships with both regional and extra-regional counterparts. The specific strategic, political and technological-capacity alignments are important factors when considering the various partnership models. In most cases, however, regional countries frame their defence-industrialisation and partnership pursuits under the banner of seeking strategic autonomy. It is unsurprising, therefore, that offset arrangements and co-development and production are among the preferable or common defence-industrial partnership models in the region.

As we have seen above, there is a long history of European defence prime contractors working with Southeast Asia's defence industry, and they have been responsive to offset and intellectual property or ToT requirements. While European–Southeast Asian defence-industrial partnerships have largely been limited to licensed production and ToT, there is evidence that some joint design and development frameworks are emerging as regional countries seek to improve their indigenous capabilities in the near future.

Such defence-industrial partnerships have enabled Southeast Asian countries to develop various domestic capabilities to varying degrees of success. They have also placed these European companies on a stronger footing for future engagement, despite the preference to diversify suppliers and reduce reliance. However, the defence market may become increasingly contested as new international suppliers, such as Israel, have also begun to engage the region and as strategic partnerships with regional players like South Korea and Japan develop, while US firms continue to have a strong presence in the region.[104]

The diversity of suppliers creates a level of competition and enables countries to demand more extensive offset requirements from foreign suppliers. However, it can increase costs by reducing inter-operability and duplicating some capabilities. It can also result in the loss of any efficiencies of scale and require multiple training and maintenance programmes. Given that full defence autarky is no longer feasible, the search for autonomy alone could come at the expense of military efficacy and defence cost-efficiency.

Moreover, given the strategic and symbolic significance of sophisticated weapons, government involvement in many defence-industrial partnerships is unavoidable across the Asia-Pacific. Government support and commitment was critical in major co-development and production programmes, such as *BrahMos* and GCAP. After all, risk is inherent in developing advanced combat systems. Doing so in collaboration with another country adds an additional layer of complexity that compounds this challenge.

With GCAP, furthermore, the partners are working to the ambitious schedule of delivering the first production-standard aircraft in 2035. Italy and the UK, however, have had the at-times bruising experience of the Eurofighter programme to draw lessons from in attempting to avoid replicating the approach and structures that caused difficulties. The GCAP International Government Organisation was agreed in December 2023, while 12 months later the industry partners, BAE Systems, Leonardo and the Japan Aircraft Industrial Enhancement (established by the Society of Japanese Aerospace Companies and Mitsubishi Heavy Industries), signed off on establishing a joint venture for the programme.[105] Key to both organisations is their decision-making and -managing capacity, rather than having to defer to their respective national structures. A lack of empowerment was at the heart of many of the travails that delayed the Eurofighter programme and increased its costs.

The lack of an initial and robust export-market strategy for joint development programmes such as *BrahMos* is another lesson that regional policymakers need to consider. Beyond the industrial capacity and technological infrastructure, defence-industrial partnerships built around joint development and production are harder to sustain without solid export-growth planning outside of the original developers. The ability to genuinely globalise production to make the joint product economically viable is yet another consideration when assessing the challenges of co-development defence-industrial partnerships.

United Aircraft Corporation – a Russian aerospace company which contributes to the country's defence autarky – at the 53rd International Paris Air Show in Paris, France, 22 June 2019

(Thierry Nectoux/Gamma-Rapho via Getty Images)

Taken together, defence-industrial partnerships across the Asia-Pacific may start with the search for autonomy among different tiered states. But in their selection of partnerships, the economic, political and strategic realities affecting all defence industrialisation and collaboration brings them to a 'concerted autonomy'. Whether and how regional policymakers can strike the balance between building domestic defence-industrial bases, developing and implementing beneficial partnerships, and ensuring military effectiveness and defence efficiency amid geopolitical uncertainties remains to be seen.

EVAN A. LAKSMANA
Shangri-La Dialogue Senior Fellow for Southeast Asian Security and Defence; Editor, *Asia-Pacific Regional Security Assessment*, IISS–Asia

ANTOINE LEVESQUES
Senior Fellow for South and Central Asian Defence, Strategy and Diplomacy, IISS

FENELLA MCGERTY
Senior Fellow for Defence Economics, IISS

ALBERT VIDAL
Research Analyst, Middle East Office, IISS–Middle East

TOM WALDWYN
Research Fellow for Defence Procurement, IISS

DOUGLAS BARRIE
Senior Fellow for Military Aerospace, IISS

NOTES

1. Ethan Barnaby Kapstein, 'International Collaboration in Armaments Production: A Second-best Solution', *Political Science Quarterly*, vol. 106, no. 4, 1991, p. 659, https://academic.oup.com/psq/article-abstract/106/4/657/7135327?redirectedFrom=fulltext.
2. Richard A. Bitzinger, 'The Globalization of the Arms Industry: The Next Proliferation Challenge', *International Security*, vol. 19, no. 2, 1994, p. 188, https://www.jstor.org/stable/2539199.
3. Richard A. Bitzinger, 'Asian Arms Industries and Impact on Military Capabilities', *Defence Studies*, vol. 17, no. 3, 2017, p. 295, https://www.tandfonline.com/doi/full/10.1080/14702436.2017.1347871.
4. *Ibid.*, p. 305.
5. 'Philippines to Acquire Missile System from India for $375 Mln', Reuters, 15 January 2022,

https://www.reuters.com/world/asia-pacific/philippines-acquire-missile-system-india-375-mln-2022-01-15/.

6 Çağlar Kurç and Stephanie G. Neuman, 'Defence Industries in the 21st Century: A Comparative Analysis', *Defence Studies*, vol. 17, no. 3, 2017, p. 219, https://www.tandfonline.com/doi/full/10.1080/14702436.2017.1350105.

7 Kapstein, 'International Collaboration in Armaments Production: A Second-best Solution', p. 657.

8 Bitzinger, 'The Globalization of the Arms Industry: The Next Proliferation Challenge', pp. 174–5.

9 Keith Hartley, 'Defence Industrial Policy in a Military Alliance', *Journal of Peace Research*, vol. 43, no. 4, 2006, pp. 473–89.

10 Marc R. Devore, 'Arms Production in the Global Village: Options for Adapting to Defense-industrial Globalization', *Security Studies*, vol. 22, no. 3, 2013, pp. 537–9, https://www.tandfonline.com/doi/full/10.1080/09636412.2013.816118.

11 Kurç and Neuman, 'Defence Industries in the 21st Century: A Comparative Analysis', p. 219.

12 Jonata Anicetti and Ulrich Krotz, 'Why States Arm and Why, Sometimes, They Do So Together', *International Studies Review*, vol. 26, no. 4, 2024, p. 6, https://academic.oup.com/isr/article-abstract/26/4/viae031/7788295?redirectedFrom=fulltext.

13 This pyramid model and the accompanying tiers are from Richard A. Bitzinger, 'New Ways of Thinking About the Global Arms Industry: Dealing with "Limited Autarky"', ASPI Strategic Insights, 2015, p. 3, https://www.aspi.org.au/report/new-ways-thinking-about-global-arms-industry-dealing-limited-autarky.

14 See Douglas Barrie and James Hackett (eds), *Russia's Military Modernisation: An Assessment* (London: IISS, 2020), https://www.iiss.org/ja-JP/publications/strategic-dossiers/russias-military-modernisation/.

15 Richard A. Bitzinger, 'New Ways of Thinking About the Global Arms Industry: Dealing with "Limited Autarky"', ASPI Strategic Insights, 2015, p. 3, https://www.aspi.org.au/report/new-ways-thinking-about-global-arms-industry-dealing-limited-autarky.

16 Henrik Heidenkamp et al., 'Foundations of International Defence Industrial Co-operation Between Western States and Emerging Powers', Royal United Services Institute, 29 May 2014, p. 1, https://www.rusi.org/explore-our-research/publications/occasional-papers/foundations-of-defence-industrial-co-operation-between-western-states-and-emerging-powers.

17 *Ibid.*, p. 2.

18 Richard Bitzinger, *Towards a Brave New Arms Industry?* (London: Routledge, 2003), p. 18, https://www.taylorfrancis.com/books/mono/10.4324/9781315000718/towards-brave-new-arms-industry-richard-bitzinger.

19 Richard A. Bitzinger, 'Defense Industries in Asia and the Technonationalist Impulse', *Contemporary Security Policy*, vol. 36, no. 3, 2015, pp. 453–72, https://www.tandfonline.com/doi/full/10.1080/13523260.2015.1111649.

20 Kurç and Neuman, 'Defence Industries in the 21st Century: A Comparative Analysis', p. 220.

21 *Ibid.*, p. 221.

22 Heidenkamp et al., 'Foundations of International Defence Industrial Co-operation Between Western States and Emerging Powers', p. 3.

23 IISS, Military Balance+, accessed 3 February 2025, https://milbalplus.iiss.org/.

24 *Ibid.*

25 Ministry of Finance, 'Revenue and Expenditure Estimates for the Financial Year 2024/2025', Government of Singapore, 16 February 2024, p. 63, https://www.mof.gov.sg/docs/librariesprovider3/budget2024/download/pdf/25-mindef-2024.pdf.

26 *Ibid.*, p. 63.

27 Constitution of the Republic of Indonesia, 'Nomor 16 Tahun 2012 Tentang Industri Pertahanan' [Law no. 16 of 2012: law on defense industry], 2012, https://www.kemhan.go.id/itjen/wp-content/uploads/migrasi/peraturan/UU0162012.pdf. There are recent ministerial regulations potentially revising those offset benchmarks.

28 Kerajaan Malaysia, 'Dasar dan Garis Panduan Program Kolaborasi Industri (Industrial Collaboration Programme – ICP) Dalam Perolehan Kerajaan' [Policies and guidelines for the industrial collaboration program (ICP) in government procurement], Malay Treasury, 2014, www.tda.my/wp-content/uploads/2022/07/PEKELILING-BAHARU-PK-1.7-DASAR-DAN-GARIS-PANDUAN-PROGRAM-KOLABORASI-INDUSTRI-INDUSTRIAL-COLLABORATION-PROGRAMME-ICP-DALAM-PEROLEHAN-KERAJAAN.pdf.

29 'Malaysia Tender Offset Policy', International Trade Administration, 25 June 2024, https://

www.trade.gov/market-intelligence/malaysia-tender-offset-policy#:~:text=The%20Industrial%20Collaboration%20Program%20(ICP,local%20economy%20and%20employment%20opportunities.

30 Office of the President of the Philippines, 'Speech by President Ferdinand R. Marcos Jr. at the Ceremonial Signing of the Self-Reliant Defense Posture Revitalization Act', 8 October 2024, https://pco.gov.ph/presidential-speech/speech-by-president-ferdinand-r-marcos-jr-at-the-ceremonial-signing-of-the-self-reliant-defense-posture-revitalization-act/; and Philippines Government Procurement Policy Board, 'Presidential Decree No. 415 March 19, 1974 Authorizing the Secretary of National Defense to Enter Into Defense Contracts to Implement Projects Under the Self-Reliant Defense Programs and for Other Purposes', https://www.gppb.gov.ph/wp-content/uploads/2023/06/Presidential-Decree-No.-415.pdf.

31 Thailand Ministry of Defence, 'นายสุทิน คลังแสง รมว.กห. เป็นประธานเปิดการหารือด้านอุตสาหกรรมป้องกันประเทศระหว่าง ไทย – สาธารณรัฐฝร' [Mr Sutin Khlangsaeng, minister of defence, presided over the opening of the defense industry discussion between Thailand and the Republic of France], 8 July 2024, https://mod.go.th/Image-Gallery/14060.aspx.

32 Vanguard, 'สทป.ร่วมกาญจนบุรีเปิดรับฟังความคิดเห็น'โครงการนิคมอุตสาหกรรม ดีทีไอ ครั้งที่ 2' [The TPA and Kanchanaburi jointly hold a public hearing on the 2nd DTI Industrial Estate Project], 30 October 2024, https://www.naewna.com/local/838298.

33 MINDEF Singapore, 'Defence Procurement', 20 January 2024, https://www.mindef.gov.sg/defence-matters/mindef-policies/defence-procurement.

34 PT Dirgantara Indonesia (Persero), 'NC212 Family', 20 January 2024, http://www.dirgantara-indonesia.com/aircraft/detail/12_nc212+family.html.

35 IISS, Military Balance+, accessed 3 February 2025, https://milbalplus.iiss.org/.

36 PT Dirgantara Indonesia (Persero), 'CN235 Family', 20 January 2024, http://www.dirgantara-indonesia.com/aircraft/detail/1_cn235+family.html.

37 Ibid.

38 Ibid.

39 Airbus, 'Indonesian Air Force Orders Four Airbus H145 Helicopters', 18 September 2024, https://www.airbus.com/en/newsroom/press-releases/2024-09-indonesian-air-force-orders-four-airbus-h145-helicopters.

40 PT Dirgantara Indonesia (Persero), 'Superpuma Family', 20 January 2024, http://www.dirgantara-indonesia.com/aircraft/detail/13_superpuma+family.html.

41 Airbus, 'Indonesian Air Force Places Order for Eight Additional H225Ms', 10 January 2019, https://www.airbus.com/en/newsroom/press-releases/2019-01-indonesian-air-force-places-order-for-eight-additional-h225ms; and Airbus, 'Indonesian Air Force Orders Four Airbus H145 Helicopters'.

42 Airbus, 'Indonesian Air Force Places Order for Eight Additional H225Ms'.

43 Airbus, 'Airbus Helicopters Delivers First Three AS565 MBe Panther to Indonesia', 21 November 2016, https://www.airbus.com/en/newsroom/press-releases/2016-11-airbus-helicopters-delivers-first-three-as565-mbe-panther-to.

44 Airbus, 'Indonesian Air Force Orders Four Airbus H145 Helicopters'.

45 Airbus Helicopters, 'PT Dirgantara Indonesia and Airbus Helicopters to Jointly Develop Local Support and Services Capabilities for Indonesia', 12 February 2014, https://www.airbushelicopters.com/website/en/press/PT-Dirgantara-Indonesia-and-Airbus-Helicopters-to-jointly-develop-local-support-and-services-capabilities-for-Indonesia_1394.html.

46 Airbus, 'Indonesian Air Force Orders Four Airbus H145 Helicopters'; PT Dirgantara Indonesia (Persero), 'PTDI and Airbus Sign Agreement to Expand Partnership in MRO of Helicopters and Military Aircraft', 2 November 2022, https://www.indonesian-aerospace.com/en/media/press_release/detail/228/ptdi-and-airbus-sign-agreement-to-expand-partnership-in-mro-of-helicopters-and-military-aircraft.

47 PT Dirgantara Indonesia (Persero), 'PTDI and Boeing Sign Strategic Agreement Strengthening Defense, Aerospace Capabilities for Indonesia', 4 November 2022, https://www.indonesian-aerospace.com/en/media/press_release/detail/236/ptdi-and-boeing-sign-strategic-agreement-strengthening-defense-aerospace-capabilities-for-indonesia.

48 PT Dirgantara Indonesia (Persero), 'PTDI and Boeing Sign Strategic Agreement Strengthening Defense, Aerospace Capabilities for Indonesia'; PT Dirgantara Indonesia (Persero), 'Sikorsky

Signs MOU with PT Dirgantara Indonesia', 4 November 2022, https://www.indonesian-aerospace.com/en/media/press_release/detail/237/sikorsky-signs-mou-with-pt-dirgantara-indonesia; and PT Dirgantara Indonesia (Persero), 'PTDI and Turkish Aerospace Sign Frame Work Agreement on Aerospace Engineering Programs', 3 November 2022, https://www.indonesian-aerospace.com/en/media/press_release/detail/229/ptdi-and-turkish-aerospace-sign-frame-work-agreement-on-aerospace-engineering-programs.

[49] Evan A. Laksmana, 'What Indonesia's Retail Approach to Defence Modernisation Means', IISS Military Balance blog, 18 September 2023, https://www.iiss.org/online-analysis/military-balance/2023/09/what-indonesias-retail-approach-to-defence-modernisation-means/.

[50] For example, the D-8: 'Brief History of D-8', D-8 Organization for Economic Cooperation, 30 January 2025, https://developing8.org/about-d-8/brief-history-of-d-8/.

[51] United Defense, '2001 Annual Report: Changing the Future of Defense', 15 April 2002, p. 10, https://www.sec.gov/Archives/edgar/vprr/0202/02024736.pdf.

[52] Defence Services Sdn Bhd, 'Trusted Name in Defence Industry with Proven Track Record', 30 January 2025, http://dssb.com.my/; and Bursa Malaysia, 'Agreements with the Government of Malaysia ("Gom") in Relation to the Military Land-based Vehicles for the Malaysian Army; and Memorandum of Understanding Between Drb-Hicom Defence Technologies Sdn Bhd ("Deftech"), A Wholly-owned Subsidiary of Drb-Hicom Berhad ("Drb-Hicom") and the Government of the Democratic Republic of Timor-Leste', 21 April 2008, https://www.bursamalaysia.com/market_information/announcements/company_announcement/announcement_details?ann_id=204532.

[53] Bursa Malaysia, 'DRB-HICOM BERHAD ("DRB-HICOM" or "COMPANY") Acceptance of Letter of Award ("Loa") from the Government of Malaysia to Drb-Hicom Defence Technologies Sdn Bhd ("Deftech") in Relation to the Manufacture, Supply and Delivery of Armoured Wheeled Vehicles', 23 February 2011, https://www.bursamalaysia.com/market_information/announcements/company_announcement/announcement_details?ann_id=144091.

[54] 'Deftech Expands Plants for AV8', The Star, 20 April 2012, https://www.thestar.com.my/business/business-news/2012/04/20/deftech-expands-plants-for-av8/.

[55] Denel, 'Denel Group Integrated Report Twenty 15/16', 2016, p. 137, http://admin.denel.co.za/uploads/103c0d0f0a51f5d9f4eeb929f3f35f22.pdf; DRB-HICOM, 'DRB-HICOM Annual Report 2021', 29 April 2022, p. 104, https://disclosure.bursamalaysia.com/FileAccess/apbursaweb/download?id=216276&name=EA_DS_ATTACHMENTS; and Kamarul Azhar, 'Cover Story: Secrecy and Complexity of Defence Procurements Provide Perfect Cover for Corruption', The Edge Malaysia, 8 September 2022, https://theedgemalaysia.com/article/cover-story-secrecy-and-complexity-defence-procurements-provide-perfect-cover-corruption.

[56] 'FNSS Completed the Serial Production; KAPLAN MT Medium Tank Platforms Are on Their Way to Indonesia', FNSS, 15 March 2022, https://www.fnss.com.tr/en/media/news/fnss-completed-serial-production-kaplan-mt-medium-tank-platforms-are-their-way-indonesia-1430.

[57] 'Presiden Menyaksikan Penyerahan 52 Unit Ranpur Pindad di Rapim TNI Polri 2024' [President witnessed the handover of 52 Ranpur Pindad units at the 2024 TNI Police Meeting], Pindad, 28 February 2024, https://pindad.com/presiden-menyaksikan-penyerahan-52-unit-ranpur-pindad-di-rapim-tni-polri-2024; and 'Wamenhan Serahkan Alpalhankam Pindad Ke Panglima TNI pada HUT ke-79 TNI' [Deputy minister of defence submits Alpalhankam Pindad to the TNI commander on the 79th anniversary of the TNI], Pindad, 3 October 2024, https://pindad.com/wamenhan-serahkan-alpalhankam-pindad-ke-panglima-tni-pada-hut-ke79-tni.

[58] 'FNSS Showcases the Newest Member of the Tracked Vehicle Family, KAPLAN APC's Conceptual Design; Joint Development and Production Program with PT PINDAD', FNSS, 22 October 2024, https://www.fnss.com.tr/en/media/news/fnss-showcases-newest-member-tracked-vehicle-family-kaplan-apcs-conceptual-design-joint-development-and-production-program-pt-pindad.

[59] Transcript of Malaysian Parliament meeting, 22 October 2009, p. 6, https://www.parlimen.gov.my/files/hindex/pdf/dr-22102009.pdf.

[60] See 'International Presence', Naval Group, 30 January 2025, https://www.naval-group.com/en/international-presence.

61 'Chronology of Scorpene Scandal', *New Straits Times*, 27 July 2024, https://www.nst.com.my/news/nation/2024/07/1082506/chronology-scorpene-scandal; and Ilah Hafiz Aziz, 'MACC Reopens Investigation into Scorpene, Discovers New Clues', *New Straits Times*, 26 July 2024, https://www.nst.com.my/news/nation/2024/07/1082210/macc-reopens-investigation-scorpene-discovers-new-clues.

62 'Menyahklasifikasi Laporan Pengauditan Audit Forensik Berkaitan Review of the LCS Programme' [Declassifying forensic audit reports related to the review of the LCS programme], Malaysian Parliament, 22 August 2022, p. 5, https://www.parlimen.gov.my/pac/review/docs-257-319.pdf.

63 Marhalim Abas, 'BHIC, BNS and Directors Sued', Malaysian Defence, 5 October 2022, https://www.malaysiandefence.com/bhic-bns-and-directors-sued/.

64 Naval Group, 'Financial Report 2020', 11 June 2021, p. 10, https://web.archive.org/web/20210919214759/https://www.naval-group.com/sites/default/files/2021-05/Financial%20Report%20Naval%20Group%202020%20EN.pdf; and 'MACC Chief: Probe into LCS Construction Never Stopped', *Malay Mail*, 25 April 2024, https://www.malaymail.com/news/malaysia/2024/04/25/macc-chief-probe-into-lcs-construction-never-stopped/130770.

65 Malaysian Parliament, 'Laporan Jawatankuasa Kira-Kira Wang Negara (Pac)' [Report of the parliamentary audit committee], September 2023, p. 9, https://www.parlimen.gov.my/pac/review/docs-271-333.pdf.

66 See 'RMN Fleet Transformation Programme #15TO5', presentation by Admiral Ahmad Kamarulzaman, 30 January 2025, https://navy.mil.my/images/widgetkit/Penerbitan/Maklumat%20Am/RMN%20Fleet%20Transformation%20Programme%2015%20to%205.pdf.

67 Sascha Bruchmann and Albert Vidal Ribe, 'The Gulf Cooperation Council States' Uninhabited and Autonomous Capabilities', IISS Online Analysis, 28 November 2024, https://www.iiss.org/online-analysis/online-analysis/2024/11/the-gulf-cooperation-council-states-uninhabited-and-autonomous-capabilities/.

68 'India & Gulf Region: First Ever Tie Up Between BEL and Saudi Company for Defence Technologies', Bharat Electronics Limited, 22 December 2021, https://bel-india.in/news-bel/india-gulf-region-first-ever-tie-up-between-bel-and-saudi-company-for-defence-technologies/.

69 'ACES Signed Strategic Agreement with CETC to Do Knowledge Transfer and Local Manufacture of Drones Payload Systems in KSA', Aerial Solutions, 3 March 2022, https://aerial-solutions.com/aces-signed-strategic-agreement-with-cetc-to-do-knowledge-transfer-and-local-manufacture-of-drones-payload-systems-in-ksa/.

70 Kim Eun-jung, 'S. Korea, Saudi Arabia Agree to Expand Defense Industry Cooperation', Yonhap News Agency, 5 February 2024, https://en.yna.co.kr/view/AEN20240205003100315.

71 'SAMI Announces Signing of MoA with Hanwha for Joint Venture Company in Saudi Arabia', Saudi Press Agency, 27 October 2019, https://www.spa.gov.sa/1939862.

72 'EDGE and Adani Defence & Aerospace Sign Landmark Cooperation Agreement in Defence & Security', EDGE, 11 June 2024, https://edgegroup.ae/news/edge-and-adani-defence-aerospace-sign-landmark-cooperation-agreement-defence-security.

73 'EDGE Signs MoU with HAL to Explore Business Cooperation', EDGE, 21 February 2023, https://edgegroup.ae/news/edge-signs-mou-hal-explore-business-cooperation.

74 Ji Da-gyum, 'S. Korea, UAE Agree to Forge Strategic Defense Industry Cooperation', *Korea Herald*, 16 January 2023, https://www.koreaherald.com/article/3041092.

75 *Ibid.*

76 'EDGE Group Company, CARACAL, Signs Agreement with Malaysia-based Ketech Asia at LIMA 2023' EDGE, 24 May 2023, https://edgegroup.ae/news/edge-group-company-caracal-signs-agreement-malaysia-based-ketech-asia-lima-2023; and 'EDGE Entity Al Tariq Signs MoU with Bharat Dynamics', EDR On-Line, 17 February 2023, https://www.edrmagazine.eu/edge-entity-al-tariq-signs-mou-with-bharat-dynamics.

77 'EDGE Entity ADSB and Sagar Defence Engineering to Explore Co-Creation of 12 Metre Vessels in India', EDGE, 23 February 2023, https://edgegroup.ae/news/edge-entity-adsb-and-sagar-defence-engineering-explore-co-creation-12-metre-vessels-india; and 'EDGE Group's LAHAB Signs MoU with Indonesia's DAHANA at Indo Defence 2022', EDGE, 5 December 2022, https://edgegroup.ae/news/

edge-groups-lahab-signs-mou-indonesias-dahana-indo-defence-2022.

78 Stephen Kalin, 'Arms Megadeal Collapsed When China, Russia Links Emerged', *Wall Street Journal*, 15 September 2023, https://www.wsj.com/politics/national-security/a-saudi-defense-contractor-courted-russia-and-china-then-its-u-s-business-partners-fled-962527ad.

79 'Saudi Arabia Will License-produce Chinese Armed Drones', Reuters, 5 October 2017, https://www.reuters.com/article/us-saudi-russia-missiles/saudi-arabia-agrees-to-buy-russian-s-400-air-defense-system-arabiya-tv-idUSKBN1CA1OD//; and Jill Aitoro, 'Russia's Rostec to Co-develop 5th-gen Fighter with UAE', DefenseNews, 20 February 2017, https://www.defensenews.com/digital-show-dailies/idex/2017/02/20/russia-s-rostec-to-co-develop-5th-gen-fighter-with-uae/.

80 'Saudi Arabia Will License-produce Chinese Armed Drones', Quwa, 24 March 2017, https://quwa.org/daily-news/saudi-arabia-will-license-produce-chinese-armed-drones/.

81 'BrahMos', CSIS Missile Defence Project, 23 April 2024, https://missilethreat.csis.org/missile/BrahMos/.

82 Petr Topychkanov, 'The BrahMos Is Just Beginning', Carnegie Endowment for International Peace, 3 July 2015, https://carnegieendowment.org/posts/2015/07/the-brahMos-is-just-beginning?lang=en.

83 'First Ever Vertical Launch of BrahMos Missile from Moving Warship', BrahMos Aerospace, 18 December 2008, https://brahmos.com/newscenter.php?newsid=62.

84 'Air Launched Weapons System', BrahMos Aerospace, https://www.brahmos.com/content.php?id=19.

85 Rajat Pandit, 'Eye on China, South Gets 1st Sukhoi Squad with BrahMos', *Times of India*, 20 June 2020, https://timesofindia.indiatimes.com/india/eye-on-china-south-gets-1st-sukhoi-squad-with-brahmos/articleshow/73400569.cms.

86 Viraj Solanki, 'India's Increased Defence and Security Engagement with Southeast Asia', IISS Online Analysis, 1 May 2024, https://www.iiss.org/online-analysis/online-analysis/2024/04/indias-increased-defence-and-security-engagement-with-southeast-asia/.

87 Matt Bassford et al., 'Sustaining Key Skills in the UK Military Aircraft Industry', RAND Europe, 31 January 2011, p. xxii, https://www.rand.org/pubs/research briefs/RB9545.html.

88 Douglas Barrie and Ben Thornley, 'Waiting in the Wings: The Asia-Pacific Air-to-air Challenge', in IISS, *Asia-Pacific Regional Security Assessment 2024* (Routledge for the IISS, 2024), pp. 124–38, https://www.iiss.org/publications/strategic-dossiers/asia-pacific-regional-security-assessment-2024/chapter-6/.

89 Akhil Kadidal, 'Update: Two Chinese Stealth Aircraft Programmes Emerge Unexpectedly', Janes Defence Weekly, 30 December 2024, https://customer.janes.com/display/BSP_82811-JDW.

90 Douglas Barrie, Karl Dewey and Fenella McGerty, '*Tempest*: Build, Buy, or Good-bye?', IISS research paper, 20 September 2024, p. 10, https://www.iiss.org/research-paper/2024/09/tempest-build-buy-or-good-bye/.

91 UK Ministry of Defence, 'Defence Industrial Strategy, Defence White Paper', December 2005, p. 84, https://www.gov.uk/government/publications/defence-industrial-strategy-defence-white-paper.

92 Douglas Barrie, 'Japan's Fighter Choice: A Repeat Order with Added Sides?', IISS Military Balance blog, 25 January 2021, https://www.iiss.org/online-analysis/military-balance/2021/01/japan-f-x-programme/.

93 UK Ministry of Defence, 'Britain to Take Leading Role in Next-generation Air Power, as Defence Secretary Launches Combat Air Strategy', 16 July 2018, https://www.gov.uk/government/news/britain-to-take-leading-role-in-next-generation-air-power-as-defence-secretary-launches-combat-air-strategy#:~:text=Setting%20out%20Britain's%20determination%20to,for%20future%20British%20air%20power.

94 Gareth Jennings, 'Analysis: UK's Post-Brexit Ambitions for Defence Aviation in Jeopardy', Janes Defence Weekly, 9 March 2018, https://customer.janes.com/display/FG_777884-JDW.

95 Douglas Barrie, 'Berlin Looks to Build Future Combat Aircraft System Consortium', IISS Military Balance blog, 19 June 2017, https://www.iiss.org/online-analysis/military-balance/2017/06/berlin/.

96 Fabrice Wolf, 'What Are the Chances of SCAF and MGCS Reaching Their Conclusion?', META-DEFFENSE.FR, 17 October 2024, https://meta-defense.fr/en/2024/10/17/scaf-megcs-peuvent-ils-arriver-a-termes/.

97 'Japan, Britain to Launch Joint Missile Research', AFP, 17 July 2014, https://sg.news.yahoo.com/japan-britain-launch-joint-missile-research-report-052535721.html.

98 UK Ministry of Defence, 'First Ever UK–Japan Foreign and Defence Ministers Meeting', 21 January 2015, https://www.gov.uk/government/news/first-ever-uk-japan-foreign-and-defence-ministers-meeting.

99 Jon Grevatt, 'Japan Nears End of X-2 Fighter Trials', Janes Defence Weekly, 6 December 2017, https://customer.janes.com/display/FG_694582-JDW.

100 Barrie, 'Japan's Fighter Choice: A Repeat Order with Added Sides?'.

101 UK Ministry of Defence, 'Joint Statement from Prime Ministers of UK, Italy and Japan: 9 December 2022', 9 December 2022, https://www.gov.uk/government/publications/joint-leaders-statement-uk-italy-japan-9-december-2022/joint-statement-from-prime-ministers-of-uk-italy-and-japan-9-december-2022.

102 Sebastian Sprenger, 'France, Germany Kick Off Race for "Quantum Leaps" in Aircraft and Tank Tech', DefenseNews, 19 June 2018, https://www.defensenews.com/global/europe/2018/06/19/france-germany-kick-off-race-for-quantum-leaps-in-aircraft-and-tank-tech/.

103 UK Ministry of Defence, 'Italy Partners with the UK on Tempest', 11 September 2019, https://www.gov.uk/government/news/italy-partners-with-the-uk-on-tempest.

104 Defence Industry Europe, 'Israeli Defence Industry Showcases Advanced Technologies at ADAS 2024 in the Philippines', 27 September 2024, https://defence-industry.eu/israeli-defence-industry-showcases-advanced-technologies-at-adas-2024-in-the-philippines/; Evan Laksmana and Max Broad, 'South Korea's Defence Relations in Southeast Asia', IISS Online Analysis, 29 September 2023, https://www.iiss.org/online-analysis/online-analysis/2023/09/south-koreas-defence-relations-in-southeast-asia/; and Jumpei Ishimaru, 'Japan's Foreign Assistance to the Philippines: Supporting Regional Security', IISS Online Analysis, 17 December 2024, https://www.iiss.org/online-analysis/online-analysis/2024/12/japans-foreign-assistance-to-the-philippines-supporting-regional-security/.

105 Tim Martin, 'GCAP Partners Form Joint Venture to Deliver Next-gen Fighter for UK, Japan and Italy', Breaking Defense, 13 December 2024, https://breakingdefense.com/2024/12/gcap-partners-form-joint-venture-to-deliver-next-gen-fighter-for-uk-japan-and-italy/.

CHAPTER 2

SIX QUESTIONS: TRUMP AND INTERNATIONAL SECURITY

This chapter seeks to answer six major questions on the extent to which President Donald Trump's second administration could reshape the international security landscape.

US President Donald Trump reviews the troops during his inauguration ceremony in Washington DC, 20 January 2025 (Greg Nash/Pool/AFP via Getty Images)

ARGUMENTS AND FINDINGS:

- The second Trump administration has come out of the gate swinging on major foreign-policy issues – from tariffs to peace deals in Europe and the Middle East.
- Trump's personal predispositions and personnel appointments may be important drivers of his foreign-policy execution, but the United States ultimately needs to wrestle with deeper-rooted structural issues in the international security landscape, including alliances and security orders in Europe and the Asia-Pacific.
- Across different regions, strategic policymakers and stakeholders may be rethinking their policies on strategic autonomy if they can no longer expect a consistent American leadership across the board.

IMPLICATIONS FOR REGIONAL SECURITY:

- How Trump's second term redefines major security questions – and how effectively his team addresses them – will have long-term consequences for regional and global security.
- If regional policymakers doubt American staying power and leadership across the board, the management of security flashpoints may be harder given that regional powers may not have the wherewithal to replace the United States' military preponderance.

The return of Trump for a second term in the White House has raised the level of anxiety among regional and global policymakers and stakeholders. The early indications suggest the Asia-Pacific is the arena the Trump team will prioritise. What the US chooses to do there will have significant consequences beyond the region. But any serious attempt to focus on China and the Asia-Pacific would be hamstrung by any lack of sustainable resolution over the war in Ukraine. The administration's focus as of March 2025 therefore has been on hammering out a Ukraine–Russia deal. But how the US pushes that deal forward will have significant implications not just for the European security order but also the strategic capital and credibility of the administration in other parts of the world, from the Middle East, South Asia to Northeast Asia.

Furthermore, the use of what perhaps can be described as coercive economic statecraft by Washington, whether through tariffs on some imported goods, or pushing for port control changes in Panama and access to rare earth minerals in Ukraine, will raise further questions regarding the international economic-security order as well. Trump's role in the Israeli–Palestinian conflict moving forward will also be an important litmus test for many across the Middle East and beyond. Some Asia-Pacific countries like Indonesia and Malaysia might even see that role as a litmus test on whether they can publicly work with the Trump administration, given how the conflict has strongly resonated in these countries.

While Association of Southeast Nations (ASEAN) member states may be sceptical of Trump's commitment to the grouping and the region, the Quad could play a more central role in the broader Asia-Pacific regional security architecture moving forward. How Washington seeks to perhaps re-energise the Quad is therefore an important question, even if the other three members – Australia, India and Japan – may have other pressing foreign-policy priorities than the Quad. The six questions below, answered by IISS experts in late March 2025, in any case underscores the depth of the structural issues and challenges confronting American foreign policy under a second Trump administration.

WILL TRUMP PRIORITISE FOREIGN OVER DOMESTIC POLICY?

On 2 September 1987, a 41-year-old real-estate developer paid more than a quarter of a million dollars to publish a full-page open letter in three American newspapers, the *New York Times*, the *Washington Post* and the *Boston Globe*.[1] Under the headline 'There's nothing wrong with America's Foreign Defense Policy that a little backbone can't cure', the letter argued that 'Japan and other nations have been taking advantage of the United States' and that the US should stop paying for their defence. The author, Donald Trump, had updated his voter registration and joined the Republican Party only two months earlier, days before travelling to Moscow to meet Soviet leader Mikhail Gorbachev to discuss a hotel project and, apparently, the issue of nuclear disarmament.[2]

Mikhail Gorbachev, then-secretary of state George Shultz, Trump and his then-wife Ivana Trump attend an event in Washington DC, 9 December 1987

(Guy DeLort/WWD/Penske Media via Getty Images)

At that stage Trump was widely expected to challenge then-vice president George H. W. Bush in the 1988 Republican presidential primary, but he did not. He changed his party registration five times between 1999 and 2012, seemingly always with an eye on the election calendar.[3] When he finally did throw his hat into the ring, joining the Republican presidential primary in 2015, reporters tallied his past positions and realised he had taken contradictory stances on nearly every major domestic policy issue: tax rates, healthcare reform, abortion and gun control.[4] A conservative policy expert characterised Trump's views as 'a total random assortment of whatever plays publicly'.[5]

On foreign policy, however, Trump's views have remained remarkably constant. As in 1987, Trump is a critic of American defence alliances, particularly with wealthy countries that in his view can afford to defend themselves. Now, as then, he sees American foreign relations predominantly through the lens of international trade balances, not in terms of security and defence. This explains his willingness to criticise NATO member countries and allies in Asia, including Japan and South Korea, based on their trade relations with the US. In this view, countries that run trade surpluses are strong and those with trade deficits are weak.

Trump entered office for a second time feeling emboldened, having overcome two impeachments, multiple criminal prosecutions and intense media scepticism. His election victory was by a wider margin than in 2016 and there was a sense at his inauguration that cultural debates and the national mood had shifted in his favour.[6]

The Trump administration will have major opportunities to influence domestic policy, but notably, the president's top priorities – immigration, tariffs, increasing energy exports and implementing a cultural reformation within the federal government – all have foreign-policy implications (see Figure 2.1). For example, US foreign aid was decimated soon after Trump took office, falling victim to the administration's desire both to shrink the government and align its activities with the values of the Republican Party. In terms of legislation, Republicans are expected to have complete control of Congress – supported by a sympathetic majority on the Supreme Court – in 2025 and 2026. Congressional majorities are slim, however, and each house is managed by an untested leader. Significant intra-party disagreements – including on taxes, entitlements, welfare, abortion and healthcare – cast

Figure 2.1: **Trump's executive orders by policy focus, 20 Jan–20 Feb 2025**

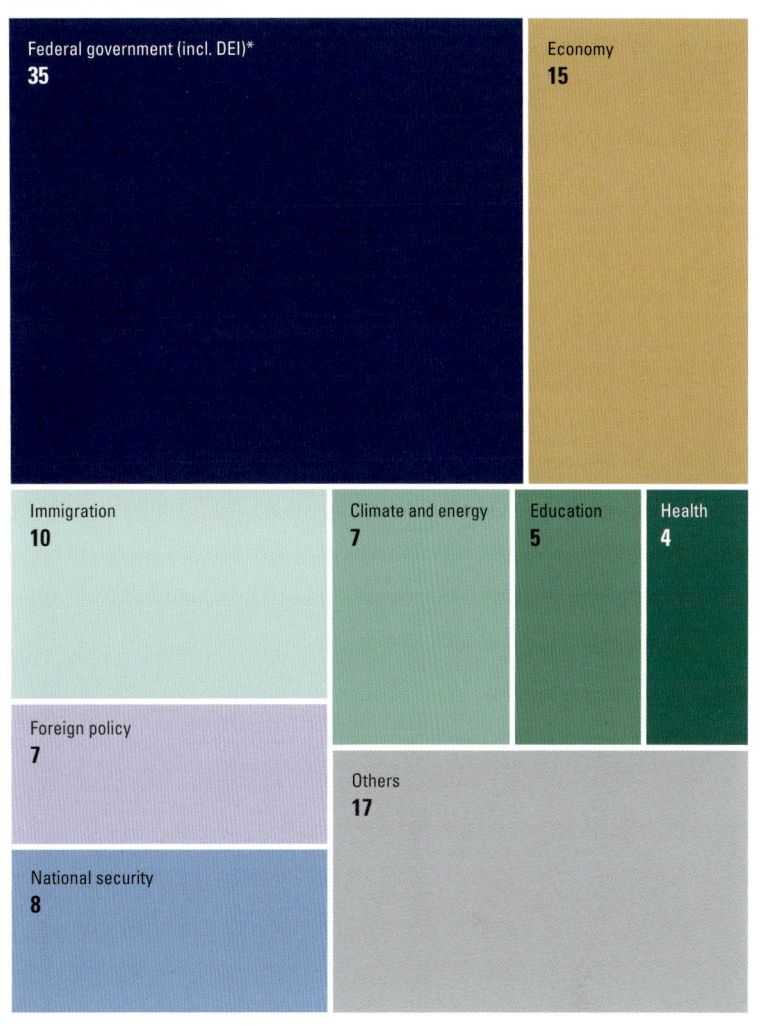

Federal government (incl. DEI)*	35
Economy	15
Immigration	10
Climate and energy	7
Education	5
Health	4
Foreign policy	7
Others	17
National security	8

©IISS

*Issues related to diversity, equity and inclusion.

Note: Data retrieved on 20 February 2025. Executive orders counted do not include nominations sent to the Senate, or pardons/grants of clemency, except when they were issued by proclamation.

Source: CNN

further doubt over the legislative victories that are obtainable before mid-term elections empower a new Congress in January 2027.

Trump's ability to act unilaterally in foreign policy suits his temperament – more so than, for example, brokering legislative compromises on domestic-policy issues. On the world stage he can receive tributes from supplicants, punish opponents, seek out leverage to use in negotiations and, most fundamentally, reform American foreign policy in ways he has been imagining for 40 years.

It is unclear whether Trump will think in terms of defining a legacy, given that he will presumably leave office in January 2029 due to constitutionally defined term limits. But he is focused on expanding the powers of the presidency and using them to reshape America's role in the world. By 1987, Trump thought that the time had come for the US to abandon its role as beneficent underwriter of a liberal and rules-based order stabilised by increasingly free trade. His early moves in 2025 have followed from this idea, with Washington pivoting sharply towards mercantilism and away from transatlantic allies, particularly regarding the defence of Ukraine. He has also expressed a preference for addressing major global challenges – including nuclear stability – on a bilateral basis involving China, or trilaterally involving China and Russia.

CAN TRUMP'S TARIFFS RESHAPE THE REGIONAL ECONOMIC-SECURITY ORDER?

Trump's economic agenda seems similar to that of his first term, not least in his preference for deploying tariffs to address the United States' chronic deficits in goods trade with the rest of the world. There is no doubt that the US now views those deficits as problematic. Particularly egregious, in Trump's view, is the trade imbalance with China, which ran up an aggregate goods-trade surplus of nearly USD1trillion in 2024.[7] But several other countries – including Germany, Japan, Mexico, South Korea and ASEAN member states – also have large trade surpluses with the US. The recent strength of the US dollar has further aggravated these imbalances. In real effective terms the US currency is now nearly as strong as it was in the early 1980s, when protectionist sentiment and concerns about the hollowing-out of domestic industry in the US was also increasing.[8]

Supporters of tariffs cite the measures initiated in the 1890s by William McKinley (president from 1897–1901), who was known as the 'Napoleon of protection' and one of Trump's favourites among his predecessors.[9] The McKinley Tariff of 1890 was designed to support US industries against competition from the British Empire and Germany.[10] The development of the US tinplate sector at the time was seen by tariff supporters as a good example of how tariffs can have a positive impact, although economists remain divided on the exact nature of the impact.[11] But for tariffs to bring benefits for the US today, they would at least need to be strategically targeted, accompanied by effective domestic industrial policies and buoyed by a weakening of the US dollar.

Trump poses with Southeast Asian leaders for a photo during the ASEAN–US Summit in Manila, 13 November 2017

(Manan Vatsyayana/AFP via Getty Images)

In their high-growth periods, China, Japan, South Korea and Taiwan showed how tariffs and industrial policy can interact effectively to support manufacturing expansion. But Trump is yet to clearly develop and articulate his broader industrial policy and expanding manufacturing would require a replay from the major economies (including China) of the 1985 Plaza Accord agreement between the then-G5 countries to allow their currencies to strengthen against the US dollar. But multilateral currency intervention looks highly unlikely today, not least given Sino-US political strains and the deflationary pressures in China, which a stronger renminbi would aggravate. There is also a risk of retaliation from countries targeted by US tariffs, as indeed happened in response to US protectionism of the 1890s.[12] Beijing has in recent years also been increasing the range of tools at its disposal to respond to economic coercion.[13]

In any case, Trump's tariffs and foreign economic policies will accelerate the reconfiguration of the global economy as countries and companies adjust to geopolitical headwinds, even if their impact on the US domestic economy is uncertain. This reordering had already started by the late 2010s and was perhaps further catalysed by economic-security policies towards China implemented during Joe Biden's presidency.[14] One example of this reconfiguration has been China's increased direct investment in ASEAN countries and India since the 2018 US–China trade war (see Figure 2.2). These investments sought to avoid US tariffs on direct exports from China while also deepening regional ties and building strategic resilience.

The ASEAN-initiated but now perhaps China-dominated Regional Comprehensive Economic Partnership mega trade bloc could provide a tailwind for deeper China–ASEAN economic integration, particularly around supply-chain reconfiguration. The substantial conclusion of the ASEAN-China Free Trade Area 3.0 upgrade negotiations in late 2024 could deepen those trends. Reports in early 2025 that some manufacturers may shift production to Southeast Asia from Mexico to avoid US tariffs also show how mobile modern supply chains could adapt to circumstances.[15]

Figure 2.2: **China and the US: economic footprint in Southeast Asia, 2019–23**

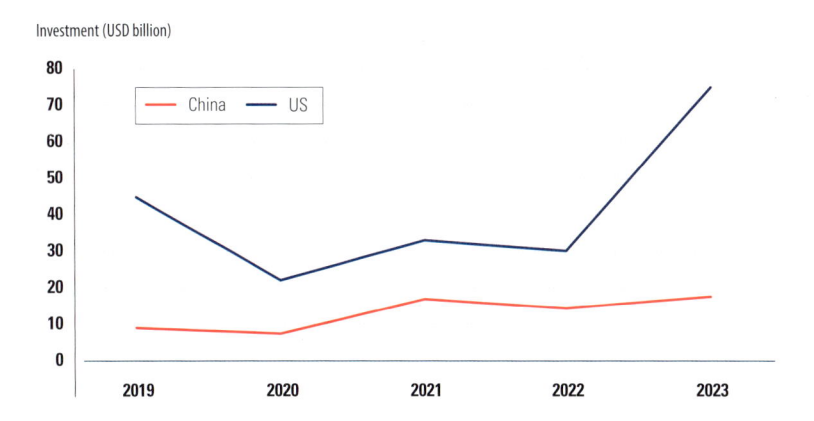

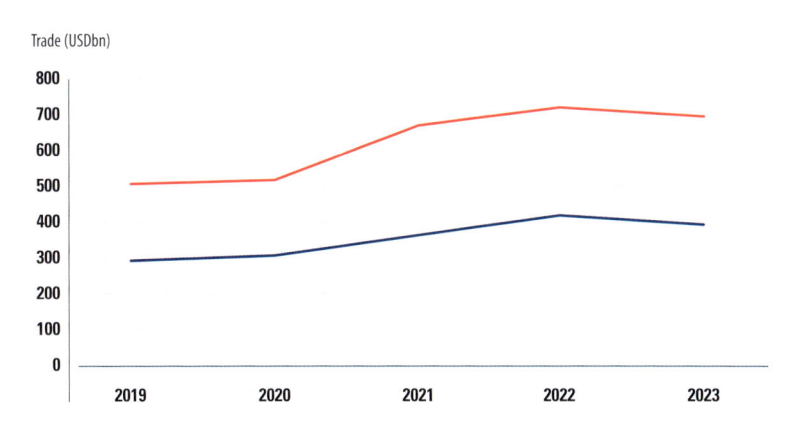

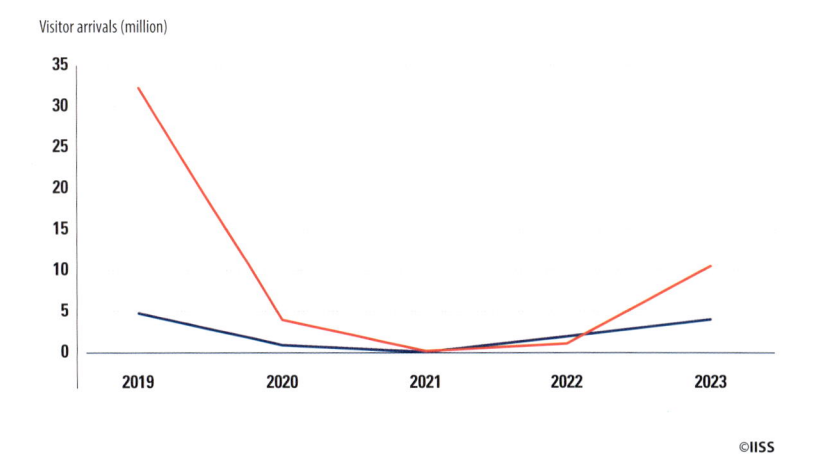

Source: ASEANstats

President of Ukraine Volodymyr Zelenskyy and US Special Envoy for Ukraine and Russia Keith Kellogg during their meeting in Kyiv, 20 February 2025

(Vitalii Nosach/Global Images Ukraine via Getty Images)

Japan and other regional countries hope that the US will one day join the Comprehensive and Progressive Agreement for Trans-Pacific Partnership (CPTPP) trade bloc, in which Japan and the UK are now the largest economies by a significant margin. But this trajectory now looks impossible given Trump's antipathy towards, and the bipartisan consensus against, trade multilateralism. Although a poor substitute for CPTPP membership, Biden's Indo-Pacific Economic Framework (IPEF) was at least a potential platform for American efforts at promoting economic governance, if not integration, in the region.

Given that Trump is almost certain to abandon the IPEF, and with the World Trade Organization increasingly moribund, the CPTPP, but particularly Japan, will shoulder a significant share of the burden of building economic governance and protecting the rules-based economic order in the region. China is also likely to step up its efforts to shape the region in its economic interests. The lack of an economic pillar had always been a weakness of the Biden administration's broader security strategy towards the Asia-Pacific, particularly given the increasing overlap between economics and national security. This strategic gap will only widen under the second Trump administration.

CAN TRUMP SECURE PEACE IN UKRAINE?

Trump's team had acknowledged before his inauguration that ending the war in Ukraine could not be accomplished very quickly. In January 2025 his special envoy to Ukraine and Russia, retired US Army lieutenant-general Keith Kellogg, suggested it would take '100 days' to get a deal to end the fighting, while National Security Advisor Mike Waltz said the president would establish ties 'in the coming months' that would lead to the end of the conflict.[16]

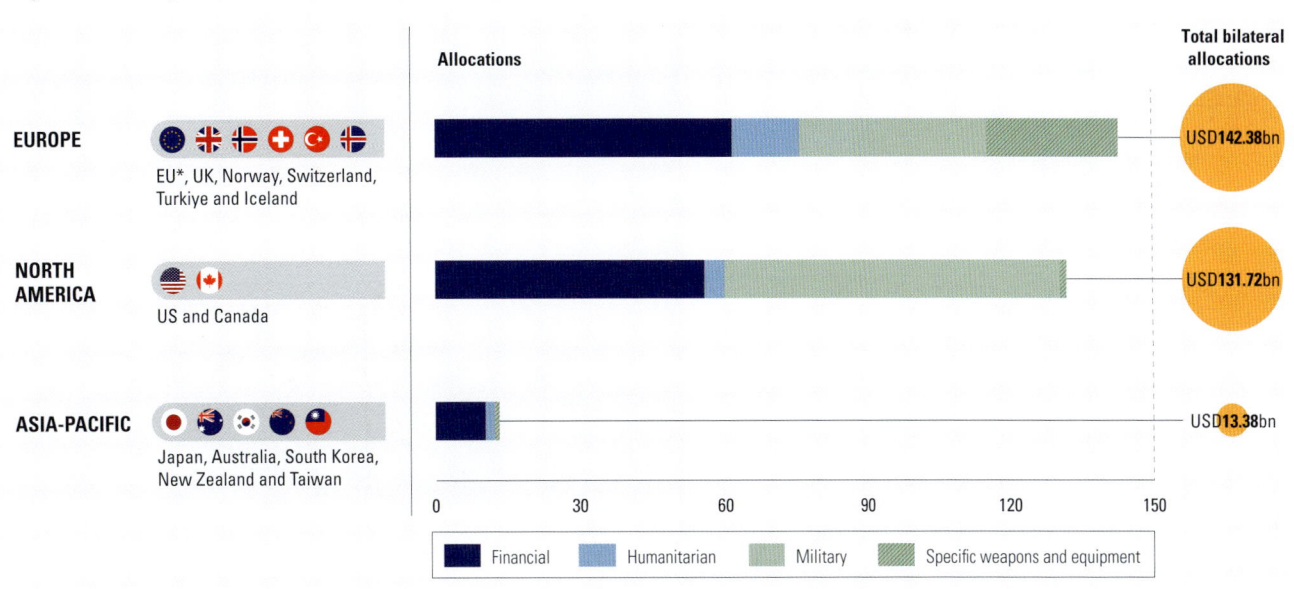

Figure 2.3: **European, North American and Asia-Pacific contributions to Ukraine since Russia's 2022 invasion (USDbn)**

Region	Countries	Total bilateral allocations
EUROPE	EU*, UK, Norway, Switzerland, Turkiye and Iceland	USD142.38bn
NORTH AMERICA	US and Canada	USD131.72bn
ASIA-PACIFIC	Japan, Australia, South Korea, New Zealand and Taiwan	USD13.38bn

Allocation categories: Financial, Humanitarian, Military, Specific weapons and equipment

*The European Union (Commission and Council), and its 27 member states. Note: Data includes bilateral contributions between 24 January 2022 and 31 December 2024.
Source: Ukraine Support Tracker, Kiel Institute for the World Economy
©IISS

In principle, this tacit acknowledgement of the challenges involved in ending Russia's protracted war against Ukraine was a good sign. It could have given the Trump administration the time to comprehensively assess the war aims and bargaining positions of both Kyiv and Moscow. It could also have enabled Trump to secure the support of European allies by aligning his strategy with their objectives. By February, however, Trump was laying the groundwork for negotiations between Russia and Ukraine without European partners.[17] Following a publicly covered tense White House meeting between President Volodymyr Zelenskyy, Trump and Vice President J.D. Vance in early March, European leaders rallied around Ukraine to find the best way to support its defensive efforts as American military aid hung in the balance (see Figure 2.3).

Nevertheless, if Trump plays his cards right, he might still manage to end the war and reach a ceasefire agreement. But to do so, he would need to negotiate from a position of strength (which he might think he could create by himself) and insist on a cessation of hostilities before beginning discussions with President Vladimir Putin; which he failed to do. He would also need to allow the Russian leader to save face by persuading Ukraine to accept a de facto, but not officially recognised, Russian occupation of parts of Ukrainian territory after the fighting had stopped.

He would also need to persuade European powers to commit forces to uphold peace in Ukraine as part of a credible security guarantee for the country. He could utilise NATO's military capabilities and the economic heft of the European Union (and others) to offer carrots and sticks to Putin and Zelenskyy. In mid-February 2025, however, Trump and his team declared that Ukrainian membership of NATO was unrealistic.[18]

In this context Trump could threaten Russia by intensifying military support for Ukraine and increasing production and exports of US oil and gas in order to drive down global energy prices. He could press Ukraine to accept a ceasefire in return for security guarantees. Instead, Trump sought to impose a deal on Ukraine's rare-earth minerals in exchange for the United States' much-needed military aid and humanitarian support.[19] And he could convince European allies that it is in their best interest to provide military and other forms of support to maintain the ceasefire arrangement, including by securing continued US commitment to Europe's defence.

However, as of late March 2025, major challenges limit Trump's chances of ending the war in a way that will be favourable both to Ukrainian and Western interests, let alone of securing lasting peace. A fundamental problem is that Russia's principal war aim remains unchanged: to eliminate Ukraine from the political map as an independent nation. And Putin has demonstrated his willingness to expend huge losses and enormous financial resources in pursuit of that objective.

NATO military forces during a static display after exercise *Steadfast Dart* at the Smardan Training Area in southeastern Romania near the border with Ukraine, 19 February 2025

(Daniel Mihailescu/AFP via Getty Images)

Another factor is that inside Russia, any compromise with Trump might be interpreted as a weakness on Putin's part. Indeed, the incentive for Putin to agree to a lasting ceasefire and to find a long-term political solution may have decreased precisely because of Trump's arrival and his goal of striking a quick deal. Furthermore, China's role in allowing Moscow to continue the war should not be underestimated. In mid-February, Beijing expressed the hope that 'all parties and stakeholders directly involved' in the war should also be part of any peace talks.[20]

Further challenges have been created by Trump's threats to withdraw defence commitments to European allies, his insistence that European forces would have to shoulder the burden of a potential peacekeeping or a peace-enforcement mission without the involvement of US troops, and his sympathy towards Russia's strong refusal to countenance Ukraine's future membership of NATO. All these positions undermine the transatlantic solidarity and burden-sharing required for a lasting ceasefire and political settlement. They also disregard the severe military-capacity limitations that European powers would face when it came to safeguarding a ceasefire agreement.[21]

Trump also faces another problem of his own making: the expectations among US voters and a Republican-controlled Congress about a speedy resolution and significant reduction of support for the Russia–Ukraine war. This could reduce his patience and levers for a comprehensive solution that meets American, Ukrainian and European interests, unless the administration and Trump's own party returns to the traditional US foreign- and defence-policy positions based on a firm US commitment and engagement in European security. In mid-February, the Republican Party seemed split on how to best support or respond to Trump's proclivities on the possible peace talks.[22] In any case, Trump's capacity to end the war and secure lasting peace in Ukraine will surely be tested and will require his ability to readjust some of his current positions.

CAN TRUMP BRING PEACE TO THE MIDDLE EAST?

On the campaign trail in 2024, Trump promised to bring peace to the Middle East, implying he would move swiftly to end the war between Israel and its Iranian-backed enemies Hamas, Hizbullah and Ansarullah (the Houthis). Trump's pressure on Israeli Prime Minister Benjamin Netanyahu and threat in December 2024 that there would be 'all hell to pay' if Hamas did not release the remaining hostages it was holding before he took office was a key factor in bringing about a ceasefire in mid-January 2025, a feat that the Biden administration had failed to accomplish for over a year.[23] But in the short-to-medium term, a lasting end to the regional conflict between Israel and the Iranian-backed groups may hinge on Trump's ability to both constrain Israel and deter Iran.

The Middle East was on the brink of an all-out war between Iran and Israel at least twice in 2024. On both occasions the onset of direct hostilities was prompted by Israeli attacks on Iranian soil. The first was the strike on Iran's consulate in Damascus on 1 April; the second was the assassination of Hamas leader Ismail Haniyeh in Tehran on 31 July, just hours after the inauguration of Iranian President Masoud Pezeshkian. On both occasions Iran responded by launching hundreds of missiles and uninhabited aerial vehicles (UAVs) indiscriminately against Israel.[24]

Trump needs to ensure that Israel abides by the terms of its ceasefire agreements in Lebanon and Gaza. Israel's numerous violations of the ceasefire agreement it concluded with Hizbullah in November 2024 – nearly 1,100 as of mid-March 2025 – risk unravelling the deal and reigniting the conflict in Lebanon.[25] Although severely degraded, Hamas may choose to abandon the ceasefire deal in Gaza if it perceives that Israel is violating its terms egregiously. After all, despite the immense military pressure it was under, Hamas managed to exercise strategic patience, by holding out for a ceasefire agreement that could eventually guaranteed its core demands, notably the full withdrawal of Israeli forces from Gaza and freedom of movement for its own personnel within the strip.

Meanwhile, an undeterred Iran that seeks to reconstitute its influence and its networks of non-state armed partners in Lebanon, Syria and Gaza would also prove highly destabilising.[26] The stunning fall of the Assad regime in December 2024 at the hands of Sunni rebel groups backed by Turkiye has dealt a massive blow to Iran's ability to resupply Hizbullah in neighbouring Lebanon. Intensified US strikes on Houthi targets in Yemen send a clear message of resolve as Trump raises the pressure on Iran and its partners while offering to negotiate with Tehran on its nuclear programme.

To deter Iran, Trump will probably need to demonstrate clear resolve. During his previous tenure he embarked on a 'maximum pressure' campaign against Tehran, including by seeking to drive down Iranian oil exports.[27] This time around,

A Zamyad pick-up truck carries an Iranian-made *Shahed* 136 UAV in downtown Tehran, 10 January 2025

(Hossein Beris/Middle East Images/AFP via Getty Images)

however, the success of a similar maximum-pressure move depends on whether Iran, in response to its recent setbacks, will choose to de-escalate or pursue the development of a nuclear weapon instead.

In any case, the long-term prospects of a lasting peace in the Middle East will hinge upon Trump's ability to work with the Palestinians, the Israelis and key Arab states to lay out a credible pathway towards a two-state solution. Trump's bizarre plan to depopulate and annex Gaza under US authority has sowed panic in the region, gutting hopes that the US under Trump would push to turn the ceasefire into a lasting peace. Although the Arab League has rejected the plan and rallied around an Egyptian counter-proposal for the reconstruction of Gaza, Trump's position may be interpreted by the extreme right in Israel as a sign of US approval for their designs to annex the West Bank.

CAN TRUMP WORK WITH INDIA TO REVITALISE THE QUAD?

In January 2025, in his new role as Trump's secretary of state, Marco Rubio's first group meeting was with the foreign ministers of the other three Quad countries. This provided reassurance to Australia, India and Japan that the Asia-Pacific would remain a priority for the new administration, following the pre-election rhetoric that implied a second Trump term would usher in a more isolationist foreign policy. The ensuing joint statement by the four Quad foreign ministers reaffirmed their 'shared commitment to strengthening a Free and Open Indo-Pacific where the rule of law, democratic values, sovereignty and territorial integrity are upheld and defended'.[28]

Significantly, the Quad foreign ministers' message to China, without naming it, was sharp: 'We also strongly oppose any unilateral actions that seek to change the status quo by force or coercion.'[29] This was in contrast to their previous joint statement, marking the 20th anniversary of the Quad on 31 December 2024, in which they had merely said they shared 'a vision of a free and open Indo-Pacific that is peaceful, stable, and prosperous, underpinned by effective regional institutions'.[30]

For India, which hosts the next Quad summit later this year, this change in language and tone suggests both opportunities and challenges. Over the past two decades the focus of the Quad has evolved from humanitarian assistance and disaster relief to fighting climate change, cancer and pandemics, while bolstering quality infrastructure, maritime-domain awareness (MDA) and counter-terrorism efforts.[31] At the 2024 summit they unveiled a 'Cancer Moonshot' and explored opportunities for shared investments in health and food security.

But if the Quad were to put increased emphasis on the security and defence elements of the arrangement, the grouping could facilitate India's acquisition of advanced military-related technology and maritime-security support from the US and help it counter Chinese presence, influence and impact in the Indian Ocean. New Delhi would likely welcome such a development at a time when China's military capabilities, including its fleet of warship, are fast expanding.

Such a move, however, could also lead to increased Chinese aggression on India's northern borders, disrupting the 'thaw' and subsequent military 'drawdown' that has taken place since the violent clashes in the Galwan Valley in Ladakh in June 2020. It would probably also put further pressure on India's defence and military ties with Russia, its long-standing and trusted defence partner, just when Putin is expected to make his first visit to India – sometime in 2025 – since the 2022 invasion of Ukraine.

Nonetheless, the four Quad countries' annual joint naval exercise, *Malabar*, could become a de facto military exercise, despite their statements to the contrary, and they may also increase their MDA cooperation. This could be enhanced by further cooperation on cyber security and intelligence assessment, with the latter perhaps moving towards intelligence sharing in the future.

US Secretary of State Marco Rubio stands alongside his Japanese, Indian and Australian counterparts in Washington DC, 21 January 2025

(Andrew Caballero-Reynolds/AFP via Getty Images)

On the bilateral front, Trump and Prime Minister Narendra Modi have gotten along well in the past. The first Trump administration sought to strengthen defence ties through low-profile but effective measures such as the signing and implementation of foundational defence agreements, including the Logistics Exchange Memorandum of Agreement.[32]

India's External Affairs Minister Dr Subrahmanyam Jaishankar was the first foreign minister to meet with Rubio for bilateral talks, in January, and Modi was the fourth foreign leader to meet Trump, in Washington DC on 13 February. Amid concern over the potential imposition of tariffs on Indian exports to the US, the Indian government's annual budget, unveiled on 1 February, lowered the import duty on Harley Davidson motorcycles from the US, a bugbear of Trump. India has also begun a proactive policy of ensuring the return of Indian illegal immigrants in the US.[33]

When India hosts the next Quad summit later this year, there will be two new leaders at the table: Trump and Japanese Prime Minister Ishiba Shigeru. If it takes place in autumn, as seems likely, there could also be a new Australian prime minister. This would provide Modi with a great opportunity to seek to nudge a new security-led but not military-dominant focus for the group specifically aimed at countering China.

CAN TRUMP AVOID A WAR WITH CHINA OVER TAIWAN?

The US–China bilateral relationship is more strained than it has ever been at any other point in the twenty-first century. The current tensions – including over trade, technology and Taiwan – are setting the tone of a relationship now characterised by deep mutual distrust and a lack of dialogue mechanisms. Joe Biden was the first US president since Jimmy Carter not to visit China. Some tactical improvements were made before Trump's inauguration, such as the resumption of the military-to-military dialogue and an agreement not to include AI in nuclear decision-making. But these moves on their own are unlikely to significantly alter the strategic direction of the two great powers during Trump's second term.

Trump's first term saw the US launch its first Indo-Pacific Strategy in 2017, which made clear that the region had become a priority for Washington. Central to this strategy was an acknowledgement that Chinese coercion and influence undermined the interests of the US and countries in the Asia-Pacific. A significant US concern has been the lack of transparency around China's fast-paced military-modernisation efforts, which reportedly include a rapid expansion of its nuclear arsenal, along with the focus on military–civil fusion and new dual-use technologies. The bilateral relationship has been further strained by reported US intelligence assessments that President Xi Jinping has ordered the People's Liberation Army to be ready to invade Taiwan by 2027.[34] The increasing pace and scale of China's military exercises around Taiwan, and its use of lawfare, have further heightened concerns about a potential 'salami slicing' strategy towards unification with Taiwan.

Xi and Trump attend a welcome ceremony in Beijing, 9 November 2017

(Thomas Peter-Pool/Getty Images)

On the economic front, Trump's focus on technological competition and rebalancing trade and investment is likely to remain a mainstay in his second term. A second trade war with China may already be taking shape through tit-for-tat tariffs announced in early 2025. Under Biden, aiming to boost its regional influence and its resilience in the face of Chinese pressure, the US invested heavily in its Asian alliances and partnerships, both militarily and, albeit to a much lesser extent, economically in terms of trade (see Figure 2.2).

From Beijing's perspective, the United States' military support for Taiwan and regional partners and allies is proof of a strategy of 'containment' that seeks to suppress China's rejuvenation and rightful rise. Washington's competitive approach towards China in economic and technology policy is also seen by Beijing as fitting that pattern. The risk of misperception and miscommunication is further increased by the fact that the military and diplomatic communication mechanisms between the US and China are limited in number and insufficiently employed.[35] Given the traditional risk aversion on both sides, a large-scale war with China over Taiwan is unlikely in the near term, although it is not impossible.

This is where the United States' and China's approaches to their respective allies and partners will be particularly important. Washington will be seeking to leverage its relationships to boost its capabilities in the Pacific theatre. In potential conflict scenarios over Taiwan, Beijing may have fewer strategic partners to count on. However, Trump's displeasure over imbalanced bilateral relationships and a perception that the US is bearing too much of a financial burden could potentially target Washington's closest partners and allies in Asia, including South Korea, Japan and indeed Taiwan itself. And yet, the United States' political relationships with these countries provide it with greater strategic support and, to some extent, a deterrent effect, in the various regional contingencies.

Meanwhile, Southeast Asian states have been considering what the potential Taiwan scenarios would mean for their own national security, and to what extent they should, or could, play a role. The centrality of China as a powerful economic partner is a reality for all Southeast Asian states, and in most cases their inclination would be to avoid taking sides in a run-up to a China–Taiwan conflict, fearing that doing so would have serious consequences. Nevertheless, Southeast Asia's importance to Washington should not be underappreciated. While Trump is unlikely to boost US influence through existing multilateral institutions such as ASEAN, personal relationships may provide opportunities for Washington to build a strong relationship with leaders such as Ferdinand Marcos Jr of the Philippines and Prabowo Subianto of Indonesia.

China on the other hand is unlikely to offer Trump an expansive trade deal, even if Beijing is still considering just how transactional Trump could be in his attempt to strike a deal. Meanwhile, key figures in Trump's administration and the Pentagon will continue to place greater importance on the Asia-Pacific than on other regions, including Europe. If Trump's initial policy appointments are any indication of a future direction of travel, the US will remain preoccupied with China as a near-peer adversary across policy domains, irrespective of temporary or tactical thaws in the relationship. The main question in the next few years will be: how much scope for tactical manoeuvring will the US and China have if they both double down on their strategic objectives, and will Taiwan be caught in the crosshairs?

PAUL FRAIOLI
Editor, *Strategic Comments* and *Strategic Signals*; Senior Fellow, IISS

ROBERT WARD
IISS Japan Chair; Director of Geo-economics and Strategy, IISS

BEN SCHREER
Executive Director; Director, Defence, Technology and Future Conflict, IISS-Europe

HASAN ALHASAN
Senior Fellow for Middle East Policy, IISS

RAHUL ROY-CHAUDHURY
Senior Fellow for South and Central Asian Defence, Strategy and Diplomacy, IISS

VEERLE NOUWENS
Executive Director, IISS–Asia

NOTES

[1] Howard Kurtz, 'Between the Lines of a Millionaire's Ad', *Washington Post*, 1 September 1987. A copy of the full-page letter is available at *New York Times*, 2 September 1987, page A28, https://timesmachine.nytimes.com/timesmachine/1987/09/02/issue.html. Trump paid USD94,801 in 1987, which in 2025 would be worth USD261,778. Howard Kurt, 'Between the Lines of a Millionaire's Ad', *Washington Post*, 1 September 1987, https://www.washingtonpost.com/archive/politics/1987/09/02/between-the-lines-of-a-millionaires-ad/9c6db9c3-f7d6-4aa4-9ec4-a312feb2639e/; and US Inflation Calendar, https://www.usinflationcalculator.com/.

[2] Michael Oreskes, 'Trump Gives a Vague Hint of Candidacy', *New York Times*, 2 September 1987, https://www.nytimes.com/1987/09/02/nyregion/trump-gives-a-vague-hint-of-candidacy.html.

[3] He registered with the Independence (Reform) Party in October 1999, the Democratic Party in August 2001, the Republican Party in September 2009, deregistered from the party in December 2011 and returned to the Republican Party in April 2012. See Joshua Gillin, 'Bush Says Trump was a Democrat Longer than a Republican "in the Last Decade"', Politifact, 24 August 2015, https://www.politifact.com/factchecks/2015/aug/24/jeb-bush/bush-says-trump-was-democrat-longer-republican-las/; and Jessica Chasmar, 'Donald Trump Changed Political Parties at Least Five Times: Report', *Washington Times*, 16 June 2015, https://www.washingtontimes.com/news/2015/jun/16/donald-trump-changed-political-parties-at-least-fi/.

[4] See Timothy Noah, 'Will the Real Donald Trump Please Stand Up?', Politico, 26 July 2015,

https://www.politico.com/story/2015/07/will-the-real-donald-trump-please-stand-up-120607.

5   *Ibid*.

6   See Ezra Klein, 'Trump Barely Won the Popular Vote. Why Doesn't It Feel That Way?', *New York Times*, 19 January 2025, https://www.nytimes.com/2025/01/19/opinion/trump-mandate-zuckerberg-masculinity.html.

7   Lynn Song, 'China's Trade Surplus Hit a Record High in 2024', ING, 13 January 2025, https://think.ing.com/snaps/chinas-trade-surplus-hit-a-record-high-in-2024.

8   St Louis Federal Reserve, 'Real Narrow Effective Exchange Rate for United States', 22 January 2025, https://fred.stlouisfed.org/series/RNUSBIS.

9   Marc-William Palen, 'The Imperialism of Economic Nationalism, 1890-1913', *Diplomatic History*, vol. 39, no. 1, January 2015, p. 164, https://academic.oup.com/dh/article-abstract/39/1/157/587117?redirectedFrom=fulltext.

10 Freddy Gray, 'Empire of Trump: the President's plan to make America greater', *Spectator*, 15 January 2025, https://www.spectator.co.uk/article/empire-of-trump-the-presidents-plan-to-make-america-greater/.

11 Douglas A. Irwin, *Clashing over Commerce: A History of US Trade Policy* (Chicago, IL and London: University of Chicago Press, 2017), pp. 273–2.

12 *Ibid*., p. 166. Interestingly, given Trump's comments before he took office on the United States' absorbing of Canada, the McKinley Tariff also gave rise to fears that the US was seeking to annex Canada.

13 Evan Medeiros, 'Xi Has a Plan for Retaliating Against Trump's Gamesmanship', *Financial Times*, 5 January 2025, https://www.ft.com/content/ca79e423-7c0f-4883-a295-6fe1c73a2819.

14 These included more tariffs on Chinese exports and controls on exports of sensitive US technology to China. See Ana Swanson and Jordyn Holman, 'Biden Administration Ratchets Up Tariffs on Chinese goods', *New York Times*, 13 September 2024, https://www.nytimes.com/2024/09/13/us/politics/biden-tariffs-chinese-goods-clothing.html; and US Bureau of Industry and Security, 'Commerce Strengthens Export Controls to Restrict China's Capability to Produce Advanced Semiconductors for Military Applications', 2 December 2024, https://www.bis.gov/press-release/commerce-strengthens-export-controls-restrict-chinas-capability-produce-advanced.

15 Harry Dempsey and David Keohane, 'Donald Trump's Mexico tariffs would shift plants to Asia, Warns Car PartsMmaker', *Financial Times*, 23 January 2025, https://www.ft.com/content/e10058e3-ffbb-4a24-9201-63e1c239ac7a.

16 Alan Cullison, 'Trump's Ukraine Envoy Has a Hard Climb to Any Peace Deal', *Wall Street Journal*, 22 January 2025, https://www.wsj.com/politics/policy/trumps-ukraine-envoy-has-a-hard-climb-to-any-peace-deal-ac728e58; and David Cohen, 'Ending Russia-Ukraine War Will Take Time and Effort, Mike Waltz Says', Politico, 12 January 2024, https://www.politico.com/news/2025/01/12/ukraine-waltz-trump-putin-russia-00197709.

17 Ray Furlong, 'Europe May Not Be "At The Table" For Ukraine Peace Talks, Trump's Envoy Says', Radio Free Europe, 15 February 2025, https://www.rferl.org/a/zelenskyy-zelenskiy-munich-ukraine-russia-war/33315648.html.

18 Asami Terajima, 'Making Sense of Trump's Plan – If There Is One – to End Russia's War in Ukraine', Kyiv Independent, 15 February 2025, https://kyivindependent.com/making-sense-of-trumps-plan-if-there-is-one-to-end-russias-war-in-ukraine/.

19 *Ibid*.

20 Liz Lee, Shi Bu and Ethan Wang, 'China Calls For All Stakeholders in Ukraine War to be in Peace Process', Reuters, 15 February 2025, https://www.reuters.com/world/china-calls-all-stakeholders-ukraine-war-be-peace-process-2025-02-15/.

21 See IISS, *Building Defence Capacity in Europe: An Assessment* (Abingdon: Routledge for the IISS, 2024), https://www.iiss.org/publications/strategic-dossiers/building-defence-capacity-in-europe-an-assessment/.

22 Connor O'Brien, 'Republicans Struggle with Unified Response to Trump's Plan for Ukraine Peace Talks', Politico, 14 February 2025, https://www.politico.com/news/2025/02/14/republican-response-trump-ukraine-peace-talks-00204447.

23 James FitzGerald, 'Trump Appears to Threaten Hamas with "All Hell to Pay" Over Hostages', BBC News, 3 December 2024, https://www.bbc.com/news/articles/c62757dd55no.

24 John Raine et al., 'Iran and Israel: Everything Short of War', IISS Online Analysis, 17 May 2024, https://www.iiss.org/sv/online-analysis/online-analysis/2024/05/iran-and-israel-everything-short-of-war/.

25 'Lebanon Reports 4 More Israeli Violations of Cease-fire Deal', Anadolu Agency, 13 January 2025, https://www.aa.com.tr/en/middle-east/-lebanon-reports-4-more-israeli-violations-of-cease-fire-deal/3448885.

26 For details on Iran's regional network, see *Iran's Networks of Influence in the Middle East* (Abingdon: Routledge for the IISS, 2024), https://www.iiss.org/publications/strategic-dossiers/iran-dossier/.

27 Mahsa Rouhi, 'Iran and America: The Perverse Consequences of Maximum Pressure', *Survival Online*, 10 March 2020, https://www.iiss.org/online-analysis/survival-online/2020/03/iran-united-states-maximum-pressure/.

28 'Joint Statement by the Quad Foreign Minister', US Department of State, 21 January 2025, https://www.state.gov/joint-statement-by-the-quad-foreign-ministers/.

29 *Ibid.*

30 *Ibid.*

31 See Samir Saran et al., 'Two Decades of the Quad: Diplomacy and Cooperation in the Indo-Pacific', Observer Research Foundation, 2024, https://www.orfonline.org/research/two-decades-of-the-quad-diplomacy-and-cooperation-in-the-indo-pacific.

32 For a wider assessment of those agreements, see Antoine Levesques, 'US–India Defence and Technology Cooperation', IISS Online Analysis, 20 July 2023, https://www.iiss.org/online-analysis/online-analysis/2023/07/us-india-defence-and-technology-cooperation/.

33 'India to Take Back Verified Illegals: PM Modi Amid US Crackdown on Immigrants', India Today, 14 February 2025, https://www.indiatoday.in/india/story/india-ready-to-take-back-illegal-immigrants-pm-modi-amid-trump-crackdown-2679834-2025-02-14.

34 Noah Robertson, 'How DC Became Obsessed with a Potential 2027 Chinese Invasion of Taiwan', Defense News, 7 May 2024, https://www.defensenews.com/pentagon/2024/05/07/how-dc-became-obsessed-with-a-potential-2027-chinese-invasion-of-taiwan/.

35 For a deeper assessment on the US–China dialogue mechanism, see Meia Nouwens, 'Middling and Muddling Through? Managing Asia-Pacific Crises', *Asia-Pacific Regional Security Assessment 2024*, ed. Evan A. Laksmana, (Abingdon: Routledge for the IISS, 2024), https://www.iiss.org/sv/publications/strategic-dossiers/asia-pacific-regional-security-assessment-2024/chapter-2/.

CHAPTER 3

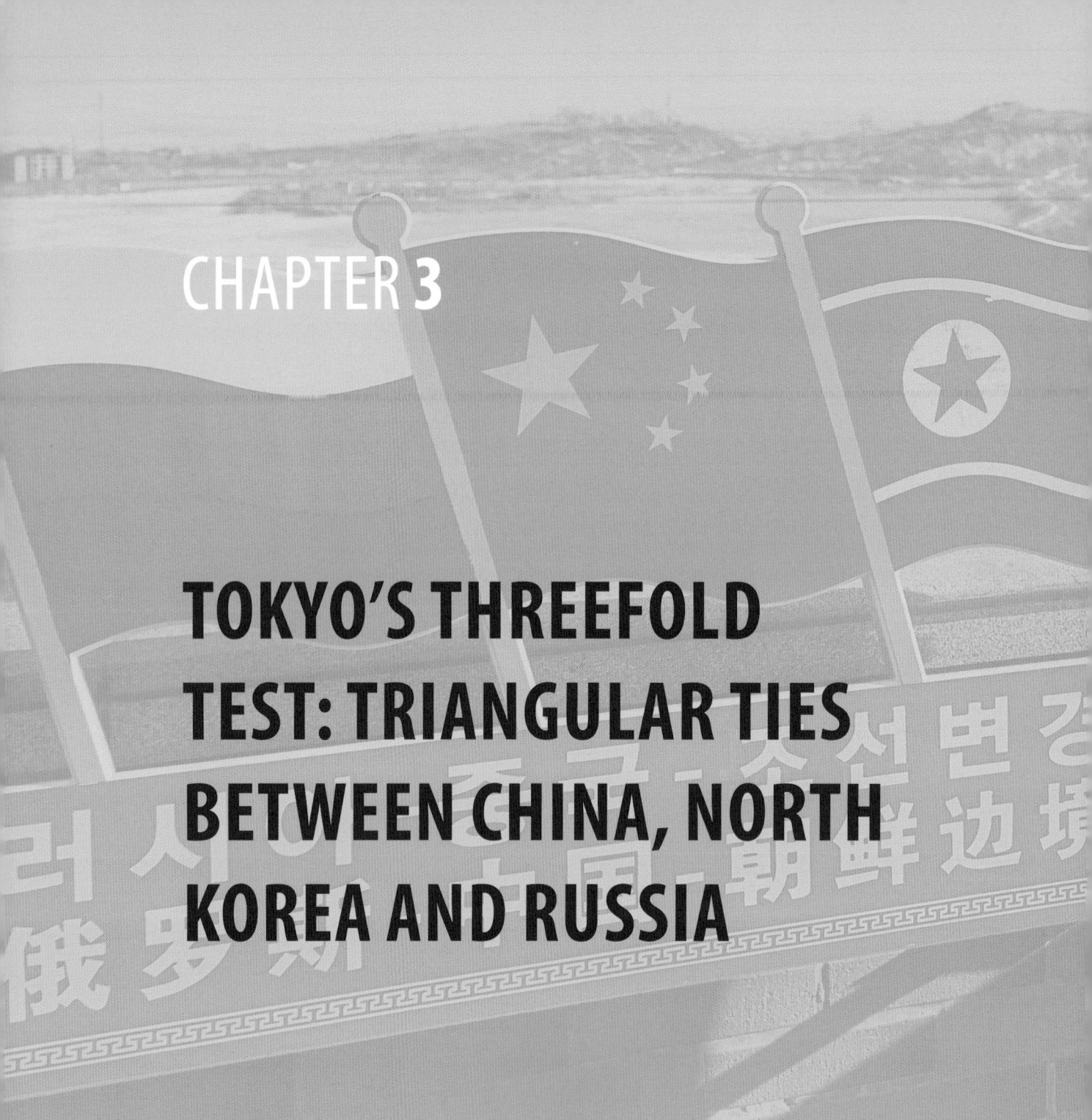

TOKYO'S THREEFOLD TEST: TRIANGULAR TIES BETWEEN CHINA, NORTH KOREA AND RUSSIA

This chapter examines how the growing triangular complexity between China, North Korea and Russia impacts Northeast Asian security and poses new challenges for Japan's strategic policy.

The flags of Russia, China and North Korea on a viewing tower on the border between the three countries in Fangchuan village near Hunchun, China (Christian Petersen-Clausen/Moment Unreleased via Getty Images)

ARGUMENTS AND FINDINGS:

- While there has been increasing convergence in the positions of China, North Korea and Russia with the war in Ukraine, their 'triangular' relationship is not yet a full 'trilateral' alliance as underlying tensions between the three countries persist.
- The complexity and unpredictability of the triangular relationship presents heightened risks to Japan's defence planning and posture as it would face a multi-layered challenge during a potential crisis or conflict.
- Japan's diplomatic approach towards China seeks common ground, in order to limit the growth of this triangular relationship, although the relationship between China, North Korea and Russia is likely to persist as the latter three's strategic competition with the United States worsens.

IMPLICATIONS FOR REGIONAL SECURITY:

- Northeast Asian security could become increasingly polarised by competing groupings – China, North Korea and Russia on the one hand and Japan, South Korea and the US on the other – and heightened strategic risks.
- Regional security assessments can no longer begin and end with US–China dynamics alone. Japan's strategic interests, posture and trajectory must be accounted for more thoroughly moving forward.

Security risks in Northeast Asia have long been assessed through a US–China lens. On the one hand, China often prefers to act alone in responding to security challenges in the region, while the US prefers to act together with its allies, such as Japan and South Korea. The recent growth in triangular ties between Japan, South Korea and the US has strengthened this regional bifurcation. But the competitive dynamic between the US and China alone is often – incorrectly – still seen as the primary driver of security risks and challenges.

Due to the dominant focus on US–China dynamics, the views and considerations of Japan as a resident Northeast Asian power can occasionally be overlooked. Tokyo, in fact, considers different security risks and benefits than Washington does when assessing its immediate environment. Indeed, Japan has been at the forefront of various security engagements with European, Northeast and Southeast Asian partners, driven to work beyond its regional environment by its own strategic assessments and perceptions.

As such, Japan has recently been confronting a new set of strategic challenges as China, North Korea and Russia have deepened their triangular bilateral defence relationships and collaborative activities. Whether and how these three countries will develop their own unified trilateral arrangement, or whether their triangular dynamics (three connected dyads) alone will increase the security risk in Northeast Asia, are questions that policymakers in Tokyo are currently seeking to answer.

TWO IS COMPANY

China's foreign affairs are largely conducted through bilateral relationship building and management. In Northeast Asia, this involves the careful management of its tense relationship with Japan, attempts to continue an economic relationship with South Korea, a balanced comprehensive partnership with Russia and continued support of North Korea, its only official ally. Each of these bilateral relationships has evolved in recent years. For Tokyo, China's deepening bilateral relationships with Russia and North Korea since Russia's 2022 invasion of Ukraine pose renewed security challenges. Japan's concern, however, precedes this, having commenced with the bilateral trends that developed between Japan and China, North Korea and Russia even before the war.

Japan and China

Japan and China's relationship has deteriorated over the last decade. Each views the other's actions as inflammatory, provocative and deliberately destabilising the security status quo. Beijing has grown increasingly frustrated with what it sees as Japan's desire to become an Asia-Pacific military power since 2016, through its relaxation of defence-related laws. This intensified in 2022 with Japan's revision of three national-security strategy documents that allowed for increased defence spending and the acquisition of counterstrike capabilities.[1] China's frustration with Japan is also linked to Japan's active support of a US-led regional order.[2] Chinese strategists list Japan's increased defence spending, strengthened military ties with NATO and securitisation of economic relationships as attempts to 'break through the restrictions of its peace constitution' and become a significant military actor.[3] A Chinese scholar has also criticised Japan's acquisition of long-range attack capabilities as an attempt to become a 'normal' regional power.[4]

Several Chinese officials believe that Japan is deepening its relationship with Taiwan in order to stoke tensions that can 'legitimise its intention to become a military power'.[5] Some in Beijing perceived this in Japan's reaction to China firing five missiles over Taiwan – which landed in Japan's exclusive economic zone – during Chinese military exercises in August 2022 after a visit by then-speaker of the US House of Representatives Nancy Pelosi. Japan's then-prime minister Kishida Fumio stated that China's military drills in response to Pelosi's visit were a 'grave problem'.[6] Although several Chinese observers mocked quotes, such as former prime minister Abe Shinzo's, that 'a Taiwan emergency is a Japanese emergency', this reveals Beijing's recognition that Japan considers Taiwan to be a matter of national security, regardless of its perceived motives.[7]

Japan's then-prime minister Kishida Fumio shakes hands with China's President Xi Jinping on the sidelines of the Asia-Pacific Economic Cooperation summit, 17 November 2022

(Japan Pool via Jiji Press/Japan Pool/Jiji Press/AFP via Getty Images)

Beijing is chagrined that, as it views it, Japan is leading support for a US-led Asia-Pacific order. Chinese strategists argue that Japan seeks to 'opportunistically profit' from its alliance, specifically to 'obtain geostrategic dividends'.[8] One Chinese academic argues that Japan 'has never been able to have a sufficient say on the international political stage' and, as such, is using such an alliance to have a greater say in the 'rules and order' of the Asia-Pacific.[9] Beijing thus perceives Japan's deepening US alliance as an opportunity to both strengthen its own regional position and 'contain' China.

Chinese scholars also consider Japan's requests for the US to commit to the application of Article V of the US–Japan Security Treaty to the Senkaku/Diaoyu islands (currently controlled by Japan) as a 'policy capture' to entangle the US and contain China.[10] One strategist predicts a scenario where the US pushes Japan to the front of the containment efforts against China and collapses Sino-Japanese relations, subsequently driving Japan to develop even closer military ties with the US and shouldering the cost of US troops. Overall, Beijing believes that Tokyo's geopolitical activities are explained by its desire to become a major military power.

Beijing, in response, seeks to exploit the differences in Japan's defence and economic relationships in order to prevent its rise as a military power and support for a US-led regional order. China aims to 'seize the main contradictions in the trilateral relationship between China, the United States and Japan' and promote the development of China–Japan relations.[11] This strategy was reflected in China's reaction to the decision by the Biden administration to block Nippon Steel from purchasing US Steel, a move branded 'incomprehensible' by the Japanese government.[12] Chinese state media ran a discussion show answering the question whether this 'was a blow to US–Japan ties' and a Ministry of Foreign Affairs spokesperson noted that China always 'upholds the principle of fair competition'.[13]

Beijing hopes that its economic relationship with Japan can prevent their bilateral ties from deteriorating. In 2024 Minister of Foreign Affairs Wang Yi described the two countries as 'important neighbours' and stated that, because of their 'highly complementary economies', they should not and will not decouple.[14] Many policymakers during the Kishida government shared this confidence, noting that despite domestic pressures, the cabinet did not support decoupling from China.

Beijing, nevertheless, is concerned that Japan wants to reduce its economic engagement with China. This would be a move away from Japan's current strategic positioning in which it relies on the US for its security and engages with China for its economy. From Beijing's perspective, ensuring that countries remain economically tied with China limits the extent to which they can pivot their security engagement towards the US. Beijing views the United States' Indo-Pacific Economic Framework more broadly as a tool to coerce Southeast Asian countries into restructuring regional production and supply chains to exclude China and to weaken Japan's economic dependencies on China. One Chinese academic argued that the 'economic linkage' can 'restrain Japan from taking excessive action on the Taiwan issue', and if Japan 'touches' China's red line on this issue the country will receive an economic 'shock'.[15]

Many Chinese analysts have thus called for China to leverage platforms, such as the Association of Southeast Asian Nations (ASEAN)-initiated Regional Comprehensive Economic Partnership, to maintain its economic ties with Japan. This objective will likely determine how Beijing manages its relationship with Japan. It will be difficult, however, to insulate these economic ties from the actions Beijing takes to advance its other historic and geostrategic concerns.

These include growing anti-Japanese sentiment among the Chinese public and party officials, as well the ambition to extend China's jurisdictional authority in its surrounding waters. Following an increasing number of coastguard intrusions by China in the waters around the Senkaku/Diaoyu islands, President Xi Jinping reportedly said in November 2023 that China needed to 'constantly strengthen' its efforts to safeguard the sovereignty of the island.[16] Some Chinese strategists also fear Japan has created 'a multidimensional joint-defence posture' on Okinawa island by deploying advanced defence forces, amphibious mobile brigades and surface-to-air units.[17]

Taken together, these factors have led China to use its economic links with Japan to impose cost on it, rather than help foster their relationship. For instance, in September 2023, China stoked nationalist outrage at Japan's release of radioactive water from the Fukushima nuclear plant into the Pacific Ocean and banned the importation of Japanese marine products.

Beijing's deepening military ties with Moscow and the growing military ties between Russia and North Korea further compound Japan's concerns about stability in its immediate region. The transfer of technology from Russia to North Korea in exchange for Pyongyang's materiel support for Russia's war effort in Ukraine has been particularly worrying for Japan. Tokyo sees this development as potentially destabilising the Korean Peninsula by providing Pyongyang with the wherewithal to modernise and expand its nuclear- and conventional-missile capabilities, and potentially its submarine technology as well. China's military cooperation with Russia on joint air or naval patrols around Japan continues to signal the strength of their relationship to Tokyo and assert their political positions. In 2024, the cooperation expanded to include a coastguard patrol (discussed below).

Russia and China

With the relationship between Russia and China labelled as becoming a 'partnership without limits' shortly before the former's invasion of Ukraine, since then it has grown even closer. At a March 2023 meeting between presidents Vladimir Putin and Xi, the latter was overheard stating that the two countries will jointly usher in 'changes – the likes of which we haven't seen for 100 years'.[18] Both countries continue to legitimate the other's national-security objectives and, over the last decade, to provide greater military utility and facilitate each other's strategic goals. These have involved a greater number of and more significant military exercises and the institutionalisation of their defence relationship across bilateral and multilateral platforms (see Figure 3.1).

On the one hand, their collaboration in the Asia-Pacific is underpinned by a shared strategic goal to undermine the US-led regional order; this is why they use regional issues to attack the United Nations Convention on the Law of the Sea or UN sanctions, for example. In March 2024, Russia used its veto to end the UN Panel of Experts' monitoring of sanctions on North Korea, while China abstained, with its spokesperson calling on states to consider Moscow's objections.

Russia and China also provide discursive legitimisation for one another's national ambitions. Beijing refers to the global sanctions against Russia as 'economic hegemonism' or 'financial terrorism' and Moscow has said that it 'opposes any form of 'Taiwanese independence' and frequently repeats the 'One China' principle.[19]

Moscow has also maintained formal neutrality on the Senkaku/Diaoyu islands, and in conversation with Putin, Xi reaffirmed that China will not take sides with either Japan or Russia over the Kuril Islands. These discursive steps help legitimise actions by Russia and China which other regional countries condemn. They also strengthen China and Russia's critique of US hegemonism and help frame their partnership to the Global South as an alternative to the US-led international order.

On the other hand, Russia and China's efforts to create a new security order in the Asia-Pacific have also inadvertently exposed the tensions within their relationship, ranging

Russian President Vladimir Putin and Xi during their meeting in Beijing, 4 February 2022

(Alexei Druzhinin/Sputnik/AFP via Getty Images)

Figure 3.1: **China and Russia: bilateral and multilateral exercises by type, 2003–24**

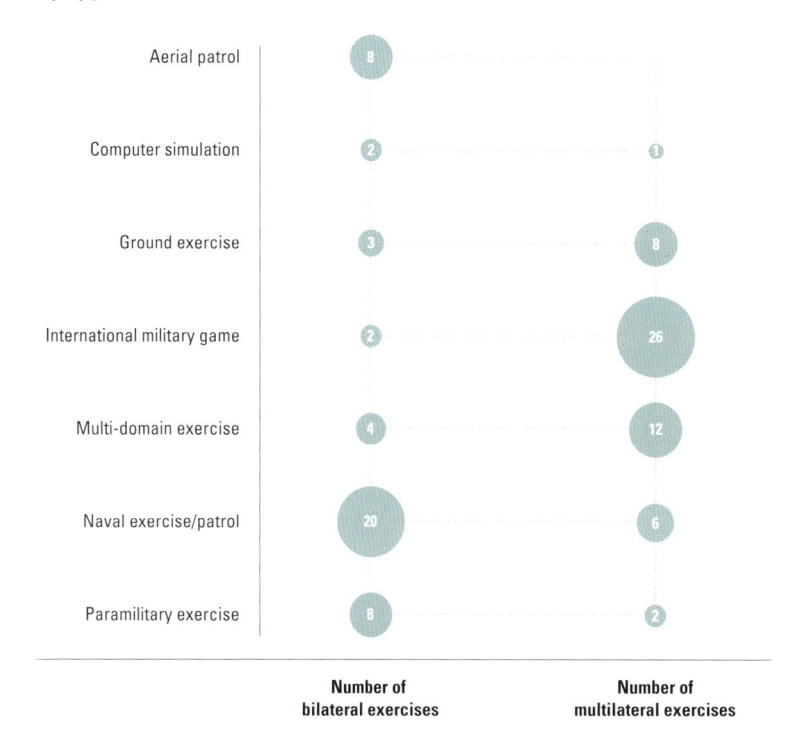

Exercise type	Number of bilateral exercises	Number of multilateral exercises
Aerial patrol	8	
Computer simulation	2	1
Ground exercise	3	8
International military game	2	26
Multi-domain exercise	4	12
Naval exercise/patrol	20	6
Paramilitary exercise	8	2

©IISS

Sources: IISS; CSIS China Power Project

from voicing concern about the deployment of North Korean soldiers to fight in Ukraine to disagreement in some of each other's national-security considerations. Such close coordination is often missing when the other's national-security ambitions are at stake. Russia has not voiced direct support for China in the country's territorial disputes with India or Vietnam, for example.[20] This is likely because both are important regional partners for Moscow, although Russia allowed Chinese coastguard vessels to sail directly into the energy-exploration blocks operated or owned by Russian firms near Vietnam at least 40 times between January 2022 and March 2023.[21] Similarly, China has not supported the involvement of North Korean troops in Ukraine and has privately voiced concern about the situation.

Although mutual discursive legitimation is therefore a common form of cooperation between Russia and China, this only happens when their regional interests align. But there are also further indications that Russia–China cooperation has shifted from legitimising each other's security ambitions to facilitating them. This is evident when comparing the changes in combined-military exercises conducted over the last two years (see Figure 3.2).

In total, there were 102 Russo-Chinese combined-military exercises from August 2003 to July 2024 – with 22 (nearly 24%) taking place since Russia's invasion of Ukraine.[22] Exercises, however, have been characterised less by a deeper (even if not total) interoperability between Russian and Chinese forces and more for their political-signalling purposes. For example, the two countries conducted a 'joint' air patrol over the Sea of Japan when the Quad leaders (Australia, India, Japan and the US) met in May 2022, where the defence chiefs of Italy, Japan and the United Kingdom signed an agreement in

Figure 3.2: **China and Russia: bilateral and multilateral exercises by year, 2003–24**

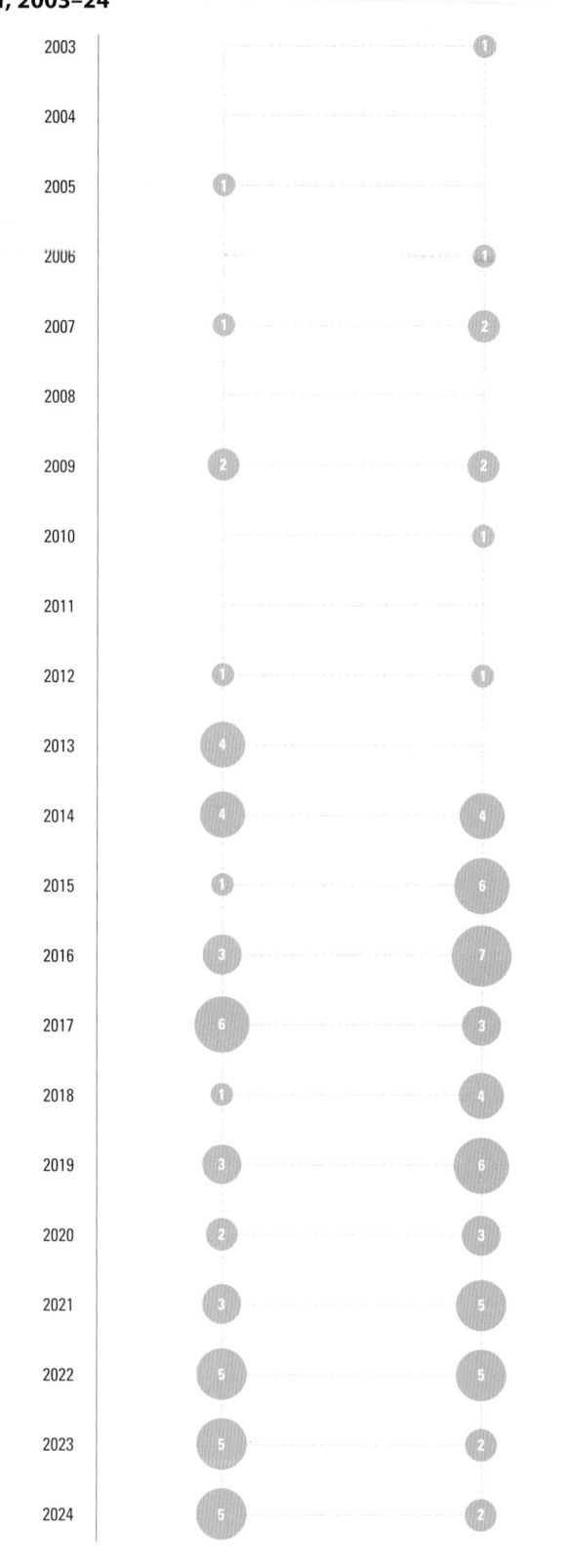

Year	Number of bilateral exercises	Number of multilateral exercises
2003		1
2004		
2005	1	
2006		1
2007	1	2
2008		
2009	2	2
2010		1
2011		
2012	1	1
2013	4	
2014	4	4
2015	1	6
2016	3	7
2017	6	3
2018	1	4
2019	3	6
2020	2	3
2021	3	5
2022	5	5
2023	5	2
2024	5	2

©IISS

Sources: IISS; CSIS China Power Project

Tokyo on producing their next-generation Global Combat Air Programme (GCAP) fighter jet (see Chapter 1 of this dossier).

More recently, however, these exercises may be preparation for scenarios when each nation provides support for the other's military operations. In September 2024, for example, the Chinese and Russian coastguards conducted their first combined drills and patrol (since signing a memorandum of understanding in April 2023). China Coast Guard vessels *Meishan* and *Xiushan* participated in drills with Russian coastguard vessels in the Sea of Japan. This was the first time this type of cooperation had taken place, and included 'maritime security threat crackdown', maritime rescue and 'joint' (or combined) patrols.[23]

While both countries value military cooperation as a form of political signalling, it is possible that these drills are laying the foundation for a deeper form of collaboration in the event of a crisis or conflict. For example, although it is unlikely that Russia would be directly involved in a Taiwan conflict, its coastguard could conduct grey-zone operations in the Sea of Japan to frustrate or block assistance from Taiwan's regional allies. Russia–China cooperation is thus possibly shifting from discursively legitimating each other's security ambitions to militarily supporting them.

China and North Korea

The relationship between China and North Korea has endured for 75 years. Despite being China's only official ally after signing a mutual defence treaty in 1961, the relationship is generally stable but at times turbulent.[24] It has been in China's national-security and strategic interest to support Pyongyang through its successive generations to prevent a unified Korea – which could be allied with the US – on its border.

A collapse of North Korea would also create instability and present a humanitarian challenge on China's borders. This is why China has remained North Korea's main trading partner for over two decades, with China's economic support accounting for almost 98% of North Korea's total imports and exports.[25] Beijing is also an important source of food, energy and medical aid to North Korea, which has suffered famine, weather catastrophes and health emergencies. China has even built infrastructure within North Korea to support the bilateral economic and trading relationship.

However, Pyongyang's doctrine of *juche* (self-reliance) has limited China's control over it. Beijing opposed North Korea's first nuclear-weapon test in 2006, criticising it as a 'flagrant and brazen' violation of international consensus.[26] This led to a period of policy shifts from Beijing: it supported nine major UN sanction resolutions on North Korea and called upon North Korea to return to negotiations in the Six-Party Talks with China, Japan, Russia, South Korea and the US.[27]

China's own strategic interests and desire to control Pyongyang – which could pursue policies which conflict with those preferred by Beijing – have driven the bilateral ties. The 2018 summit between President Donald Trump and Supreme Leader Kim Jong-un surprised Beijing and led Xi to revitalise the China–North Korea relationship. Xi made his first trip to Pyongyang the following year, a first for any Chinese leader in nearly 15 years. In 2021, China and North Korea renewed their mutual-defence treaty. Despite supporting

UN sanctions against North Korea in 2006, following North Korea's missile-testing regime in 2022 China vetoed sanctions.

However, the China–North Korea relationship has become increasingly complex as Pyongyang has taken a more confrontational stance towards South Korea. In October 2024, North Korea abandoned its reunification efforts with Seoul, identifying South Korea as a hostile state.[28] The instability of the Korean Peninsula poses a dilemma for China, which seeks to maintain the status quo in the region.

Ironically, North Korea's policy shift is a common concern for China and Japan, as reiterated at the Ninth Japan–China–ROK Trilateral Summit in May 2024.[29] Although the summit was seen as symbolic, the three governments have sought to communicate on the issue of the security and stability of the Korean Peninsula, among other topics. All three countries sought to institutionalise this triangular dialogue by arranging a foreign-ministers meeting in March 2025.[30]

Envoys from Russia, South Korea, North Korea, China, the US and Japan join hands during the Six-Party Talks in Beijing, 30 September 2007

(Andy Wong/Pool/Getty Images)

THREE IS A CROWD

A potential trilateral relationship or security arrangement between China, North Korea and Russia presents a greater security challenge to both the US and Japan than each of the three countries on their own. The risks have grown with the addition of Iran into the equation, in what the Center for a New American Security has labelled as an 'Axis of Upheaval' and H.R. McMaster has called the 'Axis of Aggressors'.[31]

Despite Beijing's claims it has curtailed the trade of dual-use goods to Russia, Chinese trade remains an essential line of support for the Russian war economy. This includes its purchase of Russian oil and gas, and the continued extensive export of Chinese technology, including semiconductors, radar and communications-jamming equipment and combat-aircraft components.

Normatively, China, North Korea and Russia share the belief that the US unjustly dominates the current international order and that the values which it projects must be rejected. Practically, however, each could present new security risks or benefits in key areas of their respective strategic interests. For China, the grouping is leveraged to support its core interests around Taiwan and its territorial ambitions. For North Korea, the grouping presents further support for its peninsular aims. For Russia, it furthers its interests in reclaiming the territory and prestige it perceives as having been lost with the fall of the Soviet Union.

However, the triangular security relationship between China, North Korea and Russia has not yet resulted in a formal trilateral alliance, even if high-level bilateral visits among the three countries persist (see Figure 3.3). To date, only Russia has suggested a trilateral naval exercise involving China and North Korea. A lack of trust and conflicting interests have prevented the three from committing to a full, treaty-level alignment with each other.

Russia and China have competing interests in Central Asia, the Arctic and even perhaps over the Russia–Ukraine war. Indeed, the war may have allowed China to broaden its engagement with Central Asia, even though it has traditionally divided this regional role with Russia. Similarly, China has signalled its interest in becoming a greater economic and strategic player in the High North, although Russia considers the Arctic to be within its own sphere of influence.[32]

But while China refuses to condemn outright Russia's invasion of Ukraine, reports suggest that several Chinese officials have become frustrated with Putin's war. In 2023, an anonymous Chinese official said Putin was 'crazy' and that China should not have 'simply followed Russia'.[33] China's envoy to the European Union, Fu Cong, stated that the war against Ukraine had put China 'in a very difficult position' and that China perceives itself to have become 'collateral damage'.[34]

China is being challenged over its ability to maintain control over Northeast Asian security dynamics within the triangular relationship with North Korea and Russia. Defence cooperation between Russia and North Korea risks destabilising the carefully constructed relationship that Beijing has maintained with Pyongyang. This is similar to Beijing's concerns in 2018, when Trump's rapprochement with Kim potentially weakened China's ability to 'control' North Korea's diplomatic activities. Beijing is now equally concerned that the Russia–North Korea relationship comes at the cost of its own level of influence over Pyongyang.

But the reasons behind these closer ties further exemplify the challenge that Beijing

Figure 3.3: **China and Russia: key bilateral high-level visits with North Korea, 2013–24**

Date	Type of visit	Engagement
May 2013	North Korea → China	Chinese
Jul 2013	China → North Korea	Chinese
2014		
Sep 2015	North Korea → North Korea	Chinese
Oct 2015	China → North Korea	Chinese
May–Jun 2016	North Korea → North Korea	Chinese
2017		
Mar 2018	North Korea → China	Chinese
Apr 2018	North Korea → China	Chinese
Apr 2018	China → North Korea	Chinese
May 2018	China → North Korea	Chinese
May 2018	China → North Korea	Chinese
Jun 2018	North Korea → China	Chinese
Jan 2019	North Korea → China	Chinese
Jun 2019	China → North Korea	Chinese
Aug 2019	North Korea → China	Chinese
Sep 2019	China → North Korea	Chinese
Oct 2019	China → North Korea	Chinese
Oct 2019	North Korea → China	Chinese
Nov 2019	China → North Korea	Chinese
Dec 2019	China → North Korea	Chinese
2020		
2021		
2022		
Jul 2023	Russia → North Korea	Russian
Jul 2023	China → North Korea	Chinese
Aug 2023	Russia → North Korea	Russian
Sep 2023	China → North Korea	Chinese
Sep 2023	North Korea → Russia	Russian
Oct 2023	Russia → North Korea	Russian
Dec 2023	North Korea → China	Chinese
Mar 2024	North Korea → China	Chinese
Apr 2024	China → North Korea	Chinese
Jun 2024	Russia → North Korea	Russian
Nov 2024	Russia → North Korea	Russian

● North Korea ● China ● Russia ▮ Chinese engagement with North Korea ▮ Russian engagement with North Korea

Sources: IISS; CSIS Beyond Parallel

faces in controlling regional events and its neighbour. There are even recent intelligence assessments that North Korea was the first to offer Russia troops to deploy to Ukraine, contrary to initial speculation that Russia, due to its weakened position following the war in Ukraine, sought North Korea's help.[35] This suggests that Pyongyang seeks to diversify its strategic partnerships beyond that with China. In return for sending its troops to Ukraine, it is likely that Pyongyang expects Russia to share military technology, although the details remain undisclosed. South Korea's National Security Adviser Shin Wok-sik said that Russia has provided North Korea with anti-aircraft missiles to reinforce its vulnerable air-defence systems.[36] Other compensations could range from surveillance satellites to submarine technology or mutual-defence guarantees; the two countries signed a bilateral treaty in June 2024 that includes a mutual-defence provision.[37]

An alleged North Korean soldier held after being captured by the Armed Forces of Ukraine, 11 January 2025

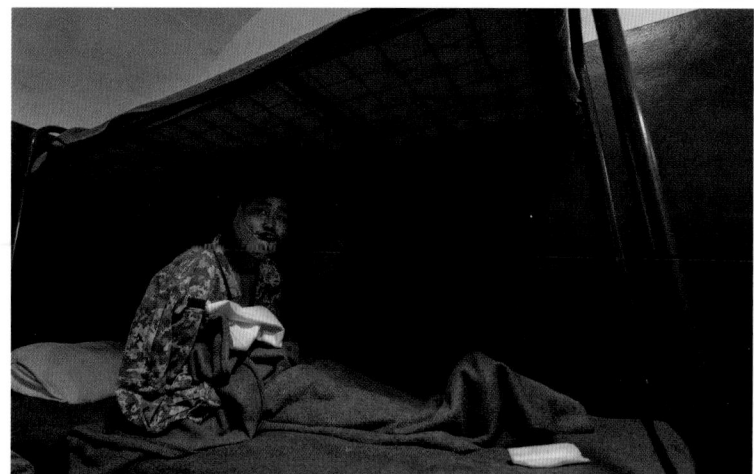

(Ukrainian President Volodymyr Zelensky's Social Media/Handout/Anadolu via Getty Images)

China's response to this changing dynamic has been cautious. In 2018, China sent Li Zhanshu, then-chairman of the Standing Committee of the National People's Congress and third-ranking member of the Politburo Standing Committee of the Chinese Communist Party (CCP), to North Korea's Founding Day celebrations. In September 2023, however, China sent Liu Guozhong, vice premier of the State Council of China and member of the Political Bureau of the Central Committee of the Chinese Communist Party, who led an unusually low-profile delegation.[38] The following year China once again sent its third-highest-ranking member of the Politburo Standing Committee of the CCP, chairman of the Standing Committee of the National People's Congress Zhao Leji, on a goodwill visit to mark 2024 as a year of friendship.[39] By then, Zhao was the highest-ranking Chinese official to have visited Pyongyang in five years.

These trips suggest that while Beijing may not look favourably on the deepening Russia–North Korea ties, it still prefers to balance its own triangular relations against what it sees as deepening minilateral ties driven by the US and its allies. Zhao's trip to Pyongyang coincided with then-US president Joe Biden's triangular summit with the Philippines and Japan. The day before, Biden and Kishida had met and pledged to advance coordination to counter challenges from China and North Korea.[40]

Japan, meanwhile, is increasingly concerned with the multilayered, interlinked security challenge of the increasingly triangular collaboration between China, North Korea and Russia. Besides the significant security risks posed by each of the dyads in the China–North Korea–Russia relationship, Japan's security environment will grow increasingly complex and challenging as the triangular ties progress. Indeed, Japan could be faced with potentially more challenging coordinated triangular dynamics between its three regional neighbours, two of whom are P5 members and another two who are collaborating in nuclear proliferation.

These concerns are not entirely new. Before Russia's invasion of Ukraine, the deputy foreign ministers of China, North Korea and Russia met in Moscow in October 2018 to discuss a coordinated trilateral approach to denuclearisation of the Korean Peninsula and called on the UN to adjust the sanctions regime against North Korea. Although the talks did not lead to the desired policy outcomes, they did set a precedent for a trilateral approach between the three countries.

Tokyo has long been concerned about Moscow and Beijing's lax enforcement of sanctions on North Korea. Japan's strategy in the late 2010s had already been described as 'to keep the North Koreans and Chinese down, the Americans in, and the Russians neutral'.[41] This may no longer be possible with China's and Russia's growing assertiveness in Southeast and Northeast Asia and North Korea's potential technology benefits from its growing ties with Russia.[42]

For now – although very much subject to change – as a rare convergence in the interests of China and Japan, both countries have expressed concern about the deepening Russia–North Korea relationship. In November 2024, National Security Secretariat then-secretary general Takeo Akiba flew to Beijing to meet with Wang and convey Japan's anxiety about the developments between Moscow and Pyongyang. However, the broader strategic lens of great-power competition through which Beijing views its own foreign relations makes any serious alignment between Japan and China which has the aim of limiting the North Korea–Russia relationship seemingly Herculean.

DOUBLING DOWN

As the triangular collaboration between China, North Korea and Russia has picked up steam, Japan has made a historic shift to develop its defence capabilities to take 'primary responsibility' for its protection. It has done so through a three-pronged approach: strengthening its deterrence and response capabilities, reinforcing its alliance with the US and enhancing its defence diplomacy with like-minded countries.[43]

The Kishida administration also took the historic decision to increase Japanese defence spending from the prevailing norm of 1% to 2% of GDP, in alignment with the 2022 National Security Strategy and Defense Buildup Program.[44] Japan also aims to acquire a 'forward-leaning denial strategy', including through the acquisition of counterstrike capabilities, to deter missile threats from China and North Korea.[45] The strategy also includes building stand-off capabilities; purchasing 400 *Tomahawk* land-attack cruise missiles from the US by 2027; and the development of hypersonic strike missiles.[46]

These policies are in line with other initiatives to enhance the Japan Self-Defense Forces' capabilities, including the conversion of the *Izumo*-class helicopter carriers to allow

Japanese and US sailors discuss *Tomahawk* missile procedures aboard USS *McCampbell* in Yokosuka near Tokyo, 28 March 2024

(Petty Officer 1st Class Charles Oki via DIVIDS)

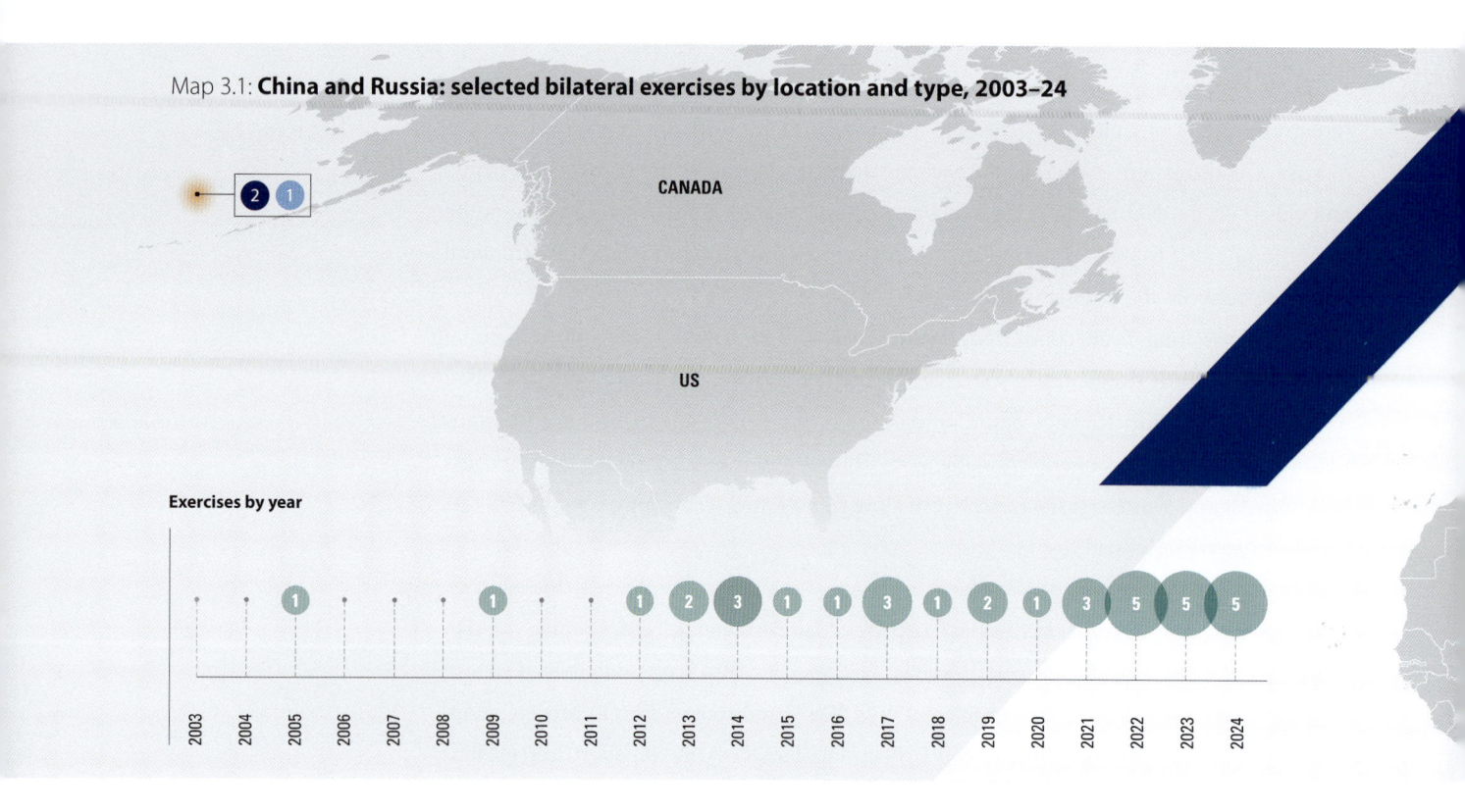

Map 3.1: **China and Russia: selected bilateral exercises by location and type, 2003–24**

them to conduct fixed-wing aircraft operations.[47] Tokyo also aims to improve its command-and-control systems and has established a Permanent Joint Headquarters in March 2025 to integrate all domains: land, sea, air, space, cyber and electromagnetic.[48] Japan is focusing on new domains such as space and cyber. In June 2023, the government adopted its first Space Security Initiative and sought to construct a satellite-constellation system consisting of small satellites to precisely monitor targets in real time.[49] Tokyo is also working towards introducing an 'active cyber defence' system to take pre-emptive action in cyberspace.[50]

Japan has even moved forward with its military preparedness for a potential Taiwan-related crisis or conflict, in addition to its traditional deterrence against North Korea's missile threat. Indeed, Japan has shifted its strategic focus to its southwestern region, an area to the south of Kyushu which stretches close to Taiwan, for a potential contingency in the area or the Senkaku/Diaoyu islands. Since 2016, Japan has enhanced its military presence in this region by deploying anti-ship and surface-to-air missiles, as well as electronic-warfare and amphibious capabilities.[51] Tokyo is also seeking to mobilise the Japan Coast Guard and police and taking a whole-of-government approach to protect critical infrastructure.[52]

So far, Japan's primary response to a triangular strategic and military relationship between China, North Korea and Russia is to remain cautious, monitor further developments and to try and engage with China on common concerns via diplomatic channels. Militarily, the triangular relationship does not require Japan to change its defence posture. Rather, it will require Japan to further expand on what it is already doing to improve its capability, capacity and readiness. This includes investing further in Japan's integrated air and missile defence, anti-submarine warfare and long-range precision strike capabilities, as well as improving Japan's magazine depth and expanding Japan's reserve force.

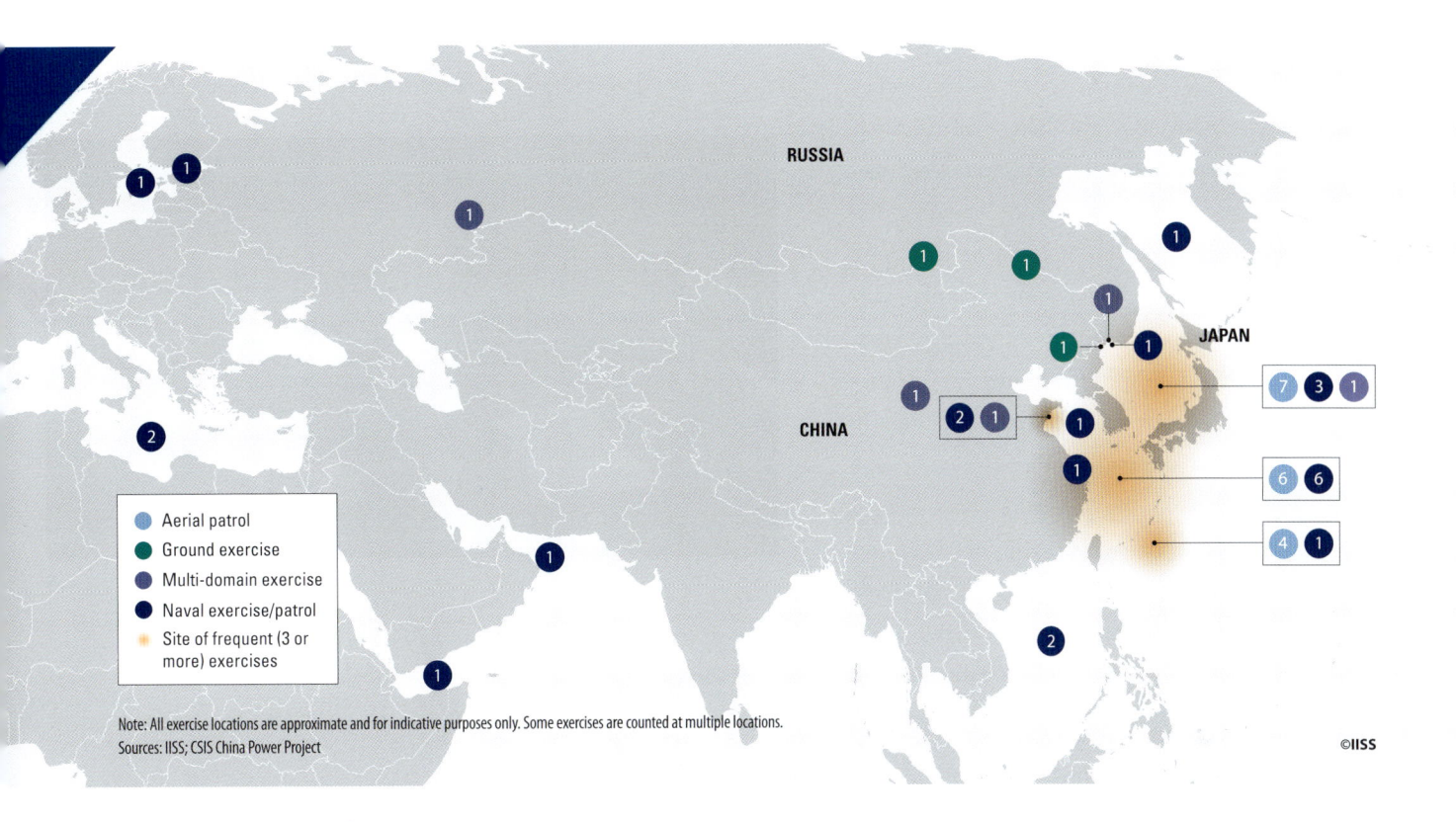

Ironclad invigorated

Tokyo is also reinforcing its alliance with the US – and seeking to play a greater role within it – to best respond to future security risks posed by a triangular collaboration between China, North Korea and Russia. The tightening of this alliance is reflected in how Tokyo's three national-security documents complement Washington's national-security and defence strategies.

A further major recent development is the United States' reconfiguring of its military command-and-control structures in Japan by upgrading the United States Forces Japan into a joint force headquarters.[53] This office will serve as a counterpart to Japan's new Permanent Joint Headquarters and enhance operational coordination and bilateral planning.

Both militaries are also deepening their joint deterrence and response capabilities. Tokyo is implementing a US-style Integrated Air and Missile Defense capability (a missile-defence network to intercept incoming missiles and a counterstrike capability to deter attacks) to be developed and operated by the two countries.[54] This, however, requires Japan to coordinate with the US on any real-time *Tomahawk* strike operations, suggesting that Tokyo's operational and political autonomy to use the capability might be limited during contingencies.[55]

Further US–Japan defence-industrial collaboration is also likely next on the list, following the regional trend of recent years (see Chapter 1 of this dossier). In December 2023, Japan made the historic policy shift of easing export restrictions on fully assembled lethal weapons, allowing the sale of *Patriot* Advanced Capability missiles to the US, with the specific aim of replenishing its stockpile (depleted by sending supplies to Ukraine).[56] In July 2024, the US and Japan also agreed to co-produce Advanced Medium-Range Air-to-Air Missiles, which will be led by the US–Japan Forum on Defence Industrial Cooperation, Acquisition and Sustainment.[57] The forum was established in April 2024 to promote greater defence-industrial collaboration.[58]

However, despite these defence-policy trends, the scale of the China–North Korea–Russia security risk requires Japan to further focus on building capability, capacity and readiness. A better integrated air- and missile-defence system, for example, may be a focus, in addition to building anti-submarine-warfare capabilities and long-range precision strikes. Japan and the US could also collaborate to build magazine depth and on the formation of a formal reserve force. Lastly, Japan and the US could increase readiness by working on larger-scale exercises that are better integrated, not just between the two allies but also with other partners, that are more frequent and employ more dynamic training regimes.

Members of the US Marine Corps and the Japan Ground Self-Defense Force engage a simulated target during exercise *Iron Fist* in Okinawa, 20 February 2025

(Lance Cpl. Raul Sotovilla via DVIDS)

The more the merrier

Japan is seeking to diversify its close partners and to build a 'multilayered network' beyond its alliance with the US.[59] This is also part of Japan's broader Free and Open Indo-Pacific framework.[60] Japan has sought to improve its relationship with South Korea and to broaden its collaboration with like-minded countries, such as the Philippines and Australia. A shared concern over Beijing's assertive behaviour in the South China Sea and the People's Liberation Army's deployments to the Pacific islands help facilitate such engagements. Japan's defence diplomacy with these countries could allow it to frame their understanding of threats in the region and lead the work towards a better coordinated defence posture.

The warming ties between Japan and South Korea under the umbrella of the Japan–South Korea–US triangular relations have played an important role in Japan's efforts to use its foreign relations to balance against China and the security concerns that it presents. The three countries' leaders held their first trilateral summit at Camp David in 2023 (and another in November 2024).[61] The summit paved the way for a joint secretariat by the end of 2024 and combined-military exercises, such as the first *Freedom Edge* multi-domain exercise, and the first joint coastguard operations in June 2024.[62] This triangular direction of travel has in part been in response to the growing China–North Korean–Russia strategic collaboration.

The Japan–Philippines–US relationship has also undergone significant development. The countries' leaders held their first trilateral summit in April 2024 amid China's increasing maritime coercion in the South China Sea.[63] The three countries are seeking to expand their trilateral coastguard exercises (which began in June 2023), and the major annual *Balikatan* exercise will include Japan for the first time in 2025.[64] Most significant perhaps is the Japan–Philippines Reciprocal Access Agreement (RAA), concluded in July 2024, which has deepened Japan–Philippines military ties and added another element to Japan–Philippines–US trilateral efforts.[65] Japan and the Philippines have been slowly broadening their practical bilateral security and defence engagement. In 2023 and 2024, Japan donated USD4m in security assistance to the Philippines and agreed to provide the Philippine Navy with rigid hull inflatable boats and additional coastal radar systems. Most recently, in 2025 Japan and the Philippines agreed to further deepen their defence ties in a response to an 'increasingly severe' security environment, in particular reference to the South and East China seas. This deepened partnership will include military exchanges, establishing a high-level strategic military dialogue and deepened information sharing.

US then-president Joe Biden holds a trilateral meeting with Philippines President Ferdinand Marcos Jr and Japan's then-prime minister Kishida Fumio, 11 April 2024

(Andrew Harnik via Getty Images)

Shared security concerns have also recently improved Japan's strategic relationship with Australia. The two countries signed an RAA in 2022, leading to increased combined-military exercises, such as Australia's first participation in the Japan–US *Keen Edge* exercise in February 2024.[66] These contribute to US-led minilateral frameworks, such as the Quad, which has aimed to expand maritime cooperation by launching the joint coastguard Quad-at-Sea Ship Observer Mission in 2025.[67] Japan may also join the second pillar of the AUKUS security partnership in 2025 in order to co-develop advanced technologies.[68]

Japan is also cooperating more with European partners on defence. Since Russia's invasion of Ukraine, Tokyo has viewed the strategic theatres in Europe and Asia as increasingly intertwined; Kishida stated in 2022 that 'Ukraine today may be East Asia tomorrow'.[69] Japan launched the joint development of next-generation fighter jets through the trilateral Italy–Japan–UK GCAP in 2022 (see Chapter 1 of this dossier) and signed an RAA with the UK in 2023.[70] Tokyo is also negotiating an RAA with France, increasingly engaging with NATO and establishing a security and defence partnership with the EU.[71] These initiatives have become increasingly critical for Japan as Russia and North Korea's mutual military support has deepened.

DUELLING GEOMETRIES?

The current security picture in Northeast Asia is becoming more complex as minilateral groupings are proliferating among the US and its allies, as well as between China and its partners. Japan continues to deepen its relationship with the US and like-minded countries, including in trilateral settings with South Korea or the Philippines and the US. While in the past China has preferred to maintain control over Northeast Asian security dynamics by pursuing bilateral relations with regional states, it has had to contend with its own minilateral groupings since Russia's invasion of Ukraine.

The relationship between China, North Korea and Russia is underpinned by a desire to change the world order into one that is anti-Western or, at the least, non-Western. However, China's relationship with North Korea and Russia is becoming more complex, with their collective relationship not yet a formalised treaty-level alliance and with each seeking to serve their own specific national interests. While the US and its regional allies grow increasingly concerned about the potential for this triangular relationship to develop into an alliance, there remain significant obstacles.

China stands to lose the most from the expanding North Korea–Russia relationship. Since 2022, China's ability to maintain control over its bilateral relations with both countries has been limited by developments in the Russia–North Korean bilateral relationship. By partnering more closely, Russia and North Korea are providing each other with an alternative to China, and in doing so are less susceptible to pressure from Beijing.

Japan's then-prime minister Kishida Fumio delivers the Keynote Address at the IISS Shangri-La Dialogue in Singapore, 10 June 2022

(IISS)

However, Beijing's need to resist what it perceives to be containment by the US and its allies is a strong driver to remain engaged with Pyongyang and Moscow. This balance between the two regional groupings is unlikely to alter unless one party changes course. In the past, deteriorating relations with Washington have led Beijing to support Pyongyang further. Conversely, China had been more willing to align with the West against North Korea's nuclear-weapons-development programmes when US–China relations were more stable.

The Trump administration, with its more hawkish approach to China so far, could present an opportunity to engage with China, along with Japan and South Korea, on the issue of its support for Russia and North Korea. Ironically, the deepening ties between Russia and North Korea could leave Beijing with fewer tools to leverage to that effect. As relations in Northeast Asia become increasingly complex and involve different multi-state strategic geometries, rather than being strictly bilateral in nature, Japan will have to be more creative in maintaining stability in Northeast Asia.

MEIA NOUWENS
Senior Fellow for Chinese Security and Defence Policy, IISS

ERIK GREEN
Research Associate, China Programme, IISS

JUMPEI ISHIMARU
Research Analyst for Japan Chair Programme, IISS

NOTES

1   Anthony Kuhn, 'Japan Lifts Longtime Restrictions to Allow Major Defense Buildup', NPR, 16 December 2022, https://www.npr.org/2022/12/16/1143017026/japan-defense-spending-weapons-buildup-rearming.

2   Linda Sieg, 'Japan Public Divided as Laws Easing Limits on Military Take Effect', Reuters, 29 March 2016, https://www.reuters.com/article/world/japan-public-divided-as-laws-easing-limits-on-military-take-

effect-idUSKCN0WV052/#:~:text=Laws%20loosening%20the%20limits%20of%20Japan's%20pacifist%20constitution,for%20the%20first%20time%20since%20World%20War%20Two.

3   Sun Li and Guan Yinghui, '学界研究动态：近期日本深度调整对华关系的动因与影响' [Academic research trends: the motivations and impacts of Japan's recent deep adjustment of relations with China], Institute of East Asian Studies, Zhejiang Gongshang University, 6 February 2024, http://dyyjy.zjgsu.edu.cn/show.asp?cid=3266.

4   Ibid.

5   Chen Xing and Wen Tianpeng, '日本涉台政策调整的路径、动因及未来走向' [The path, motivation and future trend of Japan's Taiwan-related policy adjustment], Institute of Taiwan Studies, Nanjing University, 20 October 2022, https://interpret.csis.org/translations/the-path-motivation-and-future-trend-of-japans-taiwan-related-policy-adjustment/.

6   Demetri Sevastopulo, 'US Allies Rattled by China's Aggressive Response to Nancy Pelosi's Taiwan Visit', *Financial Times*, 7 August 2022, https://www.ft.com/content/5462a57a-bd13-4313-b26b-9645b48a70ee.

7   'Former Japan PM Tells China, "A Taiwan Emergency Is a Japanese Emergency"', CNN, 1 December 2021, https://edition.cnn.com/2021/12/01/asia/abe-japan-china-taiwan-intl-hnk/index.html.

8   Chen Xing and Wen Tianpeng, 'The Path, Motivation and Future Trend of Japan's Taiwan-related Policy Adjustment', Institute of Taiwan Studies, Nanjing University, 20 October 2022, https://interpret.csis.org/translations/the-path-motivation-and-future-trend-of-japans-taiwan-related-policy-adjustment/.

9   Ibid.

10 Ibid.

11 Sun Li and Guan Yinghui, '近期日本深度调整对华关系的动因与影响' [Must grab hold of (seize) the main contradictions in the trilateral relationship between China–America–Japan], May 2023, p.67.

12 Natalie Sherman, 'Biden Blocks Japan's Nippon Steel from Buying US Steel', BBC, 3 January 2025, https://www.bbc.co.uk/news/articles/cx2vz83pg9eo.

13 'Foreign Ministry Spokesperson Guo Jiakun's Regular Press Conference on January 6, 2025', Ministry of Foreign Affairs of The People's Republic of China, 6 January 2025, https://www.mfa.gov.cn/eng/xw/fyrbt/lxjzh/202501/t20250106_11527766.html#:~:text=Guo%20Jiakun%3A%20We%20noted%20relevant,the%20health%20of%20international%20trade.

14 'China, Japan Hold High-level Political Dialogue in Beijing', State Council of the People's Republic of China, 5 November 2024, https://english.www.gov.cn/news/202411/05/content_WS67297654c6d0868f4e8ec99c.html.

15 Huang Bei and Jin Zizhen, '中日关系的改善困境与恶化限度' [The dilemma of improvement and the limit of deterioration of Sino-Japanese relations], *Quarterly Journal of International Politics*, vol. 2, 2023, https://www.cnki.net/KCMS/detail/detail.aspx?dbcode=CAPJ&dbname=CAPJLAST&filename=GJZK20230619007&uniplatform=OVERSEA&v=OW6jgKKQFKpWTEFTohU5LFEkoun4Mt-O7R0N0OmlthXJXvIIchBLlqFSWXGv-PNg.

16 'China Plans to Keep Ships Near Senkakus 365 Days in 2024', Kyodo News, 31 December 2023, https://japantoday.com/category/politics/china-plans-to-keep-ships-near-senkakus-365-days-in-2024.

17 Dzihran Mahadzir, 'Japan Stands Up Amphibious Rapid Deployment Brigade, Electronic Warfare Unit for Defense of Southwest Islands', USNI News, 1 April 2024, http://news.usni.org/2024/04/01/japan-stands-up-amphibious-rapid-deployment-brigade-electronic-warfare-unit-for-defense-of-southwest-islands.

18 Hua Xia, 'Xi, Putin Agree to Deepen Comprehensive Strategic Partnership of Coordination for New Era', Xinhuanet, 22 March 2023, https://english.news.cn/20230322/856fcc698cba4c398c2332e8607487e4/c.html; and 'China's Xi Tells Putin of "Changes Not Seen for 100 Years"', Al-Jazeera, 22 March 2023, https://www.aljazeera.com/news/2023/3/22/xi-tells-putin-of-changes-not-seen-for-100.

19 '将经济武器化将适得其反' [Weaponising the economy will backfire], *People's Daily*, 6 April 2022, http://world.people.com.cn/n1/2022/0406/c1002-32391987.html.

20 'Russia Opposes Taiwan Independence "In Any Form" – Communique', TASS, 22 August 2024, https://tass.com/politics/1832359.

21 Francesco Guarascio, 'Vietnam Sends Ship to Track Chinese Vessel Patrolling Russian Gas Field in EEZ – Data', Reuters, 27 March 2023, https://www.reuters.com/world/asia-pacific/

22 vietnam-sends-ship-track-chinese-vessel-patrolling-russian-gas-field-eez-data-2023-03-27/#:~:text=Chinese%20coast%20guard%20ships%20have,%2C%20an%20independent%20non%2Dpr.ofit.

22 Figures calculated from data collected by CSIS China Power Project, 'China–Russia Joint Military Exercises', Center for Strategic and International Studies, https://chinapower.csis.org/data/china-russia-joint-military-exercises/.

23 China Military Online, 'China Coast Guard Vessel Formation Departs for Joint Drills in Russia', 13 September 2024, http://eng.chinamil.com.cn/CHINA_209163/TopStories_209189/16338318.html. See also Meia Nouwens and Veerle Nouwens, 'China–Russia Coast Guard Cooperation: A New Dimension of China–Russia Relations?', CSIS China Power Project, 16 October 2024, https://chinapower.csis.org/analysis/china-russia-coast-guard-cooperation/.

24 Union of Soviet Socialist Republics and Democratic People's Republic of Korea, 'Treaty of Friendship, Co-operation and Mutual Assistance, Signed at Moscow, on 6 July 1961', United Nations, 23 January 1962, https://treaties.un.org/doc/Publication/UNTS/Volume%20420/volume-420-I-6045-English.pdf.

25 Ben Frohman et al., 'The China–North Korea Strategic Rift: Background and Implications for the United States', US–China Economic and Security Review Commission, 24 January 2022, https://www.uscc.gov/sites/default/files/2022-01/China-North_Korea_Strategic_Rift.pdf.

26 Kristin Huang, 'How China Responded to Previous North Korean Nuclear Tests', *South China Morning Post*, 4 September 2017, https://www.scmp.com/news/china/diplomacy-defence/article/2109692/how-china-responded-previous-north-korean-nuclear-tests.

27 'UN Security Council Resolutions on North Korea', Arms Control Association, January 2022, https://www.armscontrol.org/factsheets/un-security-council-resolutions-north-korea.

28 Hyung-Jin Kim, 'North Korea Says Its Revised Constitution Defines South Korea as "Hostile State" for First Time', AP News, 17 October 2024, https://apnews.com/article/north-korea-constitution-change-enemy-12a1ec860d84b106265d35676cb1a0b3.

29 Ministry of Foreign Affairs of Japan, 'The Ninth Japan–China–ROK Trilateral Summit', 27 May 2024, https://www.mofa.go.jp/a_o/rp/pageite_000001_00376.html.

30 'Japan to Host Trilateral Meeting with China and S. Korea in March, with Agenda Expected to Tackle Climate, N. Korea', Japan News, 23 January 2025, https://japannews.yomiuri.co.jp/politics/politics-government/20250123-234648/.

31 Andrea Kendall-Taylor and Richard Fontaine, 'The Axis of Upheaval', CNAS, 23 April 2024, https://www.cnas.org/publications/commentary/the-axis-of-upheaval; and 'Axis of Aggressors: H.R. McMaster on Defending America's Interests', Foundation for the Defense of Democracies, 26 September 2024, https://www.fdd.org/events/2024/09/26/axis-of-aggressors-hr-mcmaster-on-defending-americas-interests/.

32 Information Office of the State Council of the People's Republic of China, '中国的北极政策' [China's Arctic Policy], January 2018, https://www.gov.cn/zhengce/2018-01/26/content_5260891.htm.

33 James Kynge, Sun Yu and Xinning Liu, 'Xi Jinping's Plan to Reset China's Economy and Win Back Friends', *Financial Times*, 10 January 2023, https://www.ft.com/content/e592033b-9e34-4e3d-ae53-17fa34c16009.

34 Finbarr Bermingham, 'Chinese Ambassador Admits Russian Invasion of Ukraine Has Hurt Relations with EU', *South China Morning Post*, 23 December 2022, https://www.scmp.com/news/china/diplomacy/article/3204398/chinese-ambassador-admits-russian-invasion-ukraine-has-hurt-relations-eu.

35 Julian E. Barnes and Michael Schwirtz, 'Sending Troops to Help Russia Was North Korea's Idea, US Officials Say', *New York Times*, 23 December 2024, https://www.nytimes.com/2024/12/23/us/politics/russia-ukraine-north-korea.html.

36 'Russia Gave North Korea Anti-air Missiles in Exchange for Troops, Seoul Says', VOA, 22 November 2024, https://www.voanews.com/a/russia-gave-north-korea-anti-air-missiles-in-exchange-for-troops-seoul-says/7873098.html.

37 'Putin Signs into Law Mutual Defense Treaty with North Korea', VOA, 9 November 2024, https://www.voanews.com/a/putin-signs-into-law-mutual-defense-treaty-with-north-korea-/7858346.html; and 'North Korea Ratifies Mutual Defence Treaty with Russia', Reuters, 11 November 2024, https://www.reuters.com/world/north-korea-ratifies-mutual-defence-treaty-with-russia-2024-11-11/.

38 Jeong-Ho Lee, 'Chinese Delegation Led by Lower Rank Official to Visit Pyongyang, State Media Says', RFA, 7 September 2023, https://www.rfa.org/english/news/korea/china-pyongyang-delegate-09072023000115.html.

39 Simon McCarthy, 'China Is Sending Its Highest-level Delegation to North Korea Since 2019 to Kick Off a "Friendship Year"', CNN, 11 April 2024, https://edition.cnn.com/2024/04/10/china/china-delegation-northkorea-zhao-leji-intl-hnk/index.html.

40 Ibid.

41 James D.J. Brown, 'Japan's Strategy to Keep the North Koreans and Chinese Down, the Americans In, and the Russians Neutral', Korea Economic Institute, 29 July 2019, https://keia.org/publication/japans-strategy-to-keep-the-north-koreans-and-chinese-down-the-americans-in-and-the-russians-neutral/.

42 Gilbert Rozman, 'The China–Russia–North Korea Triangle After Kim Jong-Un's Turn to Diplomacy', Korea Economic Institute, 29 July 2019, http://www.keia.org/sites/default/files/publications/kei_jointus-korea_2019_1.0.pdf; and Andrei Lankov, 'Restitching the Triangle? North Korea Relations with China and Russia After Ukraine', Korea Economic Institute, 17 May 2023, https://keia.org/publication/restitching-the-triangle-north-korean-relations-with-china-and-russia-after-ukraine/.

43 Japan Cabinet Secretariat, 'National Security Strategy of Japan', 16 December 2022, p. 16, https://www.cas.go.jp/jp/siryou/221216anzenhoshou/national_security_strategy_2022_pamphlet-e.pdf.

44 Ibid., p. 28; and Japan Ministry of Defense, 'Defense Buildup Program', 16 December 2022, p. 49, https://www.mod.go.jp/j/policy/agenda/guideline/plan/pdf/program_en.pdf.

45 Lotje Boswinkel, 'Forever Bound: Japan's Road to Self-defence and the US Alliance', Survival: Global Geopolitics and Strategy, vol. 66, no. 3, June–July 2024, pp.105–6.

46 Japan Ministry of Defense, 'Regarding the Progress of the Projects of Stand-off Defense Capability', 18 January 2024, https://www.mod.go.jp/en/article/2024/01/299f89b-579bc56b706c608aba948a20bfe3c2335.html; Timothy Wright, 'Japan Tests New Hypersonic Glide Vehicle', IISS, 26 July 2024, https://www.iiss.org/online-analysis/missile-dialogue-initiative/2024/07/japan-tests-new-hypersonic-glide-vehicle/; and 'Japan Signs Agreement to Purchase 400 Tomahawk Missiles', Asahi Shimbun, 19 January 2024, https://www.asahi.com/ajw/articles/15118917.

47 Xavier Vavasseur, 'Japan to Test F-35B Aircraft with JS Kaga off San Diego', Naval News, 10 September 2024, https://www.navalnews.com/naval-news/2024/09/japan-to-test-f-35b-aircraft-with-js-kaga-off-san-diego/.

48 Christopher Lee, 'What Japan's Military Reorganization Means for US–Japanese Bilateral Operations', Modern War Institute, 2 April 2024, https://mwi.westpoint.edu/what-japans-military-reorganization-means-for-us-japanese-bilateral-operations/.

49 See The Space Development Strategy Headquarters of Japan, 'Space Security Initiative', June 2023, https://www8.cao.go.jp/space/anpo/kaitei_fy05/enganpo_fy05.pdf.

50 Prime Minister's Office of Japan, 'Expert Panel Toward Improving Response Capabilities in the Field of Cybersecurity', 7 June 2024, https://japan.kantei.go.jp/101_kishida/actions/202406/07cyber.html.

51 Rupert Schulenburg, 'Japan Set to Enhance Its Anti-ship Missile Inventory', IISS, 17 January 2025, https://www.iiss.org/online-analysis/missile-dialogue-initiative/2025/01/japan-set-to-enhance-its-anti-ship-missile-inventory.

52 Japan Ministry of Defense, 'Defense Buildup Program', p. 30.

53 C. Todd Lopez, 'U.S. Intends to Reconstitute US Forces Japan as Joint Forces Headquarters', US Department of Defense, 28 July 2024, https://www.defense.gov/News/News-Stories/Article/Article/3852213/us-intends-to-reconstitute-us-forces-japan-as-joint-forces-headquarters/.

54 Japan Ministry of Defense, 'Integrated Air and Missile Defense: Missile Defense Operation and Ongoing Efforts', 2023, https://www.mod.go.jp/en/d_architecture/missile_defense/index.html; and Northrop Grumman, 'Northrop Grumman and Mitsubishi Electric Collaborate to Elevate the Networking of Japan's Integrated Air & Missile Defense Systems', 16 January 2024, https://news.northropgrumman.com/news/releases/northrop-grumman-and-mitsubishi-electric-collaborate-to-elevate-the-networking-of-japans-integrated-air-missile-defense-systems.

55 Christopher B. Johnstone and Zack Cooper, 'Getting U.S.–Japanese Command and Control

56 Right', War on the Rocks, 28 June 2023, https://warontherocks.com/2023/06/getting-u-s-japanese-command-and-control-right/.

56 Takahashi Kosuke, 'Japan Eases Rules on Lethal Weapon Exports', *Diplomat*, 29 December 2023, https://thediplomat.com/2023/12/japan-eases-rules-on-lethal-weapon-exports/.

57 Jr Ng, 'Japan Seeks Large AMRAAM Order', Asian Military Review, 9 January 2025, https://www.asianmilitaryreview.com/2025/01/japan-seeks-large-amraam-order-foc/#:~:text=Japan%20has%20requested%20to%20acquire,the%20US%20Department%20of%20State; and Unshin Lee Harpley, 'Japan to Start Making AMRAAMs and Export PAC-3 Missiles', *Air and Space Forces Magazine*, 29 July 2024, https://www.airandspaceforces.com/japan-steps-up-missile-production-in-deal-with-u-s/. The US and Japan also agreed to co-produce Advanced Medium-Range Air-to-Air Missiles.

58 US Department of Defense, 'Under Secretary of Defense for Acquisition and Sustainment Travel to Japan', 5 June 2024, https://www.defense.gov/News/Releases/Release/Article/3797650/under-secretary-of-defense-for-acquisition-and-sustainment-travel-to-japan/.

59 'Japan's Kishida Advocates Wider Defense Network Ahead of US Trip', Bloomberg UK, 5 April 2024, https://www.bloomberg.com/news/articles/2024-04-05/japan-s-kishida-advocates-wider-defense-network-ahead-of-us-trip.

60 Japan, Cabinet Secretariat, 'National Security Strategy of Japan', p. 23.

61 'Trilateral Leaders' Summit of the United States, Japan and the Republic of Korea', US Embassy and Consulates in Japan, 19 August 2023, https://jp.usembassy.gov/trilateral-leaders-summit-us-japan-south-korea/; and Ministry of Foreign Affairs of Japan, 'Japan–US–ROK Summit Meeting', 15 November 2024, https://www.mofa.go.jp/region/pageite_000001_00646.html.

62 Ministry of Foreign Affairs of Japan, 'Japan–US–ROK Summit Meeting'; and US Indo-Pacific Command, 'Trilateral Statement: First Execution of Multi-domain Japan–ROK–US Exercise FREEDOM EDGE', 27 June 2024, https://www.pacom.mil/Media/News/News-Article-View/Article/3819042/trilateral-statement-first-execution-of-multi-domain-japan-rok-us-exercise-free/.

63 Ministry of Foreign Affairs of Japan, 'Japan–US–Philippines Summit', 11 April 2024, https://www.mofa.go.jp/s_sa/sea2/ph/pageite_000001_00267.html.

64 Embassy of Japan in the Philippines, 'Japan Coast Guard Conducts Trilateral Maritime Exercise with Philippines, US Coast Guards', 1 June 2023, https://www.ph.emb-japan.go.jp/itpr_en/11_000001_01181.html; and Pia Gutierrez, 'Philippines Extends Invitation to Japan to Join Balikatan 2025', ABS CBN, 17 April 2024, https://www.abs-cbn.com/news/2024/4/17/philippines-extends-invitation-to-japan-to-join-balikatan-2025-1647.

65 Ministry of Foreign Affairs of Japan, 'Signing of the Japan–Philippines Reciprocal Access Agreement', 8 July 2024, https://www.mofa.go.jp/s_sa/sea2/ph/pageite_000001_00432.html.

66 Department of Defence Australia, 'Historic Australian First for Japan's F-35As', 6 September 2023, https://www.defence.gov.au/news-events/news/2023-09-06/historic-australian-first-japans-f-35as#:~:text=A%20warm%20Northern%20Territory%20welcome,down%20at%20RAAF%20Base%20Tindal; and 'Ex. Keen Edge Concludes with Trilateral Successes', US Forces Japan, 15 February 2024, https://www.usfj.mil/Media/Press-Releases/Article-View/Article/3677748/ex-keen-edge-24-concludes-with-trilateral-successes/.

67 Prakash Panneerselvam, 'The Quad's Coast Guard Cooperation: New Dynamics in Power Politics', *Diplomat*, 17 October 2024, https://thediplomat.com/2024/10/the-quads-coast-guard-cooperation-new-dynamics-in-power-politics/.

68 Rintaro Tobita, 'Japan to Participate in AUKUS Defense Tech Tests: US Official', Nikkei Asia, 25 October 2024, https://asia.nikkei.com/Politics/Defense/Japan-to-participate-in-AUKUS-defense-tech-tests-U.S.-official.

69 The IISS Shangri-La Dialogue, IISS, 'Keynote Address – Kishida Fumio, Prime Minister, Japan', 10–12 June 2022, p. 8, https://www.iiss.org/globalassets/media-library---content-migration/files/shangri-la-dialogue/2022/

transcripts/keynote-address/kishida-fumio-prime-minister-japan-as-delivered.pdf.

70 Ministry of Foreign Affairs of Japan, 'Signing of Japan–UK Reciprocal Access Agreement', 11 January 2023, https://www.mofa.go.jp/erp/we/gb/page1e_000556.html.

71 Ministry of Foreign Affairs of Japan, 'Japan–France Foreign Ministers' Meeting', 3 May 2024, https://www.mofa.go.jp/erp/we/fr/pageite_000001_00351.html; NATO, 'Relations with Japan', 25 October 2024, https://www.nato.int/cps/en/natohq/topics_50336.htm; and European External Action Service, 'Security and Defence Partnership Between the European Union and Japan', 1 November 2024, p. 1, https://www.eeas.europa.eu/sites/default/files/documents/2024/EU-Japan%20Security%20and%20Defence%20Partnership.pdf.

CHAPTER 4

DEEP DIVE: SUBSEA WARFARE TRENDS IN THE ASIA-PACIFIC

This chapter discusses why and how the Asia-Pacific subsea domain is undergoing significant transformation and becoming of increasing strategic significance in its naval dynamics.

A nuclear-powered submarine of the People's Liberation Army Navy's North Sea Fleet prepares to dive into the sea (AFP/AFP via Getty Images)

ARGUMENTS AND FINDINGS:

- The subsea domain is undergoing transformation with the addition of new technologies, as well as the growing concern about 'seabed warfare' and the vulnerabilities of critical underwater infrastructure (CUI).
- Uninhabited platforms and systems are beginning to shape the subsea battlespace and are coupled with the heightened concerns over CUI and the prioritisation of efforts to counter threats to it.
- Renewed nuclear-deterrence concerns are also impacting the subsea environment, with China, North Korea, Russia and the United States investing in enhanced capabilities in this arena.
- There is a potential step change in China's submarine capabilities, while the US is redoubling its efforts, under some strain, to maintain its asymmetric advantage in this area.

IMPLICATIONS FOR REGIONAL SECURITY:

- How subsea battlespace trends and developments evolve will significantly shape the Asia-Pacific strategic balance over the next ten years.
- The underwater domain will become an increasingly important consideration in both defence investment and strategic calculations for major regional powers.
- While China's ambitions will guarantee significant growth in the potency of its subsea capabilities, the success or otherwise of the future programmes of the US and its allies and partners will be key to the credibility of their future deterrence postures in the region.

The subsea domain is becoming an increasingly critical arena in Asia-Pacific competitive defence dynamics, and will likely be a decisive one in any major conflict in the western Pacific. The increased potency and the proliferation of long-range precision-strike anti-ship systems have already made the Asia-Pacific naval domain an increasingly hostile and challenging battlespace for even the best-equipped surface naval forces. As such, regional navies have grown their submarine capabilities intently over the past decade.

This is unsurprising, given that submarines represent the most survivable and effective means of denying adversaries the sea or maritime space (sea denial), at least in the opening phases of a major peer-on-peer great-power conflict between China and the United States. Submarines have also become increasingly capable naval war-fighting platforms, as well as intelligence, surveillance and reconnaissance (ISR) assets and power-projection platforms with land-attack cruise missile (LACM) capabilities. These asymmetric capabilities and the advantages that they offer also make submarines more attractive to smaller regional states.

The continuing opacity of the subsurface environment and the ability of submarines to operate clandestinely also make them useful tools for grey-zone operations and 'coercive naval diplomacy'. Meanwhile, the growing concern over nuclear-force developments, proliferation, and rhetorical nuclear brinkmanship amidst ongoing conflicts and great-power frictions has made submarines even more significant as second-strike strategic nuclear platforms. It has also refocused attention on the challenging nuclear-deterrence aspects of Asia-Pacific undersea competition more than at any time since the height of the Cold War, and maybe even more so with the introduction of China and India, and potentially North Korea, as well as Russia and the US, into this game.

New technologies – especially uninhabited underwater vehicles (UUVs) and even autonomous undersea vehicles – are further transforming the character of undersea competition, frictions and potential conflict. The ambition of applying ever more artificial intelligence (AI) to the processing of undersea data also adds to the growing efforts to make the subsurface environment at least slightly more transparent for regional strategic policymakers, even if a significant body of expert opinion still questions whether the theoretical propositions behind these developments will translate into practical reality.

The ability to better survey the subsea environment and seabed is, nevertheless, becoming an increasingly significant, if not urgent, task for military planners. This is alongside the growing concern over CUI protection. All of this is taking place with a heightened awareness of the importance of traditional maritime trade routes and the need to protect them, as well as of the geo-economic significance of the subsea data-cable and pipeline networks and their potential vulnerabilities.

China's advancing submarine and undersea capabilities have been the main driver of the region's subsurface evolution. These include China's development of near-waters sea denial, the support of a growing and increasingly significant nuclear-powered ballistic-missile submarine (SSBN) force and ultimately enhanced power projection. These developments have been taking place hand in hand with Beijing's pursuit of new undersea technology. Meanwhile, the United States' once substantial advantage in platform and systems performance is under challenge, and demands across the globe are stretching its submarine force thin.

Seen in this light, the Australia–United Kingdom–United States (AUKUS) agreement, the core tenet of which is to deliver a nuclear-powered conventionally armed submarine capability for the Royal Australian Navy (RAN), could be one of the most significant future subsea-warfare developments in the region, formidable challenges notwithstanding. The role and ambitions of other regional players will also increasingly shape and shift the balance of underwater power. These include Russia, with its highly capable submarine force; North Korea, with its quest for a submarine-based nuclear-strike capability; and other regional powers, such as Indonesia, Japan, Singapore and South Korea, who seek to improve their already modernised and increasingly capable submarine and subsea arms.

China's anticipated subsea advances will make it more difficult for the US, its allies and partners to forward-operate in the western Pacific. But their responses – not least through AUKUS – should go a significant way in redressing the imbalance. In particular, the enhancements planned by some of the medium-sized players will make them powerful players in the subsea space, even with relatively small submarine forces. The potential vulnerabilities of the subsea infrastructure for some regional states brings a new aspect of uncertainty to the strategic balance and regional stability; as such, the ability to exploit advances in other subsea systems will become an increasingly important element of regional competition.

THE VERY MODEL OF A MODERN MAJOR NAVY?

The People's Liberation Army Navy's (PLAN) submarine force remains dominated by some 46 conventionally powered attack submarines (SSKs), out of a total of 58 submarines.[1] But while the majority of its boats might have been classified as ageing or obsolescent a decade ago, the fleet is slowly modernising, including all but the earliest Type-039A (*Yuan*) SSKs, some 20 of which are in service in different variants.[2] Further design improvements appear forthcoming, including X-form rudder arrangements for better manoeuvrability, and in the latest boat under construction, possibly vertical launch system (VLS) missile cells, for greater firepower.[3] However, mystery continues to surround the possibility that the first of this latest-design SSK or even some hybrid conventional/nuclear derivative of it may have sunk at its moorings at the Wuchang Shipyard in Wuhan in mid-2024.[4]

The advent of yet more capable SSKs will, nevertheless, significantly improve China's sea denial in its near waters and present a greater operational challenge to forward-deployed US naval assets, including US submarines. While the PLAN's recent submarine-force improvements have tended to be qualitative rather than quantitative, official US assessments suggest that the PLAN will have grown to 80 submarines by the middle of the next decade.[5] While this rate of expansion may not be sustainable in the long run, Beijing has made considerable expansions to and investments in its submarine industrial base.

Aside from the yard in Wuhan, China has focused on the Jiangnan Shipyard in Shanghai and the Bohai Shipyard in Huludao, where its nuclear-powered submarine production is concentrated and which has undergone significant enlargement in recent years. Despite these efforts, China still lags behind the US when it comes to nuclear-propulsion technology and submarine quieting.[6] Admiral Samuel Paparo, commander of US Indo-Pacific Command (INDOPACOM), warned in November 2024, however, that Russia may be providing submarine technology to China (and North Korea, along with missile technology) that could close some of these technology gaps with the US.[7]

China's *Yuan Wang* 1 survey ship in Dock 2 at the original site of Jiangnan Shipyard in Shanghai, 10 May 2023

(Costfoto/NurPhoto via Getty Images)

But the process of closing that gap is unlikely to be straightforward. The PLAN operates six Type-093 and -093A (*Shang* I and II) nuclear-powered attack submarines (SSNs) and six Type-094 (*Jin*) SSBNs. The greater acoustic signatures of these designs put them at a disadvantage compared to their US and other Western counterparts. Additionally, given the limited 7,000-kilometre range of their JL-2 (CH-SS-N-14) submarine-launched ballistic missiles (SLBMs), China's SSBNs had, until recently, needed to venture beyond the first island chain to put the continental US at risk. Their ability to manoeuvre stealthily and avoid detection has also been hampered by US and allied submarine and anti-submarine warfare (ASW) patrols, as well as by the limited egress points from the South China Sea, the presence of fixed undersea-monitoring networks operated by the US and Japan, and the shallowness of the other nearby waters of the Bohai Gulf, the Yellow Sea and even the slightly deeper East China Sea.[8]

The US has recently assessed that the PLAN has now equipped the Type-094 with the longer-range JL-3 (CH-SS-N-20) SLBM, which has an estimated reach of 10,000 km. This alters the strategic dynamics of the underwater battlespace. It suggests China's SSBNs can now remain within the relative safety of a protected 'bastion' in the South China Sea, reinforced by the weaponry and monitoring facilities on its occupied militarised features in the area. With a force of six SSBNs and sufficient crewing, Beijing could now sustain a continuous at-sea nuclear-deterrent posture.[9]

There are also expectations that the long-awaited next-generation Type-095 SSN, possibly equipped with VLS as a fully fledged nuclear-powered guided-missile submarine (SSGN), and the follow-on Type-096 SSBN, will appear in the coming years, if not by the end of the decade. Just how much of an improvement in capability (especially signature reduction) they will represent is unclear. The physical challenges of the near-sea water spaces will remain. But, with a greater industrial capacity at its disposal, China could significantly increase the size and potency of its nuclear-submarine force in the coming years and further shift the regional undersea-power balance and potentially break out into a greater power-projection role.

To a degree, China's subsurface capability lags behind its burgeoning surface-fleet development. Although there are few signs that the latter is slackening, the balance may shift, with indications of increased investments in the country's submarine industrial base and in the navy's submarine training, including the inauguration of a massive naval submarine academy in Qingdao in 2016. Coupled with a strong focus on more realistic yet ambitious and integrated training, this points to a greater push to integrate submarine operations with the rest of the fleet and China's other military arms, as well as for more independent submarine operations at greater range.[10] Beijing's own investment in fixed seabed sensor arrays – equated by some to a 'great underwater wall' – is another aspect of its comprehensive approach to this arena.

UNDERWATER PRESSURE

The US submarine force, perhaps the most important war-fighting capability for the US military in the Asia-Pacific, is under increasing strain from considerable capability shortfalls.[11] Some analysts, however, remain confident of the United States' submarine technological lead, which it has developed over decades.[12] Indeed, Admiral Charles Richard has described undersea capabilities as the main asymmetric advantage that the US has over China.[13]

In November 2024, the USS *Minnesota* became the first *Virginia*-class SSGN to be forward-deployed to Guam, joining four older *Los Angeles*-class boats there that will also be superseded over time.[14] The number of *Virginia*-class submarines in service now exceeds that of the older *Los Angeles*-class hulls as the US Navy continues to transition to more capable platforms.[15] While the introduction of more forward-deployed *Virginias* in the region will boost the qualitative technological lead of US submarines, a key issue will be sustaining the overall US hull numbers.

Among the growing strains on the US submarine fleet is the need to counter Russian submarine activity in the Euro-Atlantic area. Since 2016, the US Navy has advocated a force target of 66 tactical submarines (as opposed to SSBNs). The rationale underpinning this global goal is 'to hold adversaries at risk in both contested seas and open oceans'; the actual force strength, though, currently stands significantly below that, at 47.[16] Washington military planners have been concerned for some time about the prospect of a further dip in these numbers because of the post-Cold War submarine industrial-base atrophy, which led to older boats leaving service more quickly than newer ones can be brought in.

To help mitigate this 'trough' (which it is feared could reach as low as 41 hulls), the US Navy plans to refuel and extend the service

The USS *Indiana*, a nuclear-powered US Navy *Virginia*-class fast-attack submarine, leaving Florida on its maiden voyage as a commissioned submarine, 1 October 2018

(Paul Hennessy/NurPhoto via Getty Images)

lives of up to seven *Los Angeles*-class boats.[17] However, the submarine force is not expected to grow beyond 50 boats again until the early 2030s, and will not reach the target of 66 submarines until the 2050s. With some 60% of the navy's total submarine force estimated to be based in the Pacific, past INDOPACOM commanders have warned that they would have only about half the number of boats at their disposal as further *Los Angeles*-class submarines retire soon.[18]

All this has led to debates over the state of the US submarine industrial base, centred on two yards – General Dynamics' Electric Boat division and Huntington Ingalls Industries' site at Newport News Shipbuilding yard – alongside a myriad of firms in the supply chain. Despite significant increases in investment, the yards are not expected to reach the annual target output of two *Virginias* per year until 2028. This target would then have to be raised to 2.33 per year to account for the Australian boats under AUKUS, which remains a contentious policy issue in the US.[19]

That the US industry also needs to deliver the US Navy's top-priority programme, the already behind-schedule new *Columbia*-class SSBNs, exacerbates the congestion.[20] The consequent submarine-maintenance delays, which have left more than a third of the US Navy's tactical submarines out of action, compounds the problem. Submarine readiness has reached around 66% recently, still significantly below the navy's 80% target availability.[21]

Meanwhile, the planned retirement of the four modified *Ohio*-class SSGNs, each capable of housing 154 *Tomahawk* LACMs, in the late 2020s also means a major loss of offensive land-attack capability. As partial compensation, most of the latest Block V versions of the *Virginia* class being built will include an additional hull section housing a Virginia Payload Module able to carry 28 *Tomahawks*. But during recent periods of tension in the Asia-Pacific and Middle East, these vessels made high-profile overt deployments (compared to their typical modus operandi of stealth) for strategic-signalling purposes.[22] In the context of renewed concern over the balance of nuclear deterrence, the SSBN versions of the *Ohio* class have also made the occasional recent public appearance in the Asia-Pacific.[23]

Another challenge is the controversial plan from the first Trump administration to revive a nuclear-tipped sea-launched cruise-missile capability – including aboard submarines – and its potential impact on nuclear deterrence and stability in the region. Proponents argue that it would fill an important gap in theatre deterrent capabilities, particularly in the Asia-Pacific. But critics argue that it could be destabilising and point to significant trade-offs in terms of cost and diverting scarce ships and submarines from other missions. The Biden administration tried to cancel it, but the US Congress resisted, and a second Trump administration is likely to revive it. Exactly when and how is less clear.[24]

A further major improvement in US Navy submarine capability, largely driven by the demands of the Asia-Pacific theatre, is its next-generation SSN(X) design. It seeks to be

The entrance to Andersen Air Force Base at Yigo, Guam, 15 August 2017

(Ed Jones/AFP via Getty Images)

a higher-than-previous-generations performance vessel and more focused on high-intensity naval war fighting. It is also expected to be significantly larger and more expensive than existing attack submarines. However, budget constraints mean that the platform's procurement is being delayed from 2035 to the early 2040s. In the meantime, further improved versions of the *Virginia* class, which will now include a Block VIII variant, are being planned.[25]

The US Navy will likely continue to lead the submarine-technological game in the region, with further enhancements to its current and future submarines being planned, including the induction of UUVs into their armoury and the increased use of AI.[26] However, a key part of the US Navy's strategic plan for the region is its overall force-deployment posture. Until now, the US Navy's main forward-operating submarine base has been Guam. But this might change as it seeks to integrate more with key allies and partners on operations. These allies and partners, along with other players in the region, are also seeking to make their own significant submarine enhancements.

REGIONAL UNDERCURRENTS

Since the September 2021 AUKUS announcement, more details of the core plan to supply the RAN with eight nuclear-powered but conventionally armed submarines have emerged. The ongoing heated debates over the plan's affordability and feasibility notwithstanding, the UK and Australia have moved ahead with the design phase for the SSN-AUKUS submarine. It will incorporate key US propulsion and other technology and will equip the Royal Navy from the late 2030s and the RAN from the early 2040s. In the interim, Australian personnel have already begun training in the UK and US. A further key step is for the US to supply at least three and possibly up to five *Virginia*-class submarines to the RAN from 2032 onwards, until the bespoke and domestically produced SSN-AUKUS submarines start to arrive.[27]

Such an incremental approach is critical in delivering increased capabilities and enhanced deterrence as early as possible, given that the first SSN-AUKUS is a decade and a half away. But among the areas of contention over this plan are not only whether the US industrial base could satisfy the requirements of the US Navy and the RAN for *Virginia*-class submarines in the 2030s, but also whether Australia will be able to operate them effectively by then. Australia also faces a major challenge in upgrading its current *Collins*-class SSKs and sustaining them for the rest of this decade and into the 2030s.[28]

Still, some strategic benefits are already being felt by the US Navy. It has already increased its submarine port visits to Australia. In August 2024, a US Navy submarine underwent maintenance in Australia for the first time.[29] In perhaps the most significant early strategic dividend for Washington, up to four US submarines will be forward-deployed around western Australia from as early as

US Marines from Marine Rotational Force – Darwin (MRF-D) disembark from a V-22 *Osprey* during exercise *Talisman Sabre* in Townsville, Australia, 27 July 2021

(Ian Hitchcock via Getty Images)

2027 as part of Submarine Rotational Force – West (SRF-West), thus posing a significant additional operational challenge for PLAN commanders (in time a UK SSN will also periodically join SRF-West).

The ultimate outcome for the three partners could be an enhanced and better integrated overall nuclear-powered submarine force, with an enlarged nuclear-powered submarine industrial base to accompany it. But, from the outset, AUKUS has always been a project with potentially major strategic dividends accompanied by immense and sustained political, technical and financial challenges. It has already shrugged off changes of government in Australia and the UK, but a second Trump administration will bring uncertainty and unpredictability.

AUKUS will impact the Asia-Pacific underwater battlespace in another important way. It involves a second pillar of activities focused on a range of other advanced capabilities, including the development of advanced undersea technologies. This non-nuclear pillar, as predicted, has seen the greatest cooperation between the original signatories. In April 2024, the three partners announced their intention to open consultations with Canada, Japan, New Zealand and others.[30] Australia and Japan also separately agreed to enhance bilateral cooperative research on UUVs and other autonomous undersea technologies.[31]

The Japan Maritime Self-Defense Force (JMSDF) has created a formidable modern SSK fleet, with 25 boats, including two for training purposes. In terms of size it is now second only to China.[32] It has also boosted its capabilities with the arrival of the *Taigei*-class submarines with novel lithium-ion battery propulsion for extended endurance (the fifth of which was launched in October 2024), while a further follow-on class is expected to incorporate VLS missile cells later in the decade.[33] While the main force driver for Tokyo is China, concerns over North Korean and Russian regional ambitions and capabilities are also part of its strategic rationale for developing its forces (see Chapter 3 of this dossier).

South Korea, meanwhile, has equipped its KSS-III submarines with six VLS cells able to launch conventionally armed ballistic missiles – a first – while a second enlarged batch will be fitted with more cells and will also shift to lithium-ion batteries for propulsion. A third, even larger batch is set to follow.[34] While its main focus is to deter and counter North Korea, it also has China and, to some degree, delivering increased power-projection capability in mind.

Meanwhile, the launch of *Haikun*, the first boat in Taiwan's Indigenous Defence Submarine programme, in September 2023 has added to the proliferation of submarine operators in the region (see Figure 4.1).[35] The programme seeks to blunt any possible Chinese amphibious assault or blockade, although it appears to be mired in controversy over the cost of the eight new submarines and whether they could divert resources away from other relevant procurements.

Canada could be another important player as it seems determined to assert a Pacific role, potentially including through long-range submarine deployments. While it has struggled to maintain its ageing current flotilla of four *Victoria*-class (ex-UK *Upholder*) SSKs, it has unveiled an ambitious plan for 12 new conventionally powered boats with an emphasis on under-ice operations and extended endurance, with the aim to commission the first of these in 2035.[36] Whether and how these assets will be deployed to the Asia-Pacific remains unclear.

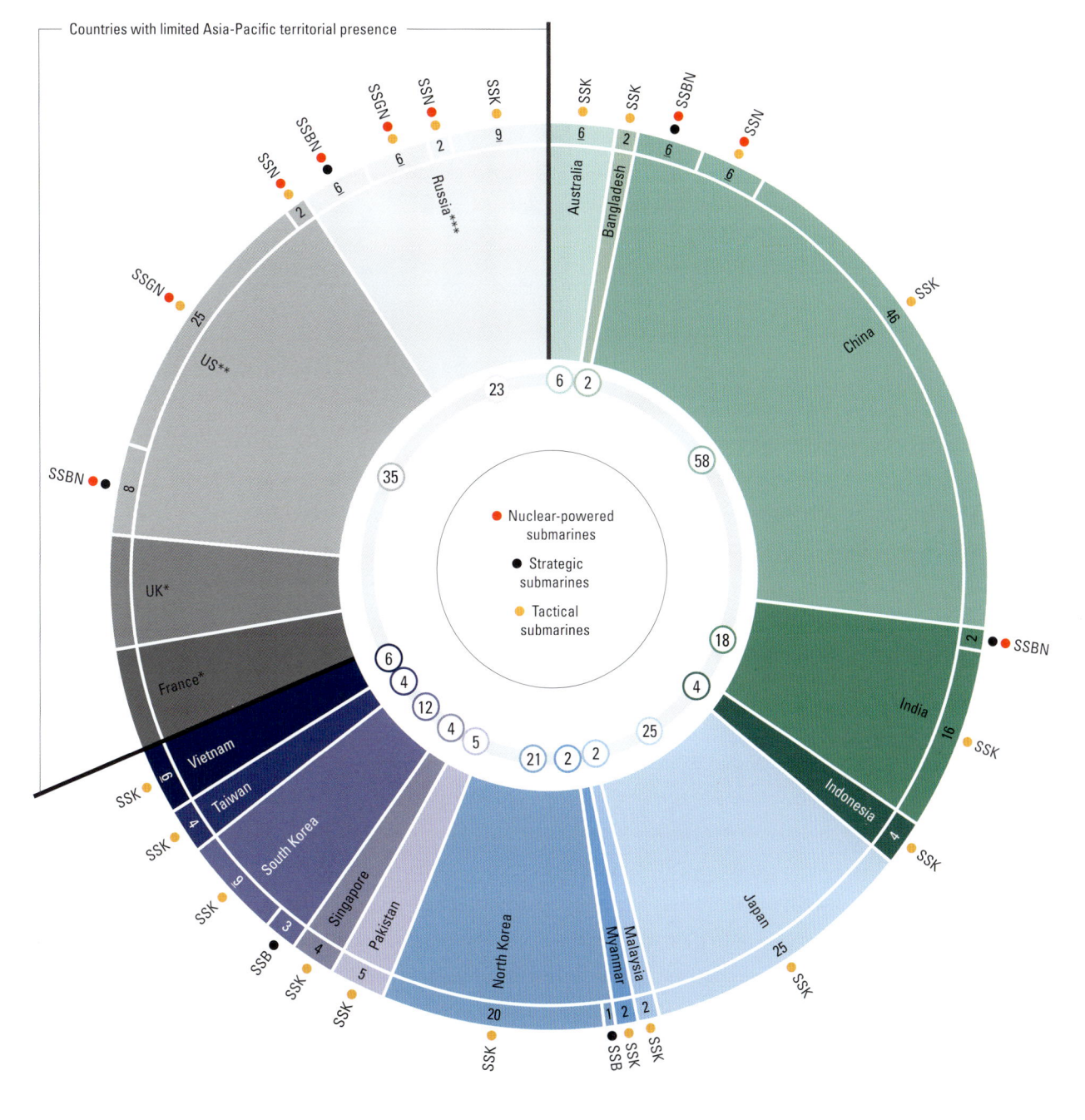

DEEP DIVE: SUBSEA WARFARE TRENDS IN THE ASIA-PACIFIC

Figure 4.1: **Asia-Pacific: submarine balance of power (selected navies)**

*France and the UK are active in the Asia-Pacific but do not base submarines there. Worldwide, France operates a fleet of 4 SSBNs and 5 SSNs, while the UK operates a fleet of 4 SSBNs and 6 SSNs. **Pacific-based submarines. ***Russian Pacific Fleet submarines.

©IISS

Note: Active inventories only; excludes coastal and midget submarines

Sources: IISS, Military Balance+, milbalplus.iiss.org; uscarriers.net

While each of these states have different security priorities, they collectively field a crucial mix of modern submarine capabilities which, if operated in an integrated way, could pose a formidable challenge to any opponent. Several Southeast Asian navies have also joined the fray, believing that even relatively modest submarine forces represent a potentially valuable asymmetric deterrent to more powerful opponents. Some are even investing in new and more capable platforms.

Vietnam led the way in 2009, with the acquisition of six Improved *Kilo*-class submarines from Russia (with the last delivered in 2017), which gave it a significant sea-denial capability. Singapore has taken delivery of the first two of four advanced Type-218SG *Invincible*-class SSKs, built by the German company TKMS. Indonesia's ambition to develop its submarine capability is focused on a plan to licence-build two French-design *Scorpène* Evolved SSKs, with a possible, although as yet unfunded, purchase of an interim off-the-shelf design to fill the gap.[37] The Philippines has also asserted its ambition to develop a submarine force as part of its strategic shift from internal to external security threats.[38] Meanwhile, Thailand has been pursuing a troubled on–off plan to purchase submarines from China.

Illustrious, one of Singapore's new Type-218SG *Invincible*-class SSKs, after its christening at the TKMS shipyard in Kiel, Germany, 13 December 2022

(Gregor Fischer/AFP via Getty Images)

The subsea environment is also heating up in the Indian Ocean. India reportedly seeks to build an indigenously designed class of SSNs, while the Indian Navy has also recently commissioned a second *Arihant*-class SSBN, although its efforts to procure new conventionally powered submarines have been marred by delays.[39] New Delhi is concerned about China's growing naval – and particularly subsea – presence in the Indian Ocean. Pakistan, meanwhile, is set to receive the first of its eight new Chinese-built *Hangor*-class SSKs, while Bangladesh and Myanmar have recently acquired submarines, although these include obsolescent Chinese-supplied boats.

One major region-wide concern is around North Korea's ambitions to create at least a rudimentary second-strike nuclear capability with a Soviet-design *Romeo*-class submarine heavily reworked as an SLBM carrier. Recently, analysts have speculated whether Pyongyang is beginning work on an SSN.[40] For the most part, however, its navy maintains a largely obsolescent but numerous fleet of coastal and midget submarines which could still pose a local challenge. In contrast, Russia remains a regional submarine power. Indeed, it has built up its Pacific Fleet submarine force to include several new *Borey*-class SSBNs and two *Yasen*-class SSGNs, as well as Improved *Kilo*-class SSKs, all of which could have a significant impact on the regional strategic naval balance.

As submarines' capabilities proliferate, there has been a revived interest and investment in ASW forces. The PLAN has made significant strides in this area, including its procurement of significant numbers of Type-054A frigates (a design being developed further). ASW nonetheless remains an area of relative weakness for the PLAN, particularly compared to the US Navy. The JMSDF has also developed as a formidable ASW force, possibly second to the US Navy in the region, with capable surface platforms and a major force of P-1 maritime patrol aircraft (MPAs).

Other major players are also investing heavily in high-end ASW capabilities. Notably, the RAN will prioritise ASW with its *Hunter*-class frigates and follow-on general-purpose frigates. A further major trend has been an increase of MPA procurements, with Australia, Canada, India, New Zealand and South Korea now operating or on the waiting list for Boeing P-8 *Poseidon* aircraft, while the US Navy is also prioritising the Asia-Pacific for deployments of these assets. The increasing requirement for persistent maritime ISR and airborne ASW is also driving interest in teaming crewed MPAs with maritime-orientated uninhabited aerial vehicles, with India and Japan adopting General Atomics' MQ-9Bs in this role.

GHOSTS IN THE GREY ZONE

The character of the subsurface battlespace has also changed significantly over the past decade with the proliferation of uninhabited maritime vehicles (UMVs) and their utility in tasks previously performed by legacy platforms. At least 40 navies worldwide now use uninhabited platforms and systems, although how they are employed within naval force structures varies considerably. Globally, the larger UMVs (which can also be optionally crewed) tend to be used in patrolling and other maritime security tasks, as in the case of Singapore's MARSEC Uninhabited Surface Vessel (USV).[41] However, the smaller, remotely operated vehicles are overwhelmingly used for military data gathering and mine warfare, as can be seen with commonly used UUV systems such as SeaFox, HUGIN and REMUS.[42]

The *Seafox* UUV, manufactured by Atlas Elektronik to locate ground and moored mines, on display at the Foyle Maritime Festival, UK, 16 July 2016

(Darron Mark/Corbis via Getty Images)

Asian countries account for approximately 27% of the total number of countries operating UMVs globally.[43] In the Asia-Pacific, China has a considerable lead in leveraging the utility of UMVs across its navy, coastguard and other state-controlled fleets. However, other smaller but technologically advanced countries, such as Singapore, are showing innovative use of a range of UMV types within their force structures. Across Asian navies, 38% of uninhabited systems are used for military data-gathering purposes (predominantly in the underwater domain) and 35% are used in mine-warfare missions.[44] As such, of uninhabited systems among Asian navies are geared towards the subsea realm, whether beneath the surface or on the ocean floor.

Uninhabited systems, however, are still largely deployed in tandem with other, legacy platforms, and are not yet due to completely replace them. Notably, the number of crewed research and surveillance vessels in the inventories of Asian navies increased from 104 to 120 between 2014 and 2024. This is due to navies seeking to better understand the subsea environment, including water conditions, currents and sea-floor contours; to support traditional submarine operations and patrols; and to probe the undersea operating space of potential opponents.

To complicate matters, there are dual-use challenges in this domain, as ostensibly purely scientific research could also serve as strategic data or even to track the navigational paths of ships or submarines. For example, the prodigious activities of Chinese oceanographic vessels in the Indian and Pacific oceans, operated by state-affiliated research organisations with close ties to the military, have drawn much attention from regional analysts and military planners.[45] The extent to which such intensified data gathering, coupled with technological means of data exploitation, will make the sea more 'transparent' remains

South Korean UUVs and other vessels on display during a ceremony at Seoul Air Base, 26 September 2023

hotly debated, but it will likely bring both new advantages and challenges to submarine operations. It also underscores the reality that the subsea space is a domain of intense intelligence activity across the Asia-Pacific – and perhaps why the underwater battlespace was dubbed 'the last great stealth domain' by First Sea Lord Admiral Sir Ben Key.[46]

The increased employment of UUVs creates new grey areas of operation (see Figure 4.2). Such systems could have a low-key footprint when it comes to intelligence gathering and a higher level of deniability (compared to missions conducted by crewed naval vessels). But, equally, they could add to the challenges of escalation management.

Over the last decade, various nations' UUVs have been recovered across the western Pacific Ocean, some even within other countries' territorial waters.[47] These include a 2016 incident when the PLAN seized a UUV operated from a US Navy ship within the South China Sea (it was subsequently returned). Chinese UUVs have been reportedly found in Vietnamese waters, as well as off at least three different sets of islands in Indonesian waters, well beyond the limits of China's claimed waters (see Map 4.1).

Up to now, these incidents have involved relatively unsophisticated systems with modest performance levels. But that could quickly change. In the Black Sea, Ukraine has strikingly demonstrated the potential of explosive-equipped USVs in combination with other systems to deliver an extremely effective sea-denial campaign. Such capabilities could migrate to the underwater space in the Asia-Pacific as well.

China has already demonstrated its potential to develop extra-large uninhabited underwater vehicles (XLUUVs), having revealed a large-displacement UUV labelled HSU001 during military parades.[48] While its operational status remains uncertain, it shows a willingness to develop larger UUVs that can carry heavier combat payloads – including ASW and offensive mine warfare – as well as conduct anti-ship missions.[49]

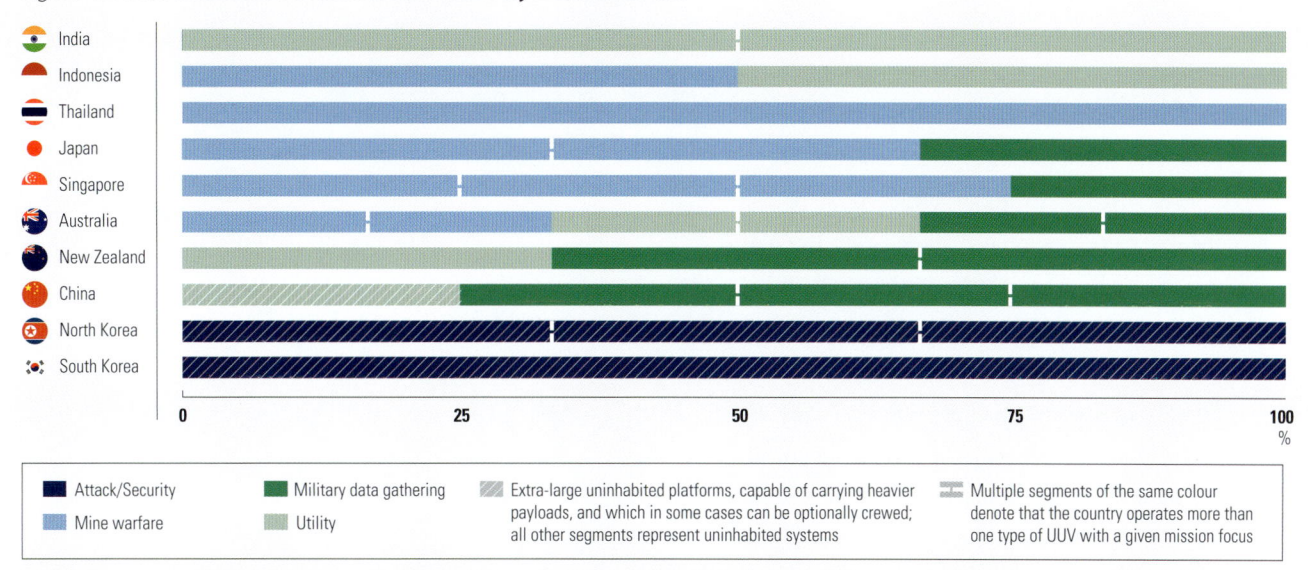

Figure 4.2: **Selected Asia-Pacific navies: UUVs by mission focus**

- Attack/Security = UUVs with an integral warhead or designed for patrol/interceptor missions; Mine warfare = UUVs used to identify or dispose of sea mines;
- Military data gathering = UUVs primarily used to collect information on the maritime environment; Utility = other or multiple mission focuses

Source: IISS, Military Balance+, milbalplus.iiss.org

©IISS

The US Navy has been pursuing its own XLUUV programme, dubbed *Orca*, for some years, and received its first prototype in December 2023.[50] Australia unveiled its *Ghost Shark* XLUUV programme in April 2024.[51] Japan and South Korea are pursuing similar programmes. While the operational timetables for these programmes remain uncertain, they will likely transform the subsea environment, although, again, likely in tandem with traditional submarines.

Mine warfare is an area that has been somewhat neglected by many Asia-Pacific navies, except by a few like China. The overall number of traditional mine-warfare vessels in Asian navies dropped from 180 to 156 from 2014–24. However, this relative neglect may be starting to change. There is growing concern about China's mine-warfare capabilities, with the PLAN operating the largest collection of mine-warfare vessels in the region.[52] Australia announced in 2023 that it was reviving a naval-mining capability.[53] Uncrewed and autonomous assets will likely play an increasing role in this future mine warfare.

WIRES ACROSS WATERS

Perhaps the most high-profile yet least visible vulnerability in the subsea space is the vast network of submarine cables (data and power) and pipelines (gas and oil) that lie on the seabed – and the rise of what has been dubbed 'seabed warfare'. Submarine communications cables, or data cables, are perhaps the most prominent element of this undersea infrastructure. There are almost 1.5 million km of these cables on the seabed, accounting for more than 95% of international data and global communications transmission.[54] These cables are also responsible for trillions of dollars' worth of financial transactions every day.

As the seafloor has always been a hazardous environment, submarine cables have suffered regular damage and required regular repair since their inception in the nineteenth century when telegraph cables were laid between England and France, Ireland and

Canada, and between Britain and other parts of the British Empire.[55] There is a great degree of reliance on this tapestry of connectors today and an increased interest in the changes in technology that put them at greater risk.

The digital nature of cables now opens them and their associated shore-based landing stations up to cyber attacks, where data can be intercepted and monitored, or the connections sabotaged (see Map 4.2). Similarly, cables can be attacked or 'tapped' by ships, submarines, divers and UUVs, in some cases at extreme depth in the remote ocean. The most high-profile recent incidents of suspected cable or pipeline sabotage have occurred in the northern Euro-Atlantic arena, although on at least two occasions a Chinese vessel has been suspected of at least some form of involvement.[56]

Worries about exposure to the vulnerabilities of CUI have been no less acute in the Asia-Pacific. Indeed, many regional bodies have recently sought to improve the resilience of undersea infrastructure. In its ICT Masterplan 2020, the Association of Southeast Asian Nations (ASEAN) outlined proposed steps to promote cooperation in improving the resilience of submarine cables. These steps include developing a framework to simplify the repair process of submarine cables, namely, by minimising the red tape required for foreign repair ships working in the waters of ASEAN member states.[57]

This was a much-needed step as submarine cables, by their very nature, transcend international and continental boundaries, with different rules and regulations in each territorial stretch of water. To complicate matters, the jurisdiction for dealing with submarine cables varies from country to country. As a result, both national and international authorities continue to grapple with what responsibilities to assign navies, coastguards, police and other maritime-security

Map 4.1: **Known Chinese UUVs found in Southeast Asia since 2016**

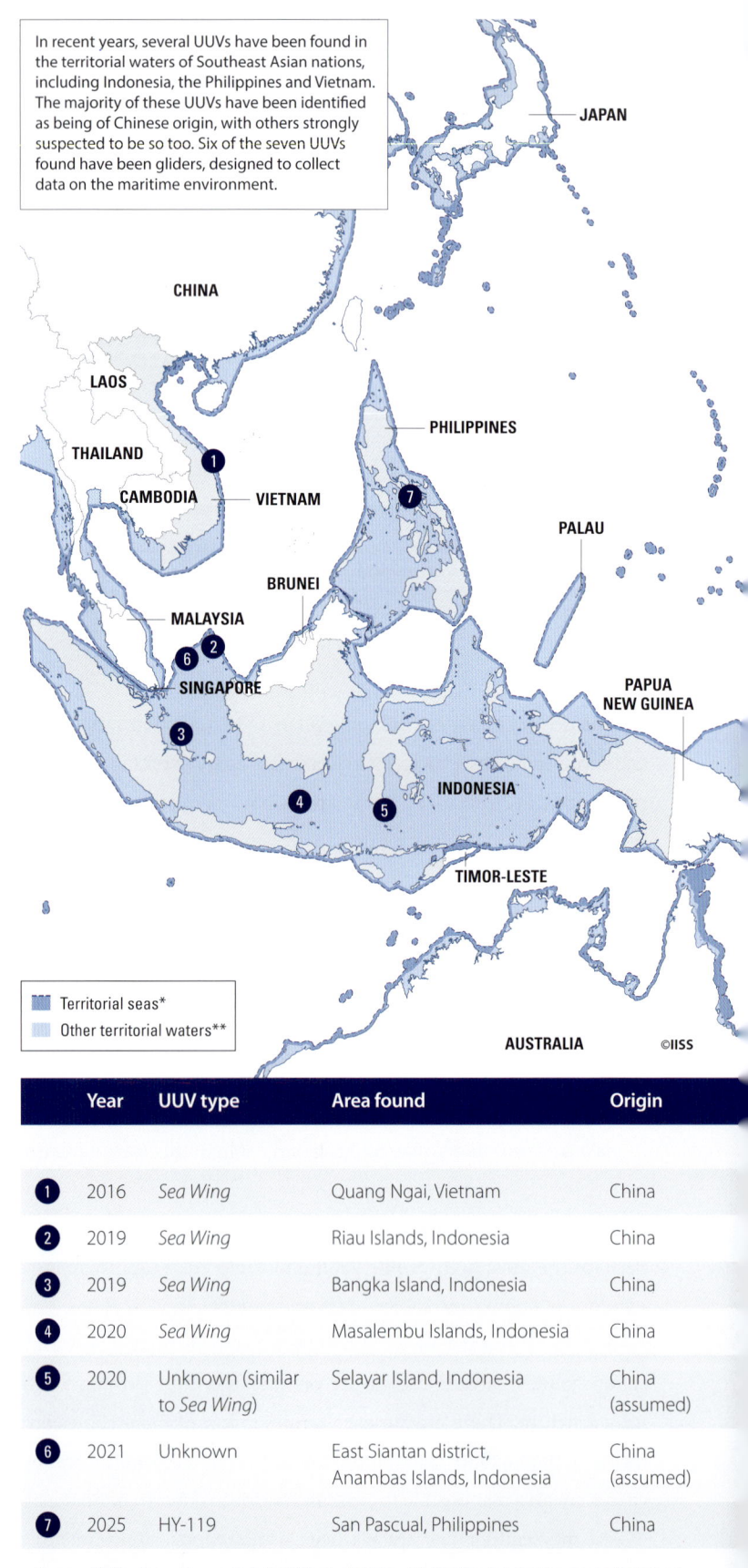

In recent years, several UUVs have been found in the territorial waters of Southeast Asian nations, including Indonesia, the Philippines and Vietnam. The majority of these UUVs have been identified as being of Chinese origin, with others strongly suspected to be so too. Six of the seven UUVs found have been gliders, designed to collect data on the maritime environment.

	Year	UUV type	Area found	Origin
1	2016	*Sea Wing*	Quang Ngai, Vietnam	China
2	2019	*Sea Wing*	Riau Islands, Indonesia	China
3	2019	*Sea Wing*	Bangka Island, Indonesia	China
4	2020	*Sea Wing*	Masalembu Islands, Indonesia	China
5	2020	Unknown (similar to *Sea Wing*)	Selayar Island, Indonesia	China (assumed)
6	2021	Unknown	East Siantan district, Anambas Islands, Indonesia	China (assumed)
7	2025	HY-119	San Pascual, Philippines	China

*From countries' baselines out to 12 nautical miles. **All waters behind countries' baselines, including internal and archipelagic waters.
Note: Map locations are plotted for illustrative purposes only. 'Area found' is approximate.

Sources: IISS; Marineregions.org

agencies, as well as the role for commercial actors in the CUI-protection efforts.[58]

Incidents involving submarine cables appear harder to address within the context of grey-zone warfare, where attribution and understanding intent are intentionally difficult. The incidents may occur under a cloak of deniability, with commercial shipping supposedly inadvertently causing damage by, for example, dragging an anchor, or seemingly innocent vessels clandestinely operating UUVs. A shortage of dedicated naval assets capable of monitoring and responding to such incidents, as well as a scarcity of submarine cable ships to undertake repairs, exacerbates the vulnerabilities.

Workers making submarine cables at a Qingdao Hanhe Cable Co. facility in Qingdao, China, 28 May 2024

(VCG/VCG via Getty Image)

While the number of submarine cables is growing globally, the number of cable-repair ships remains small; approximately 60 ships are in service and many are around 30–40 years old (see Map 4.2).[59] Only a quarter of these are routinely based in the Asia-Pacific, where it takes twice as long to repair a cable as it does in North America (30 days, versus 15), due to conflicting permit requirements (see above on ASEAN measures).[60] While militaries possess the capabilities to patrol and potentially monitor submarine-cable routes, the vastness of the Asia-Pacific waters and the multiplicity of cable routes that span them creates a Herculean challenge in terms of proactive patrolling to deter intentional attacks or to actively defend against them.

That many Asia-Pacific nations or territories are isolated islands exacerbates their vulnerability. Taiwan, for example, is heavily reliant on cables for its communications and has comparatively few landing stations that connect sea-to-shore. This has prompted worries that Taiwan could be subjected to a data blockade in the event of an attempted Chinese takeover of the island. This is not purely speculative. In 2023, Taiwanese islands experienced data outages due to Chinese non-military vessels in the area allegedly cutting cables.[61]

Smaller nations also heavily depend on submarine cables. Tonga was left without an internet connection for more than two weeks, with a third of the country's population without any connection to the outside world during that time, when an earthquake damaged cables in 2024.[62] Such vulnerabilities are not only problems to be solved, but, for a belligerent actor, potentially strategic opportunities to be exploited.

There is also an ongoing race within the Asia-Pacific for the supremacy of cable laying and cable ownership. Since 2010, more than 140 new cable routes have been laid within the Asia-Pacific, with Chinese and American companies battling for influence and control of where the routes go and over who owns them. China's HMN Technologies is a key player when it comes to cable laying in the region. The US has recently sought to block HMN's role in cable projects by threatening to sanction it, while offering grants to competitors.[63] As such, the struggle for subsea supremacy in the Asia-Pacific is not only a military battle but also an economic one.

Map 4.2: **Asia-Pacific: key undersea cables and cableships**

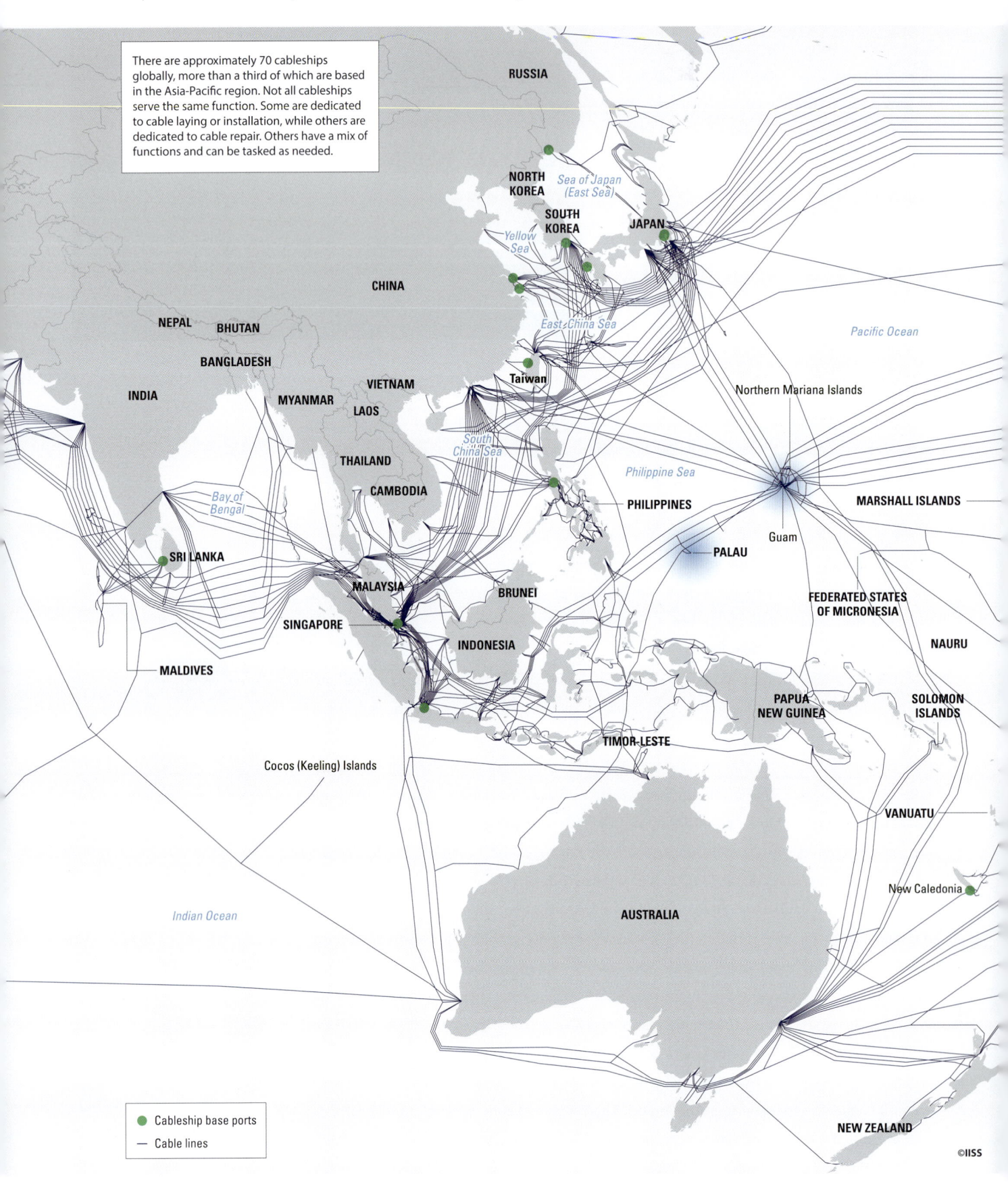

There are approximately 70 cableships globally, more than a third of which are based in the Asia-Pacific region. Not all cableships serve the same function. Some are dedicated to cable laying or installation, while others are dedicated to cable repair. Others have a mix of functions and can be tasked as needed.

- Cableship base ports
- Cable lines

©IISS

Ship name	Flag state	Operator	Base port*	Function
Ile de Re	Indonesia	OMS Group	Indonesia (Jakarta)	Installation/Repair
Teneo	Indonesia	OMS Group	Indonesia (Jakarta)	Installation/Repair
Limin Venture	Indonesia	PT Limin Marine & Offshore	Indonesia (Jakarta)	Installation/Repair
KDDI *Ocean Link*	Japan	KCS	Japan (Yokohama)	Laying/Repair
DNEX *Pacific Link*	Indonesia	DNeX Telco	Indonesia (Jakarta)	Laying/Repair
KDDI *Cable Infinity*	Japan	KCS	n.k.	Laying/Repair
Subaru	Philippines	NTT WE Marine	Japan (Yokohama)/ Philippines (Batangas)	Laying/Repair
Segero	South Korea	LS Marine Solution	South Korea (Geoje)	Laying/Repair
Lodbrog	France	OMS Group	n.k.	Installation/Repair
Reliance	Marshall Islands	SubCom LLC	New Caledonia (Nouméa)	Laying/Repair
Resolute	Marshall Islands	SubCom LLC	Taiwan (Taichung)	Laying/Repair
Responder	Marshall Islands	SubCom LLC	n.k.	Laying/Repair
Bold Maverick	Panama	S. B. Submarine Systems Co. Ltd.	China (Wujing)	Laying/Repair
Fu Hai	Panama	S. B. Submarine Systems Co. Ltd.	China (Wujing)	Laying/Repair
Fu Tai	Panama	S. B. Submarine Systems Co. Ltd.	China (Shanghai)	Installation/Maintenance
CS *Vega*	Philippines	NTT WE Marine	Philippines (Batangas)	Laying/Repair
Kizuna	Japan	NTT WE Marine	Japan (Tokyo)	Laying/Maintenance
Orion	Japan	NTT WE Marine	Japan (Nagasaki)	Laying
Kem (Project 1275)	Russia	Russian Navy	Russia (Vladivostok)	Repair
Asean Explorer	Indonesia	ASEAN Cableship Pte Ltd	Sri Lanka (Colombo)	Laying/Repair
Asean Protector	Indonesia	ASEAN Cableship Pte Ltd	Singapore	Installation
Asean Restorer	Singapore	ASEAN Cableship Pte Ltd.	Singapore	Laying/Repair
Asean Challenger	Singapore	ASEAN Cableship Pte Ltd.	Singapore	Laying/Repair
Cable Retriever	Singapore	Global Marine Systems Limited	Philippines (Batangas)	Installation/Repair
Pacific Guardian	Indonesia	Jala Nusantara Mardika	Indonesia (Jakarta)	Repair
Tian Yi Hai Gong	China	Unknown	China (Shanghai)	Laying
Zhong Hai Ke 1	China	China Comservice Marine Tech	n.k.	Laying/Repair
Dong-Lan	China	PLAN	n.k.	Laying/Repair
Nan-Lan	China	PLAN	n.k.	Laying/Repair
Global Sentinel	Marshall Islands	SubCom LLC	n.k.	Laying/Repair

*Based on known home port or repeated visits tracked through AIS data. Note: 'Ship name', 'flag state' and 'base port' are all subject to change; 'operator' is subject to change in case of changes in ownership. There may also be other ships operating in the region but without a base port there.

Sources: IISS; International Cable Protection Committee; marinetraffic.com

PERILS OF THE DEEP?

CUI vulnerabilities are a growing concern in the Asia-Pacific, and there is increased awareness of the need for a whole-of-society security resilience. As such, these vulnerabilities are set to grow in significance in the coming years. Coupled with the continuing opaqueness of the undersea space, CUI vulnerabilities will also continue to feature prominently in the arena of hybrid, grey-zone warfare among Asia-Pacific rivals.

Advanced and novel undersea technological competition will also continue to grow and will feature more and more in calculations of relative capability advantage in the naval and, particularly, subsurface space. In this area, a small but technologically advanced group of Asian players could take on an increasingly significant role. Subsurface-capability development will still be a matter of teaming crewed and uncrewed systems. But the role and importance of the latter will continue to grow and shape the subsurface domain.

In this respect, as in other aspects of naval and maritime competition, the Asia-Pacific will likely be the theatre of the greatest pacing threat heading into the future. Advances in the capabilities of modern SSKs suggest they will take on an increasingly critical role in the balance of naval capabilities in the region. The investments made by several medium powers in these platforms – and the asymmetric advantages they offer – will also bestow on them a greater deterrent capability.

However, it will still likely be the investments and progress that China, on the one hand, and the US and its key allies and partners, on the other, make in their nuclear-powered submarine capabilities that will be most telling over time in weighing the balance of subsurface and general naval power. Moreover, due to the required financial and industrial resources and support, these developments will have a significant impact on the future naval force and deterrence postures of both China and the US.

NICK CHILDS
Senior Fellow for Naval Forces
and Maritime Security, IISS

JONATHAN BENTHAM
Research Associate for Defence
and Military Analysis, IISS

NOTES

1. IISS, Military Balance+, accessed 7 February 2025, https://milbalplus.iiss.org/.
2. Johannes R. Fischbach, 'Submarine Modernisation Plans and New Sub-surface Dynamics', IISS, 7 May 2024, https://www.iiss.org/online-analysis/military-balance/2024/05/submarine-modernisation-plans-and-new-sub-surface-dynamics/.
3. H.I. Sutton, 'China Launches Its Most Sophisticated Submarine to Date', Naval News, 21 August 2024, https://www.navalnews.com/naval-news/2024/08/china-launches-its-most-sophisticated-submarine-to-date/.
4. The new platform could also possibly be a new class of small nuclear-powered boat, or some new conventional/nuclear hybrid design. Thomas Newdick, 'Chinese Submarine That Sunk Had Exotic Hybrid Nuclear Powerplant: Report', The War Zone, 2 October 2024, https://www.twz.com/sea/chinese-submarine-that-sunk-had-exotic-hybrid-nuclear-powerplant-report.
5. US Department of Defense, 'Annual Report to Congress: Military and Security Developments Involving the People's Republic of China 2023', 19 October 2023, p. 55, https://media.defense.gov/2023/Oct/19/2003323409/-1/-

6. Sarah Kirchberger, 'China Maritime Report No. 31: China's Submarine Industrial Base: State-led Innovation with Chinese Characteristics', China Maritime Studies Institute, US Naval War College, 29 September 2023, pp. 11–12 and p. 24, https://digital-commons.usnwc.edu/cgi/viewcontent.cgi?article=1030&context=cmsi-maritime-reports.

7. Peter Aitken, 'Admiral Warns Russia Will Help China Cut US Military Dominance: Here's How', *Newsweek*, 23 November 2024, https://www.newsweek.com/samuel-paparo-warns-russia-help-china-cut-military-dominance-1990633.

8. Chi Guocang, 'CMSI Translations #7: Guarantee of Strategic Security: Expert Discusses China's Strategic Nuclear Submarines Achieving Continuous Duty', China Maritime Studies Institute, US Naval War College, 30 September 2024, p. 15, https://www.andrewerickson.com/wp-content/uploads/2024/09/CMSI-Translation-7_Guarantee-of-Strategic-Security_Expert-Discusses-Chinas-Strategic-Nuclear-Submarines-Achieving-Continuous-Duty_20240930.pdf.

9. *Ibid.*, p. 15.

10. Christopher Sharman and Terry Hess, 'China Maritime Report No. 34: PLAN Submarine Training in the "New Era"', China Maritime Studies Institute, US Naval War College, 10 January 2024, p.17, https://digital-commons.usnwc.edu/cgi/viewcontent.cgi?article=1033&context=cmsi-maritime-reports.

11. Megan Eckstein, 'Harris: PACOM Needs More Subs, Long-range Missiles to Counter Chinese Threats', USNI News, 23 February 2016, https://news.usni.org/2016/02/23/harris-pacom-needs-more-subs-long-range-missiles-to-counter-chinese-threats.

12. Paul Dibb and Richard Brabin-Smith, 'Why the US Will Stay Dominant in Undersea Warfare', The Strategist, Australian Strategic Policy Institute, 26 April 2024, https://www.aspistrategist.org.au/why-the-us-will-stay-dominant-in-undersea-warfare/.

13. Oliver Parkin and Tyler Rogoway, 'Extremely Ominous Warning About China from US Strategic Command Chief', The War Zone, 6 November 2022, https://www.twz.com/extremely-ominous-warning-about-china-from-us-strategic-command-chief.

14. Lt James Caliva, 'First Forward-deployed Virginia-class Submarine Arrives in Guam', US Navy Press Office, 26 November 2024, https://www.navy.mil/Press-Office/News-Stories/Article/3978491/first-forward-deployed-virginia-class-submarine-arrives-in-guam/.

15. IISS, Military Balance+, accessed 7 February 2025, https://milbalplus.iiss.org/.

16. These exclude four elderly *Ohio*-class ex-SSBNs modified as SSGNs, and one heavily damaged and currently non-operational *Seawolf*-class SSN. IISS, Military Balance+, accessed 7 February 2025, https://milbalplus.iiss.org/. This rationale is from US Navy, 'Chief of Naval Operation Navigation Plan 2022', 26 July 2022, p. 10, https://media.defense.gov/2022/Jul/26/2003042389/-1/-1/1/NAVIGATION%20PLAN%202022_SIGNED.PDF.

17. Ronald O'Rourke, 'Navy Virginia-class Submarine Program and AUKUS Submarine (Pillar 1) Project: Background and Issues for Congress', Congressional Research Service, 5 August 2024, p. 4, https://sgp.fas.org/crs/weapons/RL32418.pdf.

18. Ben Werner, 'Indo-Pacom Commander Says Only Half of Sub Requests Are Met', US Naval Institute News, 27 March 2019, https://news.usni.org/2019/03/27/42212.

19. O'Rourke, 'Navy Virginia-class Submarine Program and AUKUS Submarine (Pillar 1) Project: Background and Issues for Congress', p. 15.

20. Ronald O'Rourke, 'Navy Columbia (SSBN-826) Class Ballistic Missile Submarine Program: Background and Issues for Congress', Congressional Research Service, 30 September 2024, pp. 39–41, https://crsreports.congress.gov/product/pdf/R/R41129/277.

21. Megan Eckstein, 'Navy's Sub Readiness Boss Unveils Steps to Teach On-time Maintenance', Defense News, 7 November 2023, https://www.defensenews.com/naval/2023/11/07/navys-sub-readiness-boss-unveils-steps-to-reach-on-time-maintenance/.

22. Nick Childs, 'Submarines Surface in More Overt Deterrence Role', IISS Military Balance blog, IISS, 19 May 2023, https://www.iiss.org/online-analysis/military-balance/2023/05/submarines-surface-in-more-overt-deterrence-role/.

23. Heather Mongilio, 'USS Kentucky Make Port Call in South Korea, First SSBN Visit in 40 Years', USNI News, 18 July 2023, https://news.usni.org/2023/07/18/uss-kentucky-calls-in-south-korea-first-ssbn-visit-in-40-years.

24. Sydney J. Freedberg Jr, 'Sub-launched Nuclear Cruise Missile Will Need "an Entirely New Industrial Base", Warns Navy Admiral', Breaking Defense, 15 November 2024, https://

breakingdefense.com/2024/11/sub-launched-nuclear-cruise-missile-will-need-an-entirely-new-industrial-base-warns-navy-admiral/.

25 Sam LaGrone, 'Naval Reactors: Virginia-class Will Extend to Block VIII, SSN(X) Start in 2040s', USNI News, 13 November 2024, https://news.usni.org/2024/11/13/naval-reactors-virginia-class-will-extend-to-block-viii-ssnx-start-in-2040s?mc_cid=6a2474a206&mc_eid=792d6ef221.

26 Vice-Admiral Robert M. Gaucher, 'Maintaining Undersea Superiority: Status Report', USNI Proceedings, October 2024, https://www.usni.org/magazines/proceedings/2024/october/maintaining-undersea-superiority-status-report.

27 A key part of the agreement, for non-proliferation and other reasons, is that the nuclear-reactor compartments for all the SSN-AUKUS boats will be constructed in the UK. Australian Government, 'Pathway to Australia's Nuclear-powered Submarine Capability', Australian Submarine Agency, 2 October 2024, https://www.asa.gov.au/sites/default/files/documents/2024-10/Nuclear_Powered_Capability_Fact_Sheet_0.pdf.

28 Colin Clark, '"Alarming" but "Not Surprising"': Australia Reportedly Left with 1 Operational Sub amid Repairs, Upgrades', Breaking Defense, 1 November 2024, https://breakingdefense.com/2024/11/alarming-but-not-surprising-australia-reportedly-left-with-1-operational-sub-amid-repairs-upgrades/.

29 Kirsty Needham, 'Australia Conducts First Maintenance of US Nuclear Submarine', Reuters, 23 August 2024, https://www.reuters.com/world/australia-conducts-first-maintenance-us-nuclear-submarine-2024-08-23/.

30 UK Government, 'AUKUS Partnership to Consult with Other Nations Including Japan on Military Capability Collaboration', 8 April 2024, https://www.gov.uk/government/news/aukus-partnership-to-consult-with-other-nations-including-japan-on-military-capability-collaboration.

31 Australian Government, 'Australia and Japan Sign Research Agreement for Undersea Warfare', 23 January 2024, https://www.defence.gov.au/news-events/releases/2024-01-23/australia-and-japan-sign-research-agreement-undersea-warfare.

32 IISS, Military Balance+, accessed 7 February 2025, https://milbalplus.iiss.org/.

33 Kosuke Takahashi, 'Japan Launches Fifth Taigei-class Submarine for JMSDF', Naval News, 4 October 2024, https://www.navalnews.com/naval-news/2024/10/japan-launches-fifth-taigei-class-submarine-for-jmsdf/.

34 Gordon Arthur, 'Submarines Resurgent', Asian Military Review, 28 November 2023, https://www.Asianmilitaryreview.com/2023/11/submarines-resurgent/.

35 Tessa Wong, 'Haikun: Taiwan Unveils New Submarine to Fend Off China', BBC News, 28 September 2023, https://www.bbc.co.uk/news/world-asia-66932808.

36 Government of Canada, 'Canada Launching Process to Acquire up to 12 Conventionally-powered Submarines', 10 July 2024, https://www.canada.ca/en/department-national-defence/news/2024/07/canada-launching-process-to-acquire-up-to-12-conventionally-powered-submarines.html.

37 Fauzan Malufti, 'Indonesia and France Discuss Key Details on Scorpène Evolved Submarines', Naval News, 20 September 2024, https://www.navalnews.com/naval-news/2024/09/indonesia-and-france-discuss-key-details-on-scorpene-evolved-submarines/.

38 'Philippines Plans to Buy Submarines to Defend Sovereignty in South China Sea – Senior Official', Reuters, 1 February 2024, https://www.reuters.com/world/asia-pacific/philippines-plans-buy-submarines-defend-sovereignty-south-china-sea-senior-2024-02-01/.

39 Rahul Singh, 'India to Ink Deal for Rafale Jets, Submarines Soon: Navy Chief', *Hindustan Times*, 3 December 2024, https://www.hindustantimes.com/india-news/india-to-ink-deal-for-rafale-jets-submarines-soon-navy-chief-101733164652391.html.

40 A.B. Abrams, 'North Korea's Nuclear Submarine Program Could Seriously Complicate a Future US War Effort', *Diplomat*, 15 October 2024, https://thediplomat.com/2024/10/north-koreas-nuclear-submarine-program-could-seriously-complicate-a-future-us-war-effort/.

41 In IISS Military Balance+ these are classified as uninhabited platforms.

42 In IISS Military Balance+ parlance these are classified as uninhabited systems.

43 'Asian' here refers to countries and territories that fall within the 'Asia' region within the IISS *Military*

Balance publication, IISS, Military Balance+, accessed 7 February 2025, https://milbalplus.iiss.org/.

44 IISS, Military Balance+, accessed 7 February 2025, https://milbalplus.iiss.org/.

45 Matthew P. Funaiole, Brian Hart and Aidan Powers-Riggs, 'Surveying the Seas', Center for Strategic and International Studies, 10 January 2024, https://features.csis.org/hiddenreach/china-indian-ocean-research-vessels/.

46 Royal Navy News, 'New Attack Submarine HMS Anson Joins the Royal Navy', 31 August 2022, https://www.royalnavy.mod.uk/news/2022/august/31/220831-hms-anson-joins-the-royal-navy-fleet.

47 H.I. Sutton, 'Underwater Drone Incidents Point to China's Expanding Intelligence Gathering', RUSI, 15 January 2021, https://rusi.org/explore-our-research/publications/commentary/underwater-drone-incidents-point-chinas-expanding-intelligence-gathering.

48 David R. Strachan, 'China Enters the UUV Fray', Diplomat, 22 November 2019, https://thediplomat.com/2019/11/china-enters-the-uuv-fray/.

49 H.I. Sutton, 'China's New Extra-large Submarine Drones Revealed', Naval News, 16 September 2022, https://www.navalnews.com/naval-news/2022/09/chinas-secret-extra-large-submarine-drone-program-revealed/.

50 Aaron-Matthew Lariosa, 'Navy Receives First of Six Prototype Extra Large Orca Underwater Drones', USNI News, 21 December 2023, https://news.usni.org/2023/12/21/navy-receives-first-of-six-prototype-extra-large-orca-underwater-drones.

51 'First Autonomous Undersea Vehicle "Ghost Shark" Prototype Ready', Australian Government, 18 April 2024, https://www.minister.defence.gov.au/media-releases/2024-04-18/first-autonomous-undersea-vehicle-ghost-shark-prototype-ready.

52 Andy Wong, 'Mine Warfare in Asia-Pacific Naval Theatre: A Clear and Present Danger', Wavell Room, 21 November 2022, https://wavellroom.com/2022/11/21/mine-warfare-in-asia-pacific-naval-theatre-a-clear-and-present-danger/.

53 'Australian Defence Force to Purchase Smart Sea Mines', Australian Government, 29 August 2023, https://www.defence.gov.au/news-events/releases/2023-08-29/australian-defence-force-purchase-smart-sea-mines.

54 See US Department of Commerce, 'Submarine Cables', National Oceanic and Atmospheric Administration, 5 March 2024, http://www.noaa.gov/submarine-cables; and TeleGeography, 'Submarine Cable Frequently Asked Questions', https://www2.telegeography.com/submarine-cable-faqs-frequently-asked-questions.

55 'Submarine Cable History', Ocean Networks Inc., https://www.submarinecablesystems.com/history.

56 Bojan Pancevski, 'Chinese Ship's Crew Suspected of Deliberately Dragging Anchor for 100 Miles to Cut Baltic Cables', Wall Street Journal, 29 November 2024, https://www.wsj.com/world/europe/chinese-ship-suspected-of-deliberately-dragging-anchor-for-100-miles-to-cut-baltic-cables-395f65d1?msockid=1edab09d35a669582b04a40b346d6833.

57 The ASEAN ICT Masterplan 2020, ASEAN, 2020, p.21, https://asean.org/wp-content/uploads/images/2015/November/ICT/15b%20--%20AIM%202020_Publication_Final.pdf.

58 Jeslyn Tan, 'Securing the Backbone: Security Challenges to and Governance of Submarine Cables in the Indo-Pacific', Melbourne Asia Review, https://melbourneasiareview.edu.au/securing-the-backbone-security-challenges-to-and-governance-of-submarine-cables-in-the-indo-pacific/.

59 Robert Clark, 'Another Telco Supply-chain Shortage: Cable Ships', Light Reading, 23 November 2022, https://www.lightreading.com/digital-transformation/another-telco-supply-chain-shortage-cable-ships.

60 Priscilla Tomaz and Julia Voo, 'Submarine Cables: The Achilles' Heel of Cyberspace in the Asia-Pacific', IISS, Cyber Power Matrix, https://www.iiss.org/cyber-power-matrix/submarine-cables-the-achilles-heel-of-cyberspace-in-the-asia-pacific/.

61 'How China and Russia Could Hobble the Internet', The Economist, 11 July 2024, https://www.economist.com/international/2024/07/11/how-china-and-russia-could-hobble-the-internet.

62 Kalafi Moala, 'Parts of Tonga Without Internet After Cables Damaged and Starlink Ordered to Cease Operations', Guardian, 16 July 2024, https://www.theguardian.com/world/article/2024/jul/16/parts-of-tonga-without-internet-after-cables-damaged-and-starlink-ordered-to-cease-operations.

63 'How China and Russia Could Hobble the Internet'.

CHAPTER 5

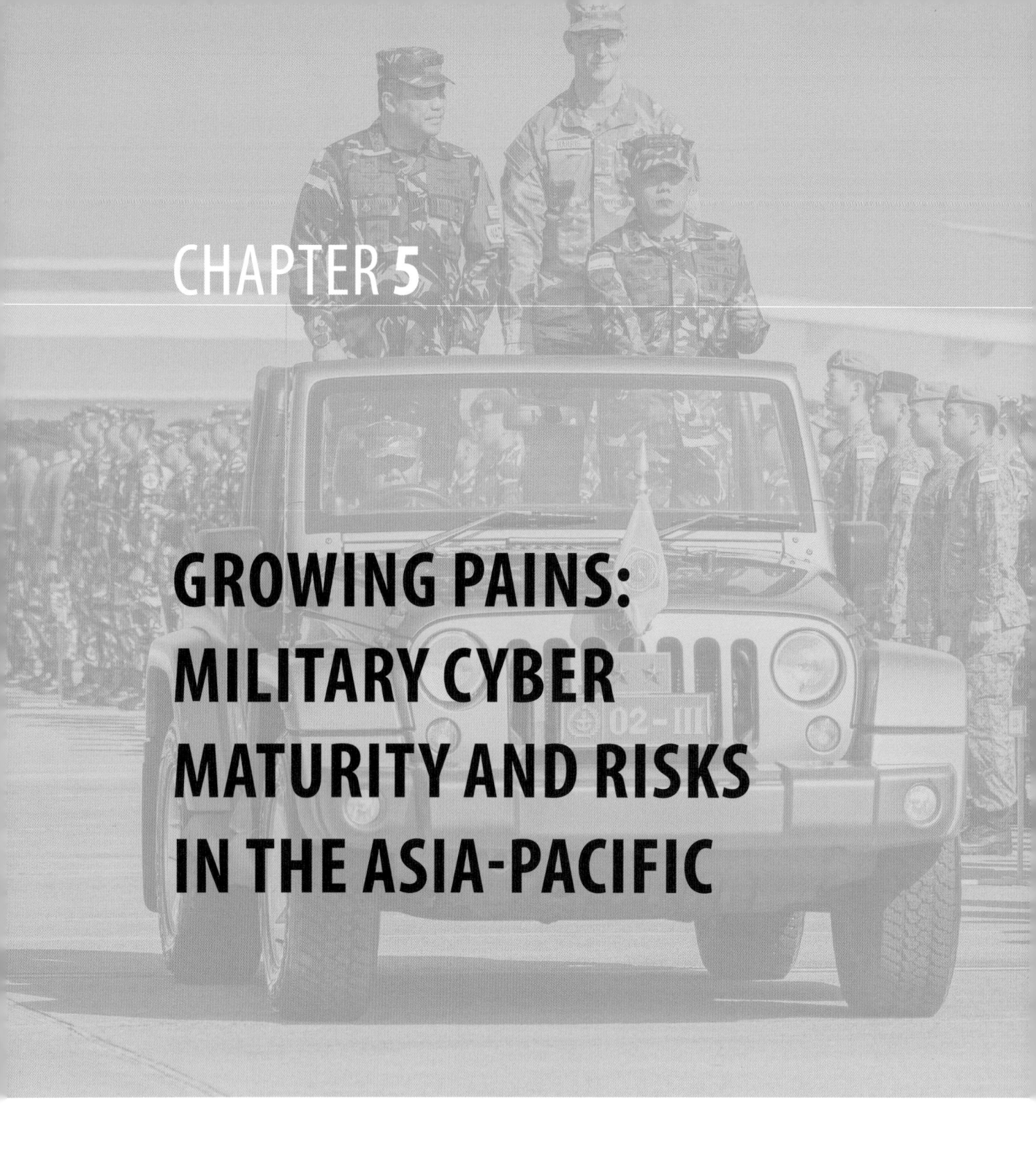

GROWING PAINS: MILITARY CYBER MATURITY AND RISKS IN THE ASIA-PACIFIC

This chapter examines how Asia-Pacific states seek to 'mature' their military cyber forces to meet the growing state and non-state threats emanating from cyberspace.

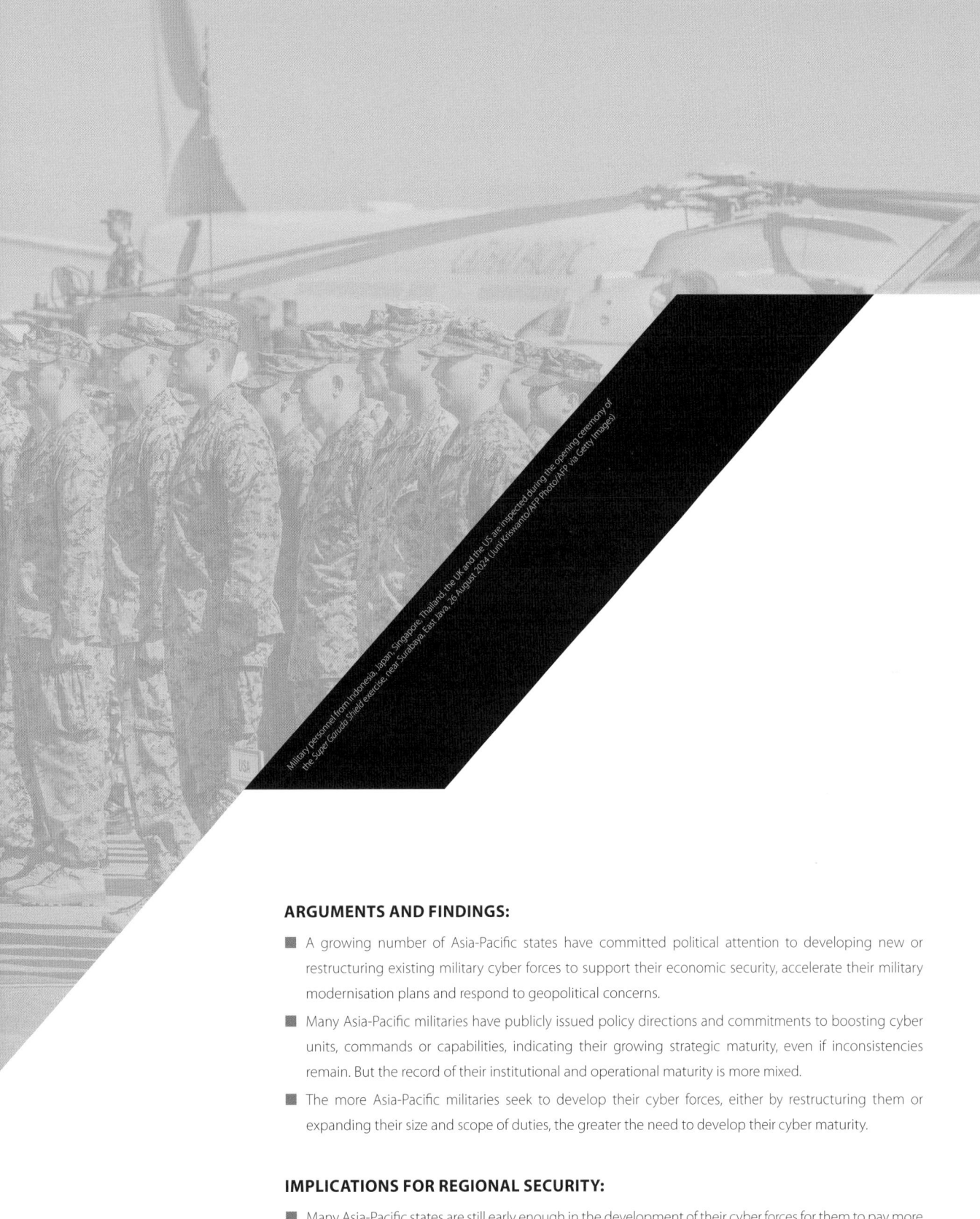

Military personnel from Indonesia, Japan, Singapore, Thailand, the UK and the US are inspected during the opening ceremony of the Super Garuda Shield exercise, near Surabaya, East Java, 26 August 2024 (Juni Kriswanto/AFP Photo/AFP via Getty Images)

ARGUMENTS AND FINDINGS:

- A growing number of Asia-Pacific states have committed political attention to developing new or restructuring existing military cyber forces to support their economic security, accelerate their military modernisation plans and respond to geopolitical concerns.
- Many Asia-Pacific militaries have publicly issued policy directions and commitments to boosting cyber units, commands or capabilities, indicating their growing strategic maturity, even if inconsistencies remain. But the record of their institutional and operational maturity is more mixed.
- The more Asia-Pacific militaries seek to develop their cyber forces, either by restructuring them or expanding their size and scope of duties, the greater the need to develop their cyber maturity.

IMPLICATIONS FOR REGIONAL SECURITY:

- Many Asia-Pacific states are still early enough in the development of their cyber forces for them to pay more attention to understanding the limitations and risks of constant competition and conflict in cyberspace.
- Failing to consider and respond to these risks could lead to a cyber-security dilemma wherein an increasing number of states will appear as 'cyber capable' and could find themselves engaging with competition and conflict dynamics with which they have not previously contended.

Cyberspace – a man-made, interconnected, virtual domain that has been integrated across several aspects of life – has evolved into a domain which states seek to use to exert influence over each other, bringing them into competition and conflict.[1] Emanating a myriad of threats, cyberspace is a domain of constant competition, and Asia-Pacific states are taking steps to ensure that their militaries, alongside other institutions, are structured to defend against and address them.[2]

But conflicts in cyberspace unfold differently from conventional military ones. Indeed, when used alone, cyber operations appear far less effective than traditional physical tools at achieving strategic outcomes during conflict; their effects are hard to anticipate and contain; their impact may be short-lived on resilient targets; and they depend on a well-prepared target environment, relying on unpatched systems and undetected vulnerabilities.[3]

Creative depiction of the world of cyberspace, focused on the Asia-Pacific

(KTSimage/iStock/Getty Images Plus via Getty Images)

States, nonetheless, continue to establish and strengthen their military cyber forces as the nature of warfare and cyber operations evolves.[4] This does not in itself guarantee that they will be successful, as there is no uniform approach for the development of cyber forces and their uses. Yet the political decisions that are currently being made on cyber forces reflect how states are beginning to perceive cyberspace and how to tackle competition and conflict within it.

Asia-Pacific states, in particular, have year-on-year become increasingly vulnerable to cyber threats.[5] Connectivity has exploded in the region in recent years and governments are committed to further development of their digital economies.[6] They are playing a larger role in global supply chains, from semiconductors to commercial commodities and the transportation of vital goods and services.[7] And crucially, the region is central to the growing geopolitical competition driven by major powers.

As such, it is unsurprising that at least 11 regional states have been either establishing, elevating or restructuring their cyber forces since 2017 (see Table 5.1). Elsewhere, the pursuit of military cyber capabilities has been driven by historical lessons and distinct national-security imperatives. Outside the region, this is clear through the United States' and United Kingdom's development of cyber-offensive capabilities as an extension of traditional signals intelligence and electronic warfare, which were then used to support counter-terrorism objectives following 9/11.

Likewise, many Asia-Pacific states have sought to enhance their intelligence-gathering through cyber means, to defend against intelligence efforts targeting them, both from within and outside the region. For example, as the region's financial and trade hub, Singapore faces significant cyber risks from state and non-state actors, targeting its finance, maritime and telecommunications sectors. India, Malaysia and Thailand now also use cyber capabilities to monitor domestic activity, such as dissidents, activists and investigative

Table 5.1: **Selected Asia-Pacific military cyber units and forces since 2017**

Military	Unit or force	Commander rank	Reporting to	Year of formation	Responsibility
Brunei	Cyber Defence Unit	Colonel	Commander, Royal Brunei Armed Forces**	2021	Cyber and information operations
China	PLA Cyberspace Force	Lieutenant-general	Central Military Commission	2024†	Cyber and information operations
India	Defence Cyber Agency	Rear admiral	Chief of Defence Staff, Indian Armed Forces	2018	Cyber operations
Indonesia	TNI Cyber Unit	Brigadier-general	Commander, Indonesian National Armed Forces (TNI)	2019	Cyber operations
Japan	JSDF Cyber Defense Command	Major-general	Commander, Joint Operations Command (J-JOC)*	2022†	Cyber operations
Malaysia	Defence Cyber and Electromagnetic Division	Rear admiral	Chief of Defence Forces, Malaysian Armed Forces	2020	Cyber operations and electromagnetic warfare
Philippines	AFP Cyber Command	Colonel	Chief of Staff, Armed Forces of the Philippines	2024	Cyber operations
Singapore	Digital and Intelligence Service	Major-general	Chief of Defence Force, Singapore Armed Forces	2022	Cyber, digital and intelligence operations
Taiwan	Information, Communications and Electronic Force Command	Lieutenant-general	Minister of National Defense	2017	Cyber operations and electromagnetic warfare
Thailand	Cyber Command Centre‡	Lieutenant-general	Chief of Defence Forces, Royal Thai Armed Forces**	2024†	Cyber and digital operations
Vietnam	Cyberspace Operations Command (Command 86)	Major-general	Ministry of National Defense***	2017	Cyber and information operations

†Year of latest iteration after unit/force restructuring. *J-JOC to be established in March 2025. **Presumed based on highest operational authority. ***The Vietnam People's Army officially describes the Command as a combat element, and the Command's party organisation reports to the Central Military Commission of the Communist Party of Vietnam. ‡Operational status uncertain.

Source: IISS

journalists.[8] The combination of external and domestic national-security considerations and the utility of cyber capabilities as an amplifier for other instruments of state power have been key drivers for the creation of cyber forces in the region.

MEASURING MATURITY

There is no uniform model to develop 'military cyber' capabilities, which can be defined as cyber-enabled operations conducted by cyber forces within a formal military structure. Different countries will have their own advantages and disadvantages, from varying international partnerships to security priorities and political infrastructures and policy ecosystems. Additionally, a state's cyber capabilities may not only sit with the military and may instead be part of another agency. These factors play out even before considering variations to military structures, doctrine and strategies. Simplistic head-to-head comparisons would be analytically misleading.

Assessing how different countries seek to develop their cyber powers can be carried out by considering the different pathways by which they attempt to 'mature' their militaries to the point where they are able to conduct cyber-enabled operations in war and low-intensity conflict, or carry out deterrent actions.[9] Specifically, there are three different dimensions of military cyber maturity to assess:[10]

1. strategic maturity: the degree to which plans, doctrines and budgets are allocated towards military cyber
2. institutional maturity: the degree to which harmonisation, preparedness and inter-operability have developed
3. capability maturity: the degree to which cyber forces have cultivated personnel and tools to conduct offensive and defensive operations.

Protesters make three-finger salutes while holding portraits of Aung San Suu Kyi during a rally in Bangkok on the third anniversary of the coup in Myanmar, 1 February 2024

(Chaiwat Subprasom/SOPA Images/LightRocket via Getty Images)

Each dimension can be further broken down into different governance and organisational factors (see Table 5.2). All states, regardless of geography, economy or the threats they face, need to resolve these issues if they seek to develop their cyber capabilities. But more importantly, these dimensions of maturity provide a preliminary benchmark to analyse how well-developed Asia-Pacific states' military cyber capabilities are.

While many states have been pursuing cyber capabilities for over 30 years, the establishment of formalised cyber forces – active military organisations which conduct cyber operations and report through a military chain of command – is relatively recent, having started in the 2010s.[11]

That different Asia-Pacific militaries have chosen similar paths of formalising cyber roles and operations has lent itself to a regional comparison and assessment. The maturity measures, in other words, allow for an understanding of how far along the Asia-Pacific region is in its military cyber-capability development, even while acknowledging that each country has unique cyber-security policy features and challenges and that cyber capabilities extend beyond the armed forces.

Civilian cyber or signals-intelligence organisations have intentionally not been included in the impact matrix. The different security actors within many Asia-Pacific security establishments – the police, military, intelligence agencies – have acrimonious relationships with each other as well as with their political leaders. As such, military cyber capabilities and the decisions surrounding them will differ from the cyber-enabled operations conducted by intelligence and law-enforcement agencies. For one thing, those organisations are unlikely to be defending an armed forces' computer systems. They are also likely to be ill-equipped to monitor offensive cyber operations during conflicts. For another, these organisations would struggle to prioritise military operations alongside their non-military objectives. But these shortcomings, perhaps more of a concern for Western security establishments where cyber capabilities have historically emerged from an espionage context, are less clear-cut within the context of the Asia-Pacific.[12]

Table 5.2: **The military cyber maturity impact matrix**

		Dimensions of maturity		
		Strategic maturity	**Institutional maturity**	**Capability maturity**
Governance factors	Senior political receptivity	Interest in cyber operations can facilitate strategic maturity; scepticism can inhibit strategic maturity.	Support from leadership can facilitate institutional maturity; obstructions can inhibit institutional maturity.	Long-term planning can facilitate capability maturity; budget constraints can inhibit capability maturity.
	Civilian–military relations	Harmonising intelligence priorities can facilitate strategic maturity.	Bureaucratic rivalry can inhibit institutional maturity.	Guarding civilian cyber capabilities from military and vice versa can inhibit capability maturity.
	Military modernisation	Late-stage reforms can facilitate strategic maturity.	Redefining existing hierarchies can facilitate institutional maturity.	Reforms to established outfits can facilitate capability maturity.
	Alliances	Variations in policy development can limit understanding, inhibiting strategic maturity.	Sharing learned experiences can facilitate institutional maturity.	Unwillingness to share technical tools can inhibit capability maturity.
Organisational factors	Operational experiences	Uncertain signalling dynamics can inhibit strategic maturity.	Demonstrated 'proof of concept' can facilitate institutional maturity.	Experiences provide feedback that can facilitate capability maturity.
	Military adaptive capability	High levels of adaptive elements can facilitate strategic maturity.	High complexity, loose coupling and low redundancy can facilitate strategic maturity.	High levels of adaptive capacity, in early stages, can facilitate capability maturity.
	Divergent cultures	Subculture clashes can inhibit strategic maturity.	Competing cultural frameworks on cyber can inhibit institutional maturity.	Inflexible military culture around talent can inhibit capability maturity.

Note: For the purposes of this chapter, only a selected set of variables (not all of them) are used.

Source: IISS

STARTS AT THE TOP

Clear and comprehensive plans around how cyber capabilities should be developed and used by military organisations are an important benchmark in developing strategic maturity. The role of political and military leaders is also critical to developing well-defined plans for the acquisition of military cyber capabilities and in securing the necessary resources and support. The role of these leaders is also crucial in establishing well-defined developmental and operational goals and guiding them towards implementation.

In practice, this involves Asia-Pacific governments and legislatures developing policy documents specifying how their various militaries view cyberspace and the scope of their actions within the domain, and whether it will also use psychological and information operations to address problems associated with it. There is also a need for the military to design doctrines that will inform how cyber capabilities are integrated into traditional military operations. Developments in strategic maturity will also see matching changes to national-security goals and budgetary priorities to enable cyber military forces to grow from defending military infrastructure to producing military effects, at scale, in cyberspace.

Military cyber-strategic maturity across Asia-Pacific states is currently uneven. Some countries, like Singapore, are generally considered by analysts to be more strategically mature, while others, such as India and Japan, are still advancing. Others still, like Indonesia and the Philippines, are less far along in developing their military cyber strategies. The process of strategically maturing military cyber forces in general requires regional states to consider key challenges.

Firstly, many regional states are often reactive towards, as opposed to proactive and preventive of, major cyber incidents. Attempts to improve military cyber-strategic maturity therefore only tend to begin after an incident. But learning from the key lessons and pushing through any necessary strategic reforms after such incidents also requires strong political and military leadership.

For Singapore, what turned out to be the catalyst incident unfolded between June and July of 2018, where a threat actor breached SingHealth, the country's largest group of healthcare institutions. While Singapore had already developed national cyber strategies and had established a civilian agency – the Cyber Security Agency – in 2015, the incident resulted in numerous strategic shifts. 'Digital Defence' was soon included within the existing national-defence strategy of 'Total Defence'.[13] The Singapore Armed Forces' (SAF) cyber units were then restructured into the Digital and Intelligence Service (DIS), which became operational in 2022.

Whereas Singapore shows that post-incident reforms can lead to strategic maturity, Indonesia has a more mixed record on this, despite seemingly being focused on developing its military cyber capabilities. It laid out cyber defence as one of the four pillars of Indonesia's defence posture in 2015 and improved on that by incorporating cyber within its 'Total Defence' doctrine in 2017.[14] The Indonesian National Armed Forces (TNI) established its Cyber Unit (Satsiber), headed by a one-star general, in the same year. By 2022, defence policymakers in Jakarta were discussing the creation of a new armed service, dubbed Cyber Force, modelled after Singapore's DIS. Analysts were sceptical of the proposed plan given the broader policy challenges around cyber personnel, resources and other political risks.[15]

Like others, Indonesia has been the target of cyber operations over the past decade, with the 'Brain Cipher' ransom attacks against its Temporary National Data Centre in Surabaya in June 2024 being particularly impactful. Poor 'cyber hygiene' and lack of backups meant that 282 public services, including immigration and airport operations, among many others, were disrupted. The attack also happened less than a month after then-president Joko Widodo launched INA Digital, the Indonesian government's tech initiative.[16] Indonesia refused to pay a USD8 million ransom and received an uncharacteristic 'mercy' from the attackers, who released the decryption tools for free. After this incident, policy discussions in Jakarta picked up.

Indonesia's reaction highlights the second challenge that hampers strategic maturity: the ability to follow through on announced reforms. This depends on the degree of support from senior political and military figures. The creation of Cyber Force was initially supported by Indonesia's then-president-elect, Prabowo Subianto. Yet a month after the new administration was sworn in during October 2024, Indonesia's new defence minister walked back the announcement, stating that the existing cyber units were adequate. Past studies, however, show that Indonesia needs to make 'changes in doctrine, technology and personnel planning' to establish a significant military cyber capability.[17]

Passengers wait at a departure board at Juanda International Airport near Surabaya, East Java, 6 April 2024

(Juni Kriswanto/AFP Photo/AFP via Getty Images)

Other Asia-Pacific countries have displayed similar inconsistencies. Thailand announced in May 2024 that it would restructure the cyber units within its armed forces, creating a Cyber Command Centre within the Royal Thai Armed Forces, an electronic-warfare division within the Royal Thai Navy's existing Cyber Command and placing network warfare units under the Defence Ministry's Department of Information and Technology Communication.[18] Despite an October 2024 deadline, the country has not publicly stated the status – completed or otherwise – of these changes.

While there is an expected and understandable secrecy around cyber developments and capabilities, inconsistencies in transparency result in confusion around the implementation of reforms. In October 2023, the Philippines announced that it would be expanding its existing Cyber Group into a 'cyber command' within the Armed Forces of the Philippines (AFP).[19] By January 2025, following a string of cyber-espionage operations, public statements confirmed that the reorganisation had occurred.[20] But the only evidence of this are minor changes to the AFP website and a social-media post from the Commander of the AFP Cyber Group stating that the reorganisation of AFP Cyber Command occurred on 26 October 2024.[21]

Limited transparency presents a challenge within some states in the region. Few public announcements are made around doctrinal changes or the implementation of new strategies, which has been observed with Indonesia's Satsiber and Singapore's DIS. India released a Joint Doctrine for Cyberspace Operations in June 2024 to provide strategic guidance to the armed forces on how the country understands and approaches military cyber operations.[22] This reflects an improvement in its overall strategic maturity, as it continues efforts that were initiated in September 2018 with the approval of the Defence Cyber Agency, a joint command that became operational in August 2021.[23]

More broadly, the unevenness of the military cyber strategic maturity across the Asia-Pacific suggests how differently political and military leaders view cyberspace and how best to combat the threats it presents. But they are also hamstrung by competing priorities and often end up taking military cyber capabilities seriously only after a major cyber incident. This weakens their strategic position in the face of future conflicts, given that developing military cyber capabilities, whether through reorganisations or the development of doctrinal thinking, takes years.

MORE, NOT MERRIER

How well a military organisation can harmonise its planning, force preparedness and ability to deliver cyber operations is a hallmark of institutional maturity. Support of a consistent nature from senior military leaders is critical in this regard. Military-leadership turnover can be a double-edged sword in that it can equally introduce new advocates or stall progress, delaying maturation. Deconflicting and harmonising the relationship between military cyber forces, civilian intelligence and law-enforcement agencies is also a key task as institutional rivalry hinders maturity efforts. Senior military leaders not only need to avoid these brakes being inadvertently applied to institutional maturity, but also need to hit the 'gas pedal' to accelerate the process.

Broader military modernisation efforts can help consolidate cyber capabilities by creating new operating procedures and improving the integration of cyber components into conventional military operations. Developing strong international partnerships or alliances can also provide unique insights and information-sharing opportunities and accelerate institutional maturity through joint exercises and inter-operability development. Operational experiences can similarly provide concrete feedback on existing structures, which can result in furthering maturity.

Across the Asia-Pacific, military cyber-institutional maturity is progressing, thanks in part to existing multilateral mechanisms and geopolitical partnerships such as the Association of Southeast Asian Nations (ASEAN) and the Quad. The ASEAN Defence Ministers' Meeting established the ASEAN Cybersecurity and Information Centre of Excellence (ACICE) in June 2021 to address cyber-security challenges.[24] The ACICE, true to ASEAN's non-interference principle, does not aim to guide states on how militaries should be structured or how to approach cyberspace; it focuses instead on information sharing, collaboration and threat awareness.

While such limitations might hinder a region-wide collective cyber-capability development, especially given that members hold different views on the military's cyber role, such multilateral efforts could gradually improve an individual military's institutional maturity by exposing it to the practices of fellow members. Similarly, the Quad, comprised of Australia, India, Japan and the US, focuses on exchanging cyber information, benefitting from its smaller membership and similar levels of cyber-infrastructure development.[25]

At the national level, however, ensuring harmonisation between existing organisations – both within the military and between civilian and military organisations – is critical. Civilian cyber agencies are often responsible for protecting the bulk of government systems targeted in cyber attacks. Politicians have blamed both Indonesia's National Cyber and Crypto Agency (BSSN) and the Philippines' Department of Information and Communication Technology for not being able to safeguard their governments' digital

US then-president Joe Biden, alongside Australian Prime Minister Anthony Albanese, Indian Prime Minister Narendra Modi and Japan's then-prime minister Kishida Fumio, speaks at a Quad summit in Wilmington, Delaware, 21 September 2024

(Brendan Smialowski/AFP via Getty Images)

infrastructure.[26] As mentioned above, the strategic maturity of military cyber units tends to be developed in the aftermath of cyber incidents. These developments often shift budgetary resources and political favour away from civilian cyber agencies towards military organisations due to the perceived national-security threat. Such shifts exacerbate bureaucratic rivalries. In Indonesia, there is even the perception that while authority is sought on cyber issues, there is a reluctance to be held responsible.[27]

In his comments delaying the establishment of the Indonesian Cyber Force, Minister of Defence Sjafrie Sjamsoeddin stated that the TNI's existing Satsiber and the Ministry of Defence's Cyber Defence Centre could fulfil the military's cyber needs.[28] This allows tensions to grow between the military's cyber units as well as those of the police, intelligence agencies and the BSSN. In maintaining the institutional status quo, budgets and resources remain split, hindering broader security objectives.[29]

As military cyber capabilities improve (discussed further below), there are questions about how they operate. There are laws and regulations in place in the US, for example, ensuring that military capabilities cannot be directed against individuals within the US, unless authorised through legal exceptions. Many Asia-Pacific countries, however, operate under a very different threat landscape that includes insurgencies, terrorism, separatist groups and political dissidents, in addition to the threats posed by transnational crime groups and nation-state actors in cyberspace. Unlike in the US, legal restrictions on deploying military capabilities and assets, including cyber, against domestic targets are likely to be flexible, if not altogether non-existent.

Aside from legal challenges, institutional developmental efforts are often hindered by the ability of senior political and military leaders to navigate, manage and ultimately rise above the bureaucratic rivalries between military cyber units and their civilian counterparts. Who has the authority and responsibility over critical national infrastructure must be agreed upon before progress can be made on military cyber-institutional maturity. Within the military, it is also necessary for cyber operations to be integrated across the organisation. India, for example, has made some advancements in this area. But the creation of new units restarts the clock of institutionalisation as new personnel, resources and remits have to be respectively allocated for and redefined.

Whether and how military cyber units can work with their civilian agencies during crises would also need to first be discovered and then institutionalised through regular joint or inter-agency exercises. Japan, for example, has announced that the Self-Defense Forces would be called on if required and would need to work well with civilian units; improved domestic drills are therefore needed. The combination of such domestic developments, as well as regional trends of collaboratively working on various cyber operations and security challenges, facilitated by regional mechanisms such as ASEAN and the Quad, has gradually driven military cyber-institutional maturity forward.

Indonesia's then-president Joko Widodo (4th l), then-defence minister and president-elect Prabowo Subianto (3rd r), and military leaders pose at the TNI's 79th-anniversary celebrations in Jakarta, 5 October 2024

(Yasuyoshi Chiba/AFP via Getty Images)

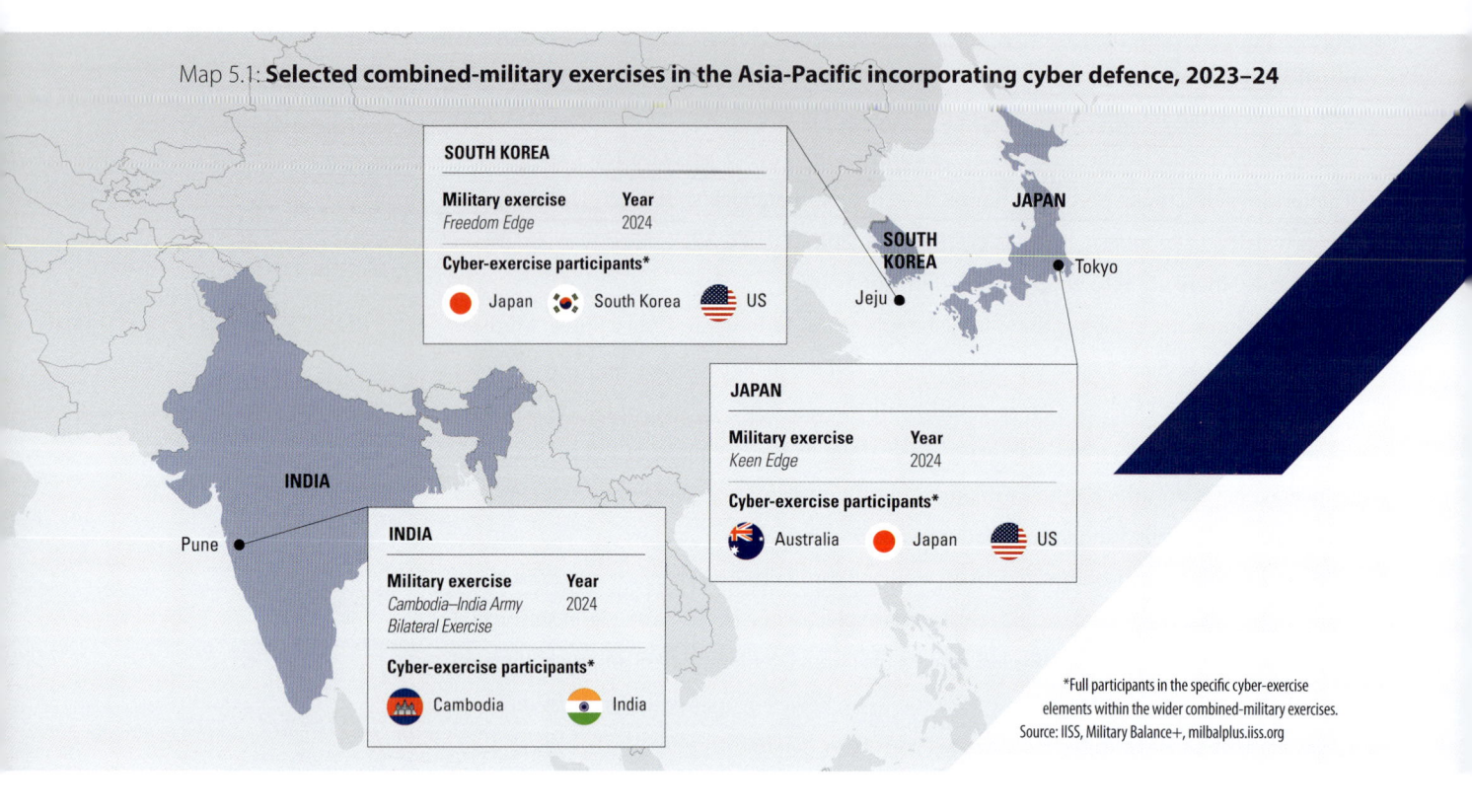

Map 5.1: **Selected combined-military exercises in the Asia-Pacific incorporating cyber defence, 2023–24**

SOUTH KOREA

Military exercise	Year
Freedom Edge	2024

Cyber-exercise participants*
- Japan
- South Korea
- US

JAPAN

Military exercise	Year
Keen Edge	2024

Cyber-exercise participants*
- Australia
- Japan
- US

INDIA

Military exercise	Year
Cambodia–India Army Bilateral Exercise	2024

Cyber-exercise participants*
- Cambodia
- India

*Full participants in the specific cyber-exercise elements within the wider combined-military exercises.
Source: IISS, Military Balance+, milbalplus.iiss.org

There are shortcomings and roadblocks to be sure. Indonesia's ransomware incident, for example, was cited as a case of a perceived abdication of responsibility and one in which the information sharing, collaboration and threat awareness espoused by the ACICE were not demonstrated during the crisis.[30] Military modernisation trends are also driven by geopolitical pressures beyond cyber security, especially when it comes to regional peers or competitors. In any case, overall military cyber-institutional maturity across the Asia-Pacific suggests that ongoing efforts continue to improve operational readiness and inter-operability between cyber forces. This will contribute towards regional security should defensive, or offensive, activities prove necessary.

PERSONNEL PATCH

Developing defensive and offensive cyber options, and having the personnel, skills and conditions to use them in line with strategic intent and organisational demands, is one of the key measures of capability maturity. Whether and how militaries develop those capabilities remains tied to the levels of strategic and institutional maturity discussed above. This maturity requires consistent leadership from senior political and military figures in allocating funding for personnel, research and technology development. How far militaries develop inter-agency arrangements and international partnerships, as well as the extent to which military modernisation plans could centralise cyber command-and-control, all impact when and how offensive and defensive capabilities can be deployed.

In recent years, many Asia-Pacific militaries seeking to develop their operational capabilities have focused on developing and recruiting skilled personnel. Augmenting military cyber forces by drawing from private-sector talent has been an effective method of jump-starting

Map 5.1

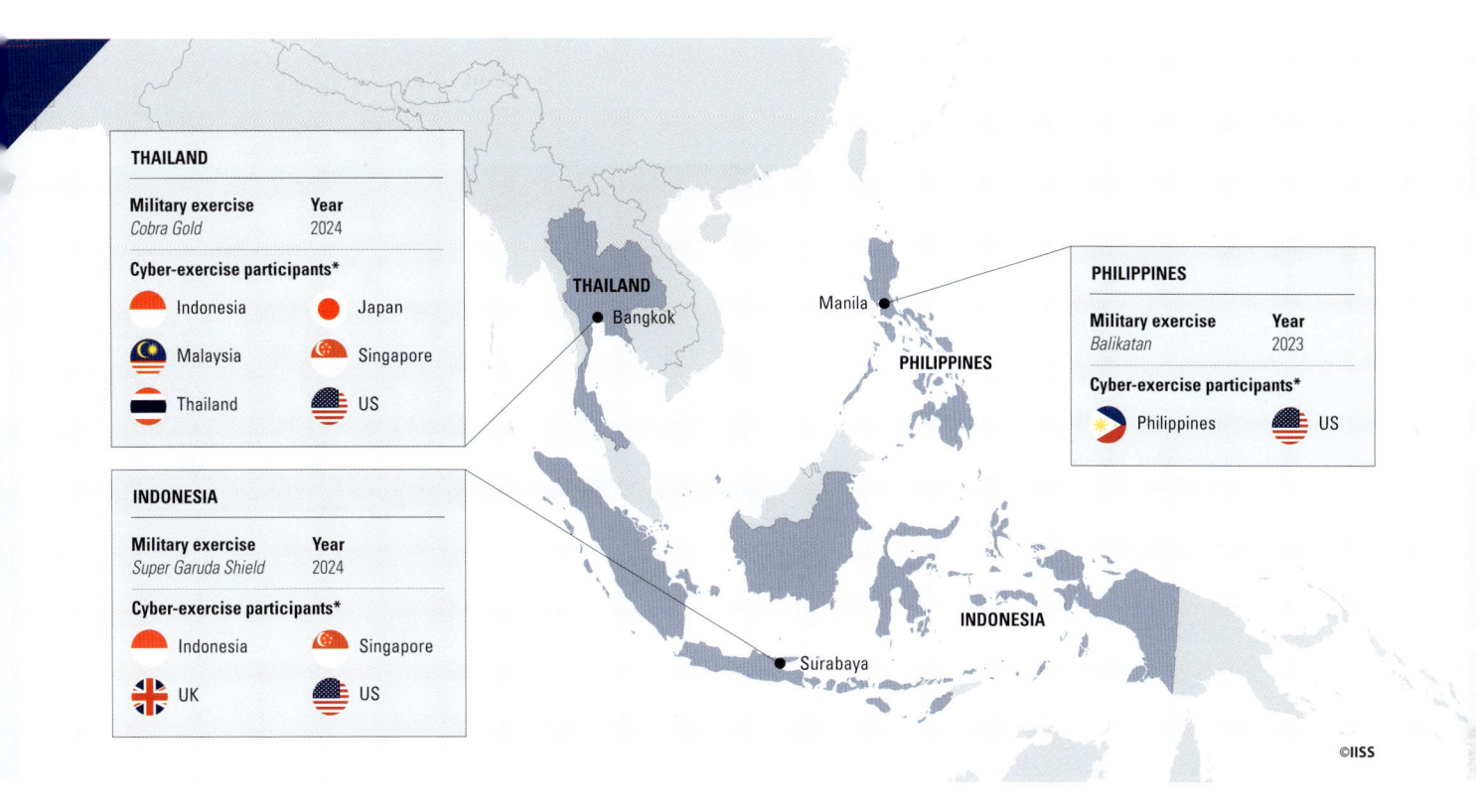

THAILAND
Military exercise	Year
Cobra Gold	2024

Cyber-exercise participants*
- Indonesia
- Japan
- Malaysia
- Singapore
- Thailand
- US

INDONESIA
Military exercise	Year
Super Garuda Shield	2024

Cyber-exercise participants*
- Indonesia
- Singapore
- UK
- US

PHILIPPINES
Military exercise	Year
Balikatan	2023

Cyber-exercise participants*
- Philippines
- US

©IISS

---

this process. Such efforts are often coupled with other capability-improvement efforts as a method to circumvent the hurdle presented by having less cyber-capable personnel.

Singapore's National Service programme includes its 'Cyber Specialist' scheme, allowing recruits to gain cyber-security skills through programmes with local universities and operational roles within the Ministry of Defence and the SAF.[31] Thailand has also sought to establish a cyber-defence academy with the aim of training between 300 and 500 specialists per year, although this remains to be implemented and does not in itself guarantee an effective cyber workforce.[32] Indonesia and Malaysia have recently sought to recruit non-military professionals into their cyber units, with Malaysia commencing studies to establish a dedicated miltiary cyber force.[33] The Philippines has started recruiting private citizens to join its army's Cyber Centre.[34]

Senior officials across the region, however, also consider that a focus on cyber-technology acquisition could help justify any increases in budgetary allocations for their small but growing cyber units or commands. Indonesia's defence minister has recently stated that the military cyber unit needs technology rather than 'a lot of people'.[35] India has even pursued the development of indigenous operating platforms for its defence systems and has commenced trials as part of an effort to improve cyber security.[36] This policy is part of the Modi government's national *Atmanirbhar Bharat* ('Make in India') push.[37]

In terms of deployable capabilities, however, regional countries still seek to learn from their allies and partners, especially through military cyber exercises. The US, in particular, has begun to organise and run cyber-defence exercises as part of a wider combined-military exercise, such as the 2024 *Cobra Gold* with Thailand and the 2023 and 2024 *Balikatan* with the Philippines (see Map 5.1). US Cyber Command has also expanded its 'Hunt Forward' initiative, deploying military cyber-security experts to support allies like Japan, the Philippines and South Korea to detect and mitigate cyber threats.[38]

The Philippines has built its military cyber strategy with substantial US support. Washington announced USD500m in foreign-military financing for the Philippines in July 2024, prioritising asymmetric and cyber capabilities.[39] Other partners of the Philippines are also chipping in: in 2023, the Philippines and Denmark signed a deal to enhance digital security and combat cyber threats proactively.[40]

South Korean and US marines line up on the beach as part of the multilateral *Cobra Gold* exercises – which also included cyber-defence exercises – in the coastal Thai province of Chonburi, 3 March 2025

(Chanakarn Laosarakham/AFP via Getty Images)

Many in the West may see these efforts as reflecting a broader strategy to address increasingly sophisticated cyber attacks, particularly those targeting critical infrastructure and originating from China, North Korea and Russia. And yet, countries within ASEAN have engaged in cyber-security exercises with China. Analysts have described these activities as efforts to learn about new cyber technology and perhaps to learn from a potential adversary.[41]

Taken together, many Asia-Pacific countries, especially those in Southeast Asia, do not yet appear to possess clear and deployable offensive cyber capabilities. Their focus remains on growing the necessary organisational infrastructure and recruiting the necessary personnel. The critical variable to consider here is the extent to which international partnerships could drive or nudge Asia-Pacific militaries to better consider their options in their pursuit of defensive and offensive cyber capabilities.

DEFENSIVE DILEMMA

Across the Asia-Pacific, states are seeking to develop their military cyber capabilities. Strategic maturity, wherein policy directions and documents are created and cyber units or commands are established, has grown in recent years. There are challenges in consistencies and resources across different countries, but the direction of travel across the region suggests that militaries are to be assigned central roles in defending cyberspace and should therefore have the necessary tools at the ready.

Despite the growing number of military-initiated cyber units, commands and forces across the Asia-Pacific, their relationship with other security, intelligence and civilian agencies tasked with cyber security – that is, the institutional maturity – remains unsettled, if not overlapping. Some countries could successfully proceed with better divisions of labour and intra-military integration of cyber capabilities, while others continue to wrestle with their maturity efforts. Regional mechanisms such as ASEAN play an important role in promoting military cyber-institutional maturity in Southeast Asia.

International partnerships and engagements help improve the military cyber-institutional maturity of many Asia-Pacific countries. They also allow regional armed forces to further develop their capability maturity – or at least identify the operational, personnel and resource gaps to be addressed. The focus for many now is to grow existing or new military cyber units, commands or forces with the necessary budget and number of personnel.

As Asia-Pacific militaries seek to develop their military cyber capabilities, the growing potential of security risks across the region must be considered. Cyber capabilities have historically been seen as non-escalatory tools due to their ability to be reset, replaced and/or restored (as opposed to the physical destruction caused by munitions); the time it takes to conduct a successful operation; the scarcity of vulnerabilities; and the inherent anonymity – and thus deniability – of such actions. But arguably, when a country develops its cyber forces, it signals to adversaries that it is prepared for cyber operations – perhaps even offensive ones, including, but not limited to, psychological or information operations.

An increase in the number of states willing to conduct offensive cyber operations, in turn, could deepen the regional-security dilemma – where actions taken in the name of defensive goals are perceived by adversaries as offensive and threatening.[42] This is where escalation dynamics in cyberspace typically experience negative feedback. Unclear thresholds on what constitutes defensive operations in cyberspace exacerbates this complexity.

In an environment where political leaders still confuse cyber-enabled espionage operations with potential military actions, there is perhaps a good reason why Asia-Pacific states hesitate to build military cyber capabilities. Political leaders inexperienced with cyber crises may also be prone to making erroneous decisions. When taken together, the growing maturity of military cyber units and capabilities across the Asia-Pacific is not necessarily risk-free or in correlation with a peaceful and stable regional-security trajectory.

The majority of countries in the region lack a well-defined doctrine for integrating military cyber forces with their conventional, longer-established services. They also lack experience in signals intelligence in comparison to China, Russia, the UK, the US and perhaps even North Korea. However, regional states will continue to pursue these capabilities because they are still viewed as a cost-effective way to exert influence against often larger or better-equipped adversaries. Short of offensive cyber operations, cyber capabilities can support better intelligence collection and operational planning.

In addition, all states must defend their military and civilian systems, including critical infrastructure, from adversaries as well as criminal groups on a daily basis. Falling behind on cyber capabilities is not a viable option. Therefore, developing cyber resilience as well as offensive capabilities – whether within the military or other security and intelligence agencies, as well as in partnership with industry – is critical for ensuring the day-to-day governing of the country, let alone for future conflicts. Domestic and regional peculiarities, such as a greater acceptance in some countries of militaries operating domestically, the absence of strong signals-intelligence capabilities, as well as the lack of an indigenous cyber industry, suggests that most states in the Asia-Pacific will tread a different path to cyber maturity to other cyber-capable states.

VIRPRATAP VIKRAM SINGH
Research Fellow, Cyber Power and Future Conflict Programme, IISS

MARINE OURAHLI
Research Analyst, Cyber Power and Future Conflict Programme, IISS

NOTES

1. Marcus Willett, 'Cyber Instruments and International Security', IISS Online Analysis, 12 March 2019, https://www.iiss.org/online-analysis/online-analysis/2019/03/cyber-instruments-and-international-security/.

2. 'Achieve and Maintain Cyberspace Superiority: Command Vision for US Cyber Command', US Cyber Command, 2018, p. 4, https://www.cybercom.mil/Portals/56/Documents/USCYBERCOM%20Vision%20April%202018.pdf; Sam Beltran, 'In Philippines, Fears of "Cyber Cold war" Amid Surge in Online Threats', *South China Morning Post*, 20 February 2025, https://www.scmp.com/week-asia/politics/article/3299488/philippines-fears-cyber-cold-war-amid-surge-online-threats.

3. Erica D. Borghard and Shawn W. Lonergan, 'Cyber Operations as Imperfect Tools of Escalation', *Strategic Studies Quarterly*, vol. 13, no. 3, Autumn 2019, pp. 131–8, https://www.airuniversity.af.edu/Portals/10/SSQ/documents/Volume-13_Issue-3/Borghard.pdf. Stuxnet, which was meticulously designed by the United States and Israel to target and permanently disable infrastructure used for Iran's nuclear-enrichment programme, was still detected in dozens of countries around the world, demonstrating the malware's capability to spread. Russia's *NotPetya* operation in 2017 was, for all intents and purposes, only intended to affect Ukraine through the use of a popular regional accounting software but quickly spread across global systems.

4. Jason Healey, 'Cyber Effects in Warfare', *Texas National Security Review*, vol. 7, no. 4, Autumn 2024, p. 49, https://tnsr.org/2024/08/cyber-effects-in-warfare-categorizing-the-where-what-and-why/#_ftnref84.

5. 'Global Cyberattacks Continue to Rise with Africa and APAC Suffering Most', Check Point, 27 April 2023, https://blog.checkpoint.com/research/global-cyberattacks-continue-to-rise/.

6. 'Global Internet Penetration Rate as of February 2025, by Region', Statista, 13 February 2025, https://www.statista.com/statistics/269329/penetration-rate-of-the-internet-by-region/.

7. Gautam Kumra and Jeongmin Seong, 'Asia: The Epicenter of Global Trade Shifts', McKinsey & Company, 3 September 2024, https://www.mckinsey.com/featured-insights/future-of-asia/asia-the-epicenter-of-global-trade-shifts.

8. Bill Marczak et al., 'Running in Circles: Uncovering the Clients of Cyberespionage Firm Circles', Citizen Lab, 1 December 2020, https://citizenlab.ca/2020/12/running-in-circles-uncovering-the-clients-of-cyberespionage-firm-circles/; 'Thailand: Dismissal of Landmark Case a Critical and Alarming Setback in Fight Against Unlawful Use of Spyware', Amnesty International, 21 November 2024, https://www.amnesty.org/en/latest/news/2024/11/thailand-dismissal-of-landmark-case-a-critical-and-alarming-setback-in-fight-against-unlawful-use-of-spyware/; and 'India: Damning New Forensic Investigation Reveals Repeated Use of Pegasus Spyware to Target High-profile Journalists', Amnesty International, 28 December 2023, https://www.amnesty.org/en/latest/news/2023/12/india-damning-new-forensic-investigation-reveals-repeated-use-of-pegasus-spyware-to-target-high-profile-journalists/.

9. Jason Blessing and Greg Austin, 'Assessing Military Cyber Maturity: Strategy, Institutions and Capability', IISS, p. 9, https://www.iiss.org/globalassets/media-library---content--migration/files/research-papers/2022/assessing-military-cyber-maturity_strategy-institutions-and-capability.pdf.

10. Blessing and Austin, 'Assessing Military Cyber Maturity: Strategy, Institutions and Capability', p. 10.

11. See Jason Healey and Robert Jervis, 'How to Reverse Three Decades of Escalating Cyber Conflict', Atlantic Council, 24 March 2021, https://www.atlanticcouncil.org/blogs/new-atlanticist/how-to-reverse-three-decades-of-escalating-cyber-conflict/; and Jason Blessing, 'The Global Spread of Cyber Forces, 2000–2018', paper presented to the 13th International Conference on Cyber Conflict, Tallinn, Estonia, May 2021, https://ccdcoe.org/uploads/2021/05/CyCon_2021_Blessing.pdf.

12. Joshua Rovner, 'Cyber War as an Intelligence Contest', War on the Rocks, 16 September 2019, https://warontherocks.com/2019/09/cyber-war-as-an-intelligence-contest.

13. IISS, 'Cyber Capabilities and National Power Volume 2', 7 September 2023, p. 111, https://www.iiss.org/globalassets/media-library---content--migration/files/research-papers/2023/09/cyber-

capabilities-and-national-power-vol-2/
cyber-capabilities-and-national-power_volume-
2_10-singapore.pdf.

14 IISS, 'Cyber Capabilities and National Power: A Net Assessment', 28 June 2021, p. 144, https://www.iiss.org/globalassets/media-library---content--migration/files/research-papers/cyber-power-report/cyber-capabilities-and-national-power---indonesia.pdf.

15 See the discussion in Christian Guntur Lebang, 'Navigating the Cyber Future: Does Indonesia Need a Cyber Military Force?', *Jakarta Post*, 6 January 2024, https://www.thejakartapost.com/opinion/2024/01/06/navigating-the-cyber-future-does-indonesia-need-a-cyber-military-force.html.

16 See discussion of the incident and Indonesia's cyber capacity in Yanuar Nugroho, 'Indonesia's National Data Centre Ransomware Attack: A Digital Governance Failure?', *Fulcrum*, 8 August 2024, https://fulcrum.sg/indonesias-national-data-centre-ransomware-attack-a-digital-governance-failure/.

17 'Cyber Capabilities and National Power: A Net Assessment', p. 145.

18 'Military to Set Up Cyber Command Centre by October', The Nation, 25 May 2024, https://www.nationthailand.com/news/general/40038311; and Rojoef Manuel, 'Thailand to Open Cyber Command Center in October', The Defense Post, 27 May 2024, https://thedefensepost.com/2024/05/27/thailand-cyber-command-center.

19 Sebastian Strangio, 'Philippine Military to Create "Cyber Command" to Combat Online Attacks', *Diplomat*, 20 October 2023, https://thediplomat.com/2023/10/philippine-military-to-create-cyber-command-to-combat-online-attacks.

20 'AFP Strengthens Counter-espionage and Cyber Defense', Security Matters, 21 January 2025, https://securitymatters.com.ph/2025/01/21/afp-strengthens-counter-espionage-and-cyber-defense; and 'Philippines Fortifies Cyber Defense, Partnering with Japan, U.S. and Others', Indo-Pacific Defense Forum, 19 January 2025, https://ipdefenseforum.com/2025/01/philippines-fortifies-cyber-defense-partnering-with-japan-u-s-and-others/.

21 'AFP Organization', Armed Forces of the Philippines, https://www.afp.mil.ph/about-us/organization/afp-organization; and Joey Fontiveros, LinkedIn, November 2024, https://www.linkedin.com/posts/joey-fontiveros-mpm-devsec-icd-ceh-sans-cobit-ccna-cnd-442b9275_onecyber-protectdefend-activity-7260456126171762689-7MpJ/.

22 'CDS Gen Anil Chauhan Releases Joint Doctrine for Cyberspace Operations', Ministry of Defence of India, 18 June 2024, https://pib.gov.in/PressReleasePage.aspx?PRID=2026240.

23 Sudhi Ranjan Sen, 'India to Set Up 3 New Agencies, Including Cyber and Space, to Boost Defence Capabilities', *Hindustan Times*, 16 October 2018, https://www.hindustantimes.com/india-news/india-to-set-up-3-new-agencies-including-cyber-and-space-to-boost-defence-capabilities/story-umuS4UOsDavcoMhHkUjuWN.html; and 'GOI in Final Stage of Formulating National Cyber Security Strategy', *Statesman*, 4 August 2021, https://www.thestatesman.com/india/goi-national-cyber-security-strategy-1502990178.html.

24 Fitriani, 'New Structures for ASEAN Cyber Defence and Information Sharing', 5 December 2023, https://www.iiss.org/online-analysis/online-analysis/2023/09/new-structures-for-asean-cyber-defence-and-information-sharing/.

25 Jasmine Moheb, 'No Teeth, No Problem: The Quad's Influence in Southeast Asia', China Focus, 5 May 2023, https://chinafocus.ucsd.edu/2023/05/05/no-teeth-no-problem-the-quads-influence-in-southeast-asia/.

26 'DICT "Negligence" Hit in PhilHealth Cyber Attack: Castro Tells Ivan Uy to Act, Not Make Excuses', POLITIKO, 10 October 2023, https://politiko.com.ph/2023/10/10/dict-negligence-hit-in-philhealth-cyber-attack-castro-tells-ivan-uy-to-act-not-make-excuses/headlines/.

27 'Indonesia's Cybersecurity Level Low, BSSN Needs Reinforcement: Expert', KeamananSiber, 13 November 2024, https://www.keamanansiber.com/2024/11/indonesias-cybersecurity-level-low-bssn.html.

28 'Defense Minister Sjafrie: The Formation of the TNI Cyber Force Needs to Be Viewed Proportionally', VOI, 26 November 2024, https://voi.id/en/news/437219.

29 Alex Firmansiyah Rahman, Syaiful Anwar and Arwin Datumaya Wahyudi Sumari, 'Analisis Minimum Essential Force (MEF) Dalam Rangka Pembangunan Cyber-Defense' [Analysis of minimum essential force (MEF) in the context of cyber-defence development], *Jurnal Pertahanan &*

Bela Negara, vol. 5, no. 3, 2018, pp. 63–85, https://jurnal.idu.ac.id/index.php/JPBH/article/view/370.

30 Comments made during the 2024 RSiS Digital Defence Symposium, 24–25 July 2024.

31 Lim Min Zhang, 'Mindef Offers New Short-term Cyber-specialist Scheme for NSFs to Boost Cyber-security Fight', *Straits Times*, 12 February 2018, https://www.straitstimes.com/singapore/mindef-offers-new-short-term-cyber-specialist-scheme-for-nsfs-to-boost-cybersecurity-fight.

32 Wassana Nanuam, 'New Military Unit to Enhance Cyber Warfare Ability', *Bangkok Post*, 26 May 2024, https://www.bangkokpost.com/thailand/general/2799266/new-military-unit-to-enhance-cyber-warfare-ability.

33 'Cyber Capabilities and National Power: A Net Assessment', p. 145; Chief Chapree, 'Malaysian Armed Forces May Recruit Hackers in the Near Future', Soyacincau,13 February 2024, https://soyacincau.com/2024/02/13/malaysian-armed-forces-may-recruit-hackers/; and Luqman Hakim and Fuad Nizam, 'Malaysian Armed Forces Mulls Dedicated Cyber Unit, Study Underway', *New Straits Times*, 16 January 2025, https://www.nst.com.my/news/nation/2025/01/1161696/updated-malaysian-armed-forces-mulls-dedicated-cyber-unit-study-underway.

34 Julia Ornedo, 'The Philippine Army Is Recruiting Young Tech Civilians to Fight Cyber Attacks', Rest of World, 21 November 2024, https://restofworld.org/2024/philippines-civilian-tech-cyber-attacks.

35 Nicholas Ryan Aditya and Novianti Setuningsih, 'Soal Satuan Siber, Menhan: Dibutuhkan Teknologinya, Bukan Orangnya yang Banyak' [On cyber unit, defence minister: we need technology, not the numerous people], *Kompas*, 4 February 2025, https://nasional.kompas.com/read/2025/02/04/18243811/soal-satuan-siber-menhan-dibutuhkan-teknologinya-bukan-orangnya-yang-banyak.

36 Mayank Singh, 'India Defence Ministry to Install "Maya OS" for Cybersecurity', *New India Express*, 9 August 2023, https://www.newindianexpress.com/nation/2023/Aug/09/india-defence-ministry-to-installmaya-os-for-cybersecurity-2603454.html.

37 Ladhu R. Choudhary, 'India's Military Modernization Efforts Under Prime Minister Modi', Stimson, 22 May 2024, https://www.stimson.org/2024/indias-military-modernization-efforts-under-prime-minister-modi/.

38 Robert Lemos, 'Japan, Philippines & US to Share Cyber Threat Intel', Dark Reading, 11 April 2024, https://www.darkreading.com/cybersecurity-operations/japan-philippines-us-forge-cyber-threat-intelligence-sharing-alliance.

39 'Joint Statement on the Philippines–United States Fourth 2+2 Ministerial Dialogue', US Department of Defense, 30 July 2024, https://www.defense.gov/News/Releases/Release/Article/3854902/joint-statement-on-the-philippines-united-states-fourth-22-ministerial-dialogue.

40 Rojoef Manuel, 'Philippines, Denmark to Expand Cyber Defense Partnership', The Defense Post, 26 October 2023, https://thedefensepost.com/2023/10/26/philippines-denmark-expand-cyber-defense/.

41 Han Noy, 'China Hosts Military Exercises with 5 ASEAN Members', VOA, 17 November 2023, https://www.voanews.com/a/china-hosts-military-exercises-with-5-asean-members/7360416.html.

42 Jason Healey, 'A Nonstate Strategy for Saving Cyberspace', Atlantic Council, 2017, p21, https://www.atlanticcouncil.org/wp-content/uploads/2015/08/AC_StrategyPapers_No8_Saving_Cyberspace_WEB.pdf

CHAPTER 6

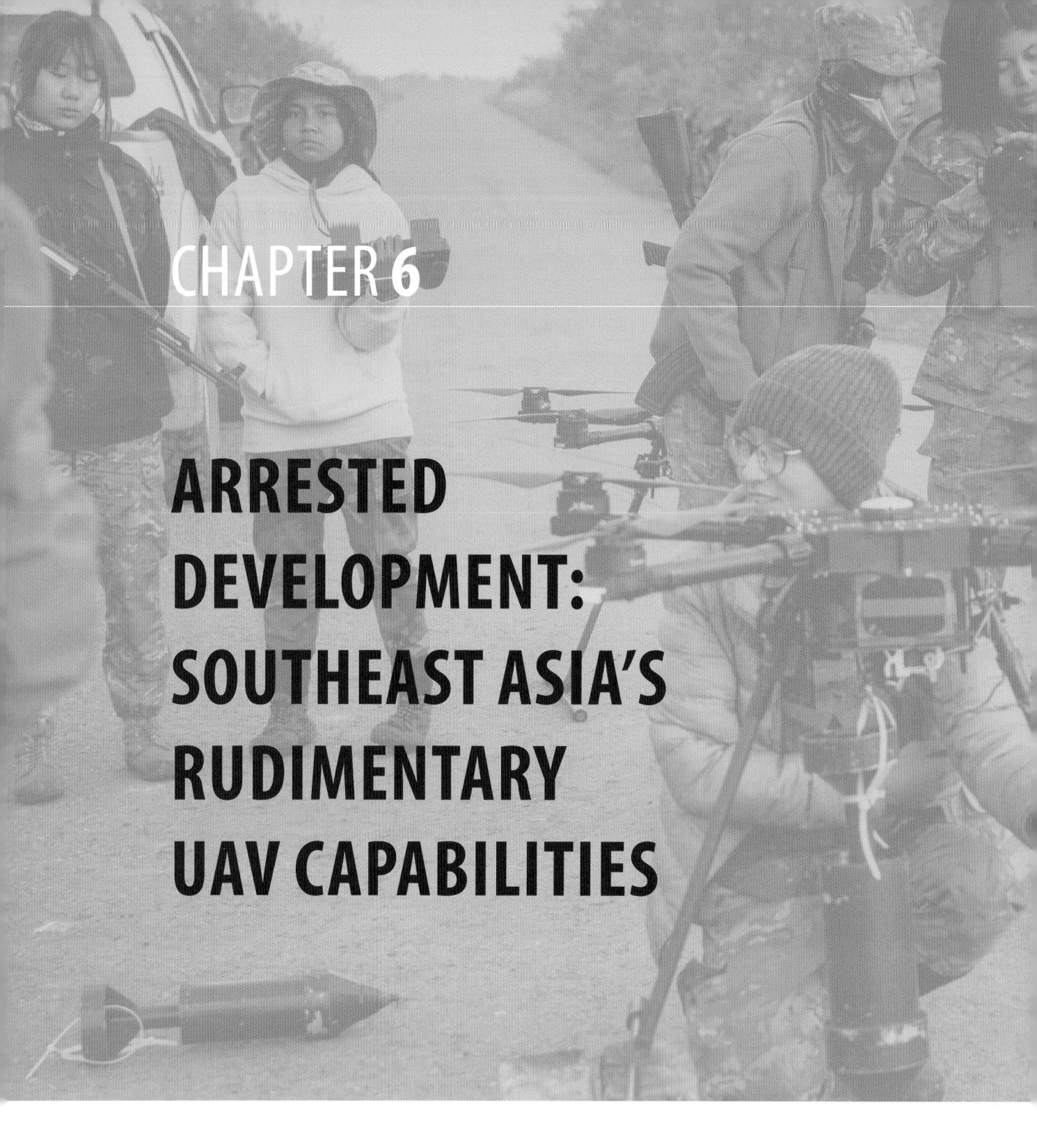

ARRESTED DEVELOPMENT: SOUTHEAST ASIA'S RUDIMENTARY UAV CAPABILITIES

This chapter examines the development and diffusion of military uninhabited-aerial-vehicle (UAV) programmes across four key Southeast Asian states and the lessons drawn from contemporary conflicts.

Members of the Mandalay People's Defence Forces preparing to release a UAV amid clashes with the Tatmadaw in northern Shan State, 11 December 2023 (STR/AFP via Getty Images)

ARGUMENTS AND FINDINGS:

- State-led programmes to develop UAVs in Indonesia, Myanmar, the Philippines and Thailand are primarily rooted in their experiences of battling insurgent movements. These operational histories still act as the primary filters to any lessons to be drawn from contemporary conflicts in Ukraine and the Middle East.

- The overall threat posed by non-state armed groups across Southeast Asia has largely subsided in recent years, outside of Myanmar. Regional analysts and policymakers consequently tend to overlook the potential for UAVs to stoke internal armed conflict.

- UAV operations have shifted to focus on the risk of regional contingencies, including in the South China Sea. However, the dynamics of UAV warfare within Myanmar may also offer operationally salient lessons for other regional militaries.

- The competing demands, as well as the resource and technical constraints, that Indonesia, Myanmar, the Philippines and Thailand face, have led to the uneven development of and incomplete or ill-defined doctrinal approaches to UAV warfare.

IMPLICATIONS FOR REGIONAL SECURITY:

- Southeast Asian states' success – or otherwise – in fully developing well-rounded UAV programmes could improve their maritime-domain and overall situational awareness when fully integrated into their broader military modernisation programmes.

- Southeast Asian states developing military UAV capabilities could potentially impact intra-state armed conflicts and inter-state tensions, especially over disputed waters like the South China Sea.

The use of UAVs has proliferated across multiple domains in Southeast Asia, during both peace and wartime. Throughout 2024, Indonesia, the Philippines and Thailand made further investments in their domestic production and overseas sourcing of various UAVs and, to a lesser extent, counter-UAV (C-UAV) systems. In Myanmar, home to the region's most intense armed conflict, both state and non-state actors have made rapid and concerted efforts to acquire and deploy UAVs onto the battlefield, with profound consequences.

Philippine soldiers arrive at a military camp in Marawi on the southern island of Mindanao, 25 May 2017

(Ted Aljibe/AFP via Getty Images)

The proliferation of UAVs across Southeast Asia may appear to coincide with the widespread and documented use of these systems in major conflicts, such as the Russia–Ukraine war and the Israel–Hamas war. Southeast Asian leaders have also suggested that these conflicts carry relevant lessons.[1] However, Southeast Asian UAV-procurement and -development programmes were already gaining some momentum prior to the onset of either of these conflicts, and the predominant strategic and operational contexts of the region are vastly different to those in Europe or the Middle East. Therefore, the urge to take the lessons offered by Ukraine or Gaza at face value risks distracting from adapting said lessons to better suit the Southeast Asian context.

Notably, UAV programmes in Indonesia, the Philippines and Thailand are largely rooted in their experiences of fighting domestic insurgencies. Outside of Myanmar, the threat and intensity of major armed insurgencies have decreased across most of the region for almost a decade. The Philippines' decades-long Islamist insurgency in the south, which saw major cities under siege in the past, has recently died down, culminating in the creation of the Bangsamoro Autonomous Region in Muslim Mindanao in 2019.[2] A communist insurgency in the south persists, but is also dwindling in scale.[3] Thailand faces a partially frozen Islamist insurgency in its southern provinces, while Indonesia continues to combat poorly equipped Papuan non-state actors fighting for an independent West Papua.[4]

The decline in major insurgencies might have partly reduced the Southeast Asian militaries' urgency to innovate. More limited defence budgets (until recently) do not help either. However, UAVs can also lower the barrier to armed insurgency and can even be a valuable tool for non-state armed groups. Although several Southeast Asian militaries have considered how they can deploy UAVs against non-state actors, they have dedicated little attention to developing their own C-UAV capabilities.

Instead, the Philippines and, to a lesser degree, Indonesia have begun shifting their focus to the South China Sea. The Philippines' stand-off with China in the Second Thomas Shoal has expanded to the Sabina and Scarborough shoals, with even President Ferdinand Marcos directing the armed forces to shift away from internal security to external territorial defence.[5] Chinese vessels, meanwhile, continue to encroach upon the waters surrounding Indonesia's Natuna Islands, which border the South China Sea, leading the Indonesian military to increase its presence in the area.[6] With regard to UAVs, the general response has been to acquire larger platforms to improve their intelligence, surveillance and reconnaissance (ISR) capabilities.

Overall, key state actors in Indonesia, the Philippines and Thailand primarily view UAVs as an emergent tool to incorporate into their existing doctrines and military postures, whether in the context of counter-insurgency or potential future inter-state conflicts. This outlook stands in contrast to the decisive and revolutionary ways state and non-state armed actors have incorporated UAVs into their operations. In Myanmar, for example, UAVs have given some non-state actors greater military capabilities. This, in turn, has allowed them to capture large parts of the country and alter the security landscape of both Myanmar and its immediate neighbourhood, including Thailand and China.

As demonstrated in Myanmar, the proliferation of inexpensive and readily available UAVs could influence pre-existing approaches to both the counter-insurgency and national-security strategies of Southeast Asian states. However, regional armed forces have yet to fully adapt their UAV-procurement patterns and doctrines in accordance with such developments (see Table 6.1). Instead, the general pattern is one of disparate development and incomplete doctrinal thinking. Resource limitations and technical constraints only worsen the situation.

FARAWAY LESSONS

There are two main lessons that can be drawn from UAV operations in Ukraine and the Middle East that could be salient to Southeast Asia, although they should be carefully thought through. Firstly, the Armed Forces of Ukraine have deployed larger fixed-wing UAVs to conduct ISR and ground attack missions. These complemented or replaced the more conventional platforms often used in these roles. In the initial stages of the Russia–Ukraine war, for example, Ukrainian fixed-wing armed UAVs, predominantly Baykar's *Bayraktar* TB2, made headlines for destroying Russian armoured fighting vehicles.[7] Later, smaller, as well as first-person view (FPV) UAVs, began to take on such roles, filling some of the space previously occupied by larger fixed-wing UAVs.[8]

The ability of low-cost UAVs to fulfil such roles presents an alternative – if limited – approach to ISR and ground-attack missions for states that otherwise struggle with resource constraints, including those in Southeast Asia. In Ukraine, smaller UAVs and FPV UAVs carrying explosives and ISR payloads have been allowed to independently identify and destroy targets without additional higher-command approval.[9] Their widespread distribution also allows a broader battlefield view previously only offered by more traditional fixed-wing UAVs. Larger fixed-wing one-way attack (OWA) UAVs can also be used for conducting long-range attacks on key infrastructure behind enemy lines.[10]

UAVs can also aid forces operating in difficult terrain. For example, some Israeli UAVs are specifically modified for operations in dense urban environments, where buildings can be a hazard and also limit satellite navigation and radio communications. Indeed, the Israel Defense Forces have employed signal repeaters to extend the reach of radio signals.[11]

Israel has also developed systems to re-gather global navigation satellite system (GNSS) signals and to limit their jamming.[12] These dynamics are relevant to Southeast Asian states operating against insurgent threats in remote, dense jungles and possibly against maritime threats spanning vast waters.

Secondly, the widespread deployment of UAVs by all sides in Ukraine and the Middle East has demonstrated an urgent requirement for C-UAV systems. 'Soft-kill' C-UAV systems aim to disconnect the UAV from the operator and/or disrupt its navigation systems.[13] These platforms are employed in Ukraine and the Middle East in various forms, including vehicle-based systems with multiple detection sensors and electronic-warfare capabilities or smaller handheld jamming systems. They are less expensive and, as such, the most common C-UAV platforms.

In contrast, 'hard-kill' C-UAV systems, consisting of air- and missile-defence systems, in Ukraine and the Middle East are prioritised to protect against UAVs flying towards key cities and critical infrastructure, given their cost and more limited supply. Israel's layered air-defence system is intended to be able to counter multiple OWA UAV attacks, that have been employed by Hamas, various Iraqi Shia militias, Hizbullah and Ansarullah (the Houthis).[14] In Southeast Asia, fully understanding how C-UAV requirements influence air- and missile-defence system procurements is challenging, given existing gaps in air- and missile-defence requirements more broadly.

A Ukrainian soldier gets ready to fly an Airlogix surveillance UAV outside of Kyiv, 9 November 2022

(Paula Bronstein via Getty Images)

GROUNDED LEARNING

During the siege of Zamboanga City in 2013, the Philippine Army (PA) conducted tests of the small fixed-wing UAVs *Raptor* and possibly *Knight Falcon*.[15] During the siege of Marawi in 2017, the PA made extensive use of Chinese commercial off-the-shelf quadcopters, manufactured by DJI, for ISR missions.[16] They were also used in an artillery-spotter role to aid manoeuvre forces and to communicate with civilians trapped within the city.[17] Hard-won lessons from these sieges led to significant reforms within the Armed Forces of the Philippines.

Both the PA and the Philippine Marine Corps (PMC) began prioritising the acquisition of small handheld and vertical take-off and landing (VTOL) UAVs, such as Elbit Systems' THOR and *Skylark*, recognising their utility in the urban combat environment.[18] Meanwhile, the Philippine Air Force (PAF), already operating larger and longer-range fixed-wing UAVs, acquired the fixed-wing Elbit Systems *Hermes* 450 and *Hermes* 900 to support the army, marines and police in counter-insurgency operations, including by conducting persistent ISR missions over Islamist and communist insurgent hotspots in the south.[19]

As these insurgencies have died down and tensions in the South China Sea have grown, the PAF has shifted the focus of its UAV operations towards the latter and the maritime domain more broadly. In 2018, new UAV hangars were built on the islands of Palawan and Luzon to facilitate more operations in the South China Sea.[20] As is the case with Indonesia, UAV operations over the South China Sea are not limited to the monitoring of foreign vessels, but also to help secure offshore oil and natural-gas platforms.[21]

In this new context, the Philippine Navy (PN) as well as the Philippine Coast Guard (PCG) are supporting the PAF. In 2022, the PN activated its first UAV unit and began operating the US-donated Insitu *ScanEagle* 2, which the PAF also operates and can be launched from naval vessels.[22] The PN has been especially keen on developing doctrinal concepts on the use of UAVs and uninhabited platforms more broadly.[23] As the PN and many other Southeast Asian navies often find it difficult to use their ships to cover the vast expanses of their waters, land-based and ship-borne UAVs can assist in this regard.

A Philippine military chaplain blesses a *ScanEagle* 2 UAV during a ceremony at a military air base in Manila, 13 March 2018

(Ted Aljibe/AFP via Getty Images)

UAV capabilities, nevertheless, still vary between the armed services. While the PA and PMC have first-hand experience and arguably a more well-defined practice for tactical unit and counter-insurgency-related UAV operations, their experiences may not be as easily transferable to the maritime domain and external defence, given the difference in expanse between the two contexts. Interestingly, the PA and PAF have begun developing or testing FPV UAVs similar to those found in Ukraine and Gaza.[24] The PAF has also begun developing cheap, small fixed-wing and rotary-wing UAVs, likely capable of carrying munitions, in the same vein as the small UAVs found on the front lines of the aforementioned conflicts.[25] How these new UAVs will be adopted to the South China Sea context remains unclear.

Ukraine has used FPV UAVs to support operations in the maritime domain. Most recently, in January 2025, Ukrainian uninhabited surface vessels (USVs) were reportedly used to launch FPV UAVs against land-based targets such as air-defence systems.[26] In December 2024, they were previously used to attack gas platforms in the Black Sea.[27] On the other hand, in September 2024, Russia launched FPV UAVs from helicopters, reportedly against Ukrainian USVs.[28] Given their short operational range, FPV UAVs required additional support. However, when other platforms can provide support, in the form of a launch platform or a signal extender, their operational range can be extended, offering a new versatile tool for operations in the maritime domain.

Both the PN and PCG are still in the preliminary stages of developing their UAV capabilities and doctrine, despite their large appetite to deploy them.[29] Moreover, their recently acquired UAVs have more limited range and endurance than the PAF's UAVs, although they can be operated from seaborne vessels. The PN seeks to extend this range; it is even considering the development of OWA UAV capabilities as a novel, cost-effective maritime-strike capability.[30] More broadly, it is considering how UAVs can be used to augment conventional capabilities to deny access to Philippine waters.[31]

In any case, given its limited resources, Manila is likely to continue leveraging the UAV capabilities of its treaty ally, the United States. In 2023, a US Army medium altitude long endurance (MALE) General Atomics MQ-1C *Gray Eagle*, reportedly operating out of Edwin Air Base in Zamboanga, was spotted flying over the BRP *Sierra Madre*, the marooned landing ship in the Second Thomas Shoal.[32] In June 2024, following a request by the Philippines, the US Marine Corps' MALE General Atomics MQ-9A *Reapers* began a rotational deployment to Cesar Basa Air Base in Pampanga.[33] During the 2024 *Balikatan* exercise, the US Marine Corps demonstrated how the Survice TRV-150Cs, a type of electric VTOL UAV, can be used for resupply missions on the island of Palawan – in essence, how UAVs can be employed to transport supplies to difficult locations such as the *Sierra Madre*.[34] Since then, the PMC has reportedly begun development on a VTOL UAV for supply transport.[35]

By comparison, the Philippines' C-UAV capabilities and doctrine remain relatively underdeveloped, even after the significant use of UAVs by enemy forces during the siege of Marawi. Preceding the siege, insurgents infiltrated the city and amassed a large contingent of combatants, weapons and UAVs.[36] Using commercial off-the-shelf DJI models, insurgents monitored troop movements and identified patterns in the PA's tactics, including a tendency to temporarily withdraw prior to an airstrike, thereby identifying strike targets and allowing for their own orderly retreats.[37] UAVs were used to help identify ambush sites when expertly combined with knowledge of local terrain. Propaganda broadcasts of combat footage recorded on UAVs were also common.[38]

Since the siege, the Philippine state forces have employed some C-UAV systems, including vehicle-based systems and handheld systems typically operated by the police forces, to protect VIPs and large events such as the 2019 Southeast Asian Games and the 2024 State of the Nation Address.[39] The PAF previously considered procuring an electronic-warfare suite for the *Hermes* 900, which could have been used to jam smaller UAVs flying closer to the ground. The programme was eventually cancelled in 2024, perhaps due to the ongoing conflict in Gaza and Elbit Systems' consequent capacity.[40] In 2019, the PN considered C-UAV capabilities to protect offshore natural-resource processing facilities.[41] In the same year, Indonesian energy firms have also tested C-UAV systems, owned by the Ministry of Defense, to protect natural-resource refineries.[42] These examples suggest the Philippines' appetite to deploy bits and pieces of C-UAV capabilities across different state security agencies, but it is less clear the extent to which their concept of operations is well developed.

PATCHY PROGRESS

Indonesia's UAV-development programmes share many similarities with the Philippines' and Thailand's. Indonesia's earliest indigenous UAV-development programmes may have been driven by the need to map and navigate the difficult terrain along the border regions in Kalimantan and Papua. The latter is a known hotspot for insurgent activities. However, maritime incidents in the waters surrounding the Natuna Islands, which border the South China Sea, have pushed Indonesia to invest in longer-range UAVs. The 'Policy for the Implementation of National Defence 2020–2024' document further emphasised the importance of these capabilities.[43] Indonesian defence leaders have since backed these plans in recent years.

The Indonesian Army's (TNI-AD) topographic directorate has employed commercial off-the-shelf UAVs to map difficult terrain in the border regions in Kalimantan and Papua since the 2010s.[44] These small UAVs were lent to army combat units possibly involved in counter-insurgency operations in Papua.[45] Small UAVs, including those manufactured by DJI, are typically sent ahead of foot patrols or to identify key targets, which may be why the TNI-AD seeks to acquire more of them.[46] Security forces have also reportedly deployed the armed rotary-wing Ziyan *Blowfish* A3 in Papua as well.[47] However, unlike insurgents in Myanmar, the Philippines and Thailand, Papuan insurgents have not – as of writing – developed their own UAV or C-UAV capabilities.

Indonesian police scouting a remote jungle airstrip in Tanah Hitam village near Jayapura, Papua province, 25 May 2009

(STR/AFP via Getty Images)

Fixed-wing UAVs such as Bhinneka Dwi Persada's *Rajawali* 720 and the National Institute of Aeronautics and Space's (LAPAN) fixed-wing LSU series were tested for border-security operations from the mid-2010s onwards, but it is unlikely any of these platforms ever entered service.[48] The fixed-wing Bhinneka Dwi Persada *Rajawali* 330 (a licence-produced version of UMS Skeldar's F-330) and the Indonesian fixed-wing Carita Boat *Elang Laut* 25 reportedly entered service in the mid- to late 2010s, but have seldom been seen since.[49] Since the 2020s, the TNI-AD has tested larger UAVs to fulfil an artillery-spotter role, including NEXIN's hybrid-VTOL PTTA and the rotary-wing Alpha Unmanned Systems A900.[50]

The Indonesian Air Force (TNI-AU) also started its UAV-development programmes in the 2010s. The indigenously designed, fixed-wing *Wulung*, manufactured by Dirgantara Indonesia (DI), was among the first TNI-AU programmes which began in 2013 to help with border- and maritime-surveillance operations.[51] While the UAV reportedly entered service in 2018, its unit assignment and basing remain unclear. Reports suggest that 75% of the *Wulung*'s components are manufactured locally; however, some of its most critical components – its electronics, flight-control system and ISR payload – are still imported.[52]

The TNI-AU's most high-profile UAV programme is the DI-manufactured MALE *Elang Hitam*, which was intended to be a dedicated maritime-surveillance UAV. Development began in 2015 and was due to be completed by 2022, with an armed variant due to be developed by 2024. However, while a first prototype without an ISR payload was unveiled in 2019, the COVID-19 pandemic caused funding difficulties and development delays. Technical

Table 6.1: **Southeast Asia: specifications of selected indigenously designed UAVs**

Country	Designation	Service	Status	Manufacturer	Endurance	Range	MTOW
Indonesia	*Elang Hitam*†	Air force	Cancelled*	DI	24 hour	250 km	1,300 kg
	Wulung	Air force	Operational*	DI	3h	120 km	125 kg
	Elang Laut 25	Army	Operational*	Carita Boat	8h	600 km	120 kg
	PTTA	Army	In development	NEXIN	n.k.	147 km	n.k.
	Rajata^	Army*	In development	DAHANA	15min	30 km	2.5 kg
	LSU-02	Army/navy	Trialled*	National Institute of Aeronautics and Space (LAPAN)	5h	n.k.	15 kg
Philippines	Knight Falcon	Army	Operational*	Philippine Army	2.5h	35 km	n.k.
	Raptor	Army	Operational*	Philippine Army	n.k.	7 km	n.k.
Thailand	U1	Air force	Operational	RV Connex	12h	100 km	140 kg
	KB-5E^	Air force	In development	Royal Thai Air Force Academy	n.k.	150 km	n.k.
	KB-10G^	Air force	In development	Royal Thai Air Force Academy	n.k.	500 km	40 kg
	D-Eyes 02	Army/navy	In development	Defence Technology Institute (DTI)	1h	10 km	5.6 kg
	D-Eyes 03	Army	In development	DTI	4h	40 km	16.9 kg
	DP 20††	Army	In development	Aero Technology Industry Company (ATIL)	20h	250 km (LOS); 2,000 km (SATCOM)	750 kg
	DP 20-A**††	Army	In development	ATIL	36h	250 km (LOS); 2,000 km (SATCOM)	1,500 kg
	DP 16**	Army	In development	ATIL	10h	250 km	360 kg
	DP 18A**	Army	In development	ATIL	12h	150 km	300 kg
	Siam UAV	Army	In development	DTI	40m	2 km	n.k.
	Falcon-V FUVEC	Navy	In development	TOP Engineering Corporation	4h	150 km	n.k.
	MARCUS	Navy	In development	Naval Research and Development Office (NRDO)	1h	15 km	24 kg
	MARCUS-B/C	Navy	In development	NRDO	2.5h	180 km	55 kg

*Reported/service status unclear. **Armed. †Synthetic aperture radar. ‡Signals intelligence. ^One-way attack. LOS = line-of-sight range; MTOW = maximum take-off weight; SATCOM = satellite-communications range

Source: IISS

limitations meant only 40% of the UAV's components were locally manufactured.[53] By 2022, it was announced that the programme funds were to be reallocated towards civilian UAV programmes, but the status of the programme as a whole remains unclear.[54]

The TNI-AU also operates one MALE UAV design. It procured six of China Aerospace Science and Technology Corporation's (CASC) armed CH-4Bs in 2019, which are now stationed in Ranai, Natuna. The TNI-AU's other large fixed-wing UAV, the Aeronautics Defense Systems' *Aerostar*, is stationed in West Kalimantan.[55] It also acquired Turkish Aerospace Industries' *Anka*-S in 2023. DI is set to assemble six of the 12 procured *Anka*-Ss, with Turkish Aerospace Industries to offer additional training for the company's engineers.[56] The TNI-AU has also shown interest in the *Bayraktar* TB2.[57]

Both Chinese and Turkish UAVs are generally seen as cost-effective, with fewer end-user restrictions and backed with some defence offset projects. However, Turkish UAVs have the advantage over Chinese UAVs in terms of reliability and being combat tested in Nagorno-Karabakh and Ukraine.[58] Indonesia chose the Turkish UAVs partly perhaps for these reasons. Taken together, these foreign acquisitions suggest that Indonesian military leaders understood the growing importance of MALE UAVs for maritime surveillance while recognising the country's defence-industrial limitations.

A China Aerospace Science and Technology Corporation CH-4 UAV performs at the 13th China International Aviation & Aerospace Exhibition in Zhuhai, Guangdong province, 29 September 2021

(VCG/VCG via Getty Images)

However, the multiplicity of UAV platforms procured, and the large number of foreign suppliers, highlight a larger logistical and inter-operability problem common across the Indonesian military. In this regard, Indonesia risks ignoring what is an important lesson from Ukraine: the value of domestically produced UAVs, which has made Ukraine less dependent on foreign assistance and allowed for rapid modifications to meet front-line requirements. To mitigate this problem, Indonesia seems to have taken a sort of halfway approach: procuring UAVs from countries with technology transfer as a key condition. Recent deals signed by Turkish and Indonesian firms, on possible joint ventures and UAV co-production, further highlights this new approach.[59] In the long term, this will bolster its ambitions to field more indigenously designed UAVs.[60]

More broadly, the UAV procurements above, coupled with the TNI-AU's establishment of a UAV-training squadron that operates a licensed-produced version of the French LH Aviation fixed-wing LH-D in 2023, suggest the Indonesian military's recognition of the platform's importance before and after the wars in Ukraine and Gaza.[61] The lessons drawn from those contemporary conflicts perhaps shaped – and may even gave new rationales for – the TNI-AU's pre-existing UAV programmes. However, it is less likely that those conflicts alone were necessary and sufficient to initiate and drive Indonesia's UAV programmes across different armed services.

The Indonesian Navy (TNI-AL) similarly activated its own UAV-training squadron, operating the rotary-wing Schiebel S-100 *Camcopter* and procuring the hybrid-VTOL *Poseidon* H6 from the Cypriot company Swarmly in 2023.[62] The VTOL capabilities of both UAVs suggest their use for shipborne operations. Supporting this possibility, the TNI-AL previously tested the LAPAN LSU-02 as an anti-ship-missile spotter during the military's 2013 tri-service joint exercise, launching the UAV from the deck of a frigate.[63] By 2018, the TNI-AL inducted the US-donated Insitu *ScanEagle* 2 and the ECA Group's rotary-wing

STERNA IT180 to detect ships' magnetic signatures.[64] The TNI-AL's interest in the *Anka*-S and the high altitude long endurance (HALE) Baykar *Bayraktar Akinci*, however, suggests it also seeks to conduct persistent maritime-surveillance missions similar to those conducted by the TNI-AU's UAVs.[65]

Lastly, the military is beginning to experiment with various C-UAV capabilities. Beyond protecting VIPs, the TNI-AD is developing prototypes for a C-UAV system. In 2024, it awarded a contract to a local company for a vehicle-based C-UAV system.[66] At the 2024 military-anniversary parade, small quadcopter UAVs flew with a VIP convoy, dropping fake munitions on would-be attackers as other UAVs were crashed into the attacking vehicles, followed by a swarm of the attackers' own small quadcopter UAVs being shot down by soldiers using handheld C-UAV systems.[67] Local company PT Pindad developed the handheld system, the SPS-1, as well as a vehicle-based system, the *Maung* MV3.[68] Similarly, the TNI-AU's special forces have been developing organic C-UAV capabilities, given their critical-infrastructure and air-base defence mandate. They deployed their vehicle-based and handheld C-UAV systems to protect the 2023 ASEAN Summit.[69]

The 2024 parade offers insight into Indonesian thinking on UAV doctrinal development, although it is too early to judge whether those tactical demonstrations will form the foundational concept of operations for UAVs more broadly. After all, a significant number of the UAVs paraded are unlikely to have entered service and may even still be in testing. However, the display of OWA UAVs, swarm UAVs and UAVs capable of carrying munitions highlights that Indonesia is paying attention to the developments coming out of recent conflicts. Conceptual innovation, however, does not equal operational implementation or combat effectiveness.

TEAMING UP

Thailand has launched a series of ambitious UAV-development programmes, bolstered by significant Chinese backing, to support its border-security and counter-insurgency operations in the south. The Royal Thai Army (RTA) and the Defence Technology Institute (DTI) have been major driving forces behind these projects. However, perhaps recognising the threat of small-UAV proliferation likely to emerge during counter-insurgency operations and from border-security challenges, Thailand has invested more readily in C-UAV capabilities.

Indeed, the RTA was an early adopter of UAV capabilities in Southeast Asia, operating the fixed-wing Israeli Aerospace Industries' *Searcher* as an artillery spotter from the late 1990s.[70] Since then, the RTA has frequently conducted ISR missions with *Searcher*s and *Hermes* 450s, likely in support of border-security and counter-insurgency operations in the southern provinces given the endurance and range of these platforms.[71] These operational mandates, combined with the RTA's domestic political dominance, have contributed to the accumulation of larger fixed-wing UAVs typically only operated by Southeast Asian air forces.

DTI has also been a major driving force behind indigenous UAV-development programmes, serving as the main coordinator between the armed services and industry partners (see Figure 6.1). DTI's D-Eyes series, started in the 2010s, were among Thailand's earliest indigenous UAV-development programmes.[72] While the quadcopter D-Eyes 01 is unlikely to have entered service, the D-Eyes 02 has been in testing with the RTA, the Royal Thai Marine Corps (RTMC) and the Royal Thai Air Force (RTAF) since the 2020s. The RTA and the RTMC are testing the platform for border-surveillance operations while the RTAF is testing the platform for air-base defence operations.[73] In a similar vein, since 2017, the quadcopter *Siam* UAV was tested by the RTA Special Forces under Internal Security Operations Command (ISOC) Region 4, the overall command responsible for counter-insurgency operations in the southern provinces.[74]

Thai soldiers stand in formation during an inspection ceremony at Chulabhorn military camp in the southern province of Narathiwat, 22 April 2018

(Madaree Tohlala/AFP via Getty Images)

However, the RTA's ambitions are not limited to small UAVs. In 2022 Aero Technology Industry (ATIL) unveiled the DP series, which includes the VTOL DP 6, the armed fixed-wing DP 16 and its follow-up the DP 18A, as well as the MALE fixed-wing DP 20 and its armed variant the DP 20-A.[75] These UAV series are intended to bolster Thailand's armed-UAV and MALE-UAV capabilities. The latter had been lacking until recently and its armed-UAV capabilities are still non-existent. These indigenous designs are also intended for possible export as Thailand seeks to become a global UAV exporter.[76] Indeed, at the Bali International Air Show last year ATIL announced a partnership with Indonesian firm Len Industri to develop an Indonesian variant of the DP 18A.[77]

Thailand has sought Chinese support for these programmes. In fact, ATIL is a joint venture between Thailand's National Science and Technology Development Agency and China's Beihang UAS Technology. The DP 20 and DP 20-A are reportedly modified variants of the Beihang CY-9 (more commonly referred to as the Harbin BZK-005), incorporating a new tail and radome with a synthetic-aperture radar to penetrate the dense foliage of southern Thailand. While reports suggest 'most' of the DP 20 and DP 20-A's components are locally manufactured, Thailand may have received support from China in developing the platforms' propulsion, flight-control, sensor and weapons-integration systems (components most countries struggle with when developing their own UAVs).[78]

Chinese support likely began around 2016, when Thailand signed a bilateral defence-industrial-cooperation agreement, including for UAVs.[79] This support may stem from two factors. Firstly, the military coups in 2006 and 2014 strained relations between Thailand and the United States.[80] Consequently, over the past decade, Thailand has sought closer political-economic ties with China, and, as such, investment from the latter has grown significantly.[81] These ties may have opened the door for defence-industrial cooperation, which Washington was often less keen on developing with Thailand.[82] Secondly, since 2010, China has become a major exporter of ISR and armed UAVs. As previously mentioned, Chinese UAVs are known to be cost-competitive and come with few end-user restrictions, and in some cases they allow for licensed production or some form of technology transfer.[83]

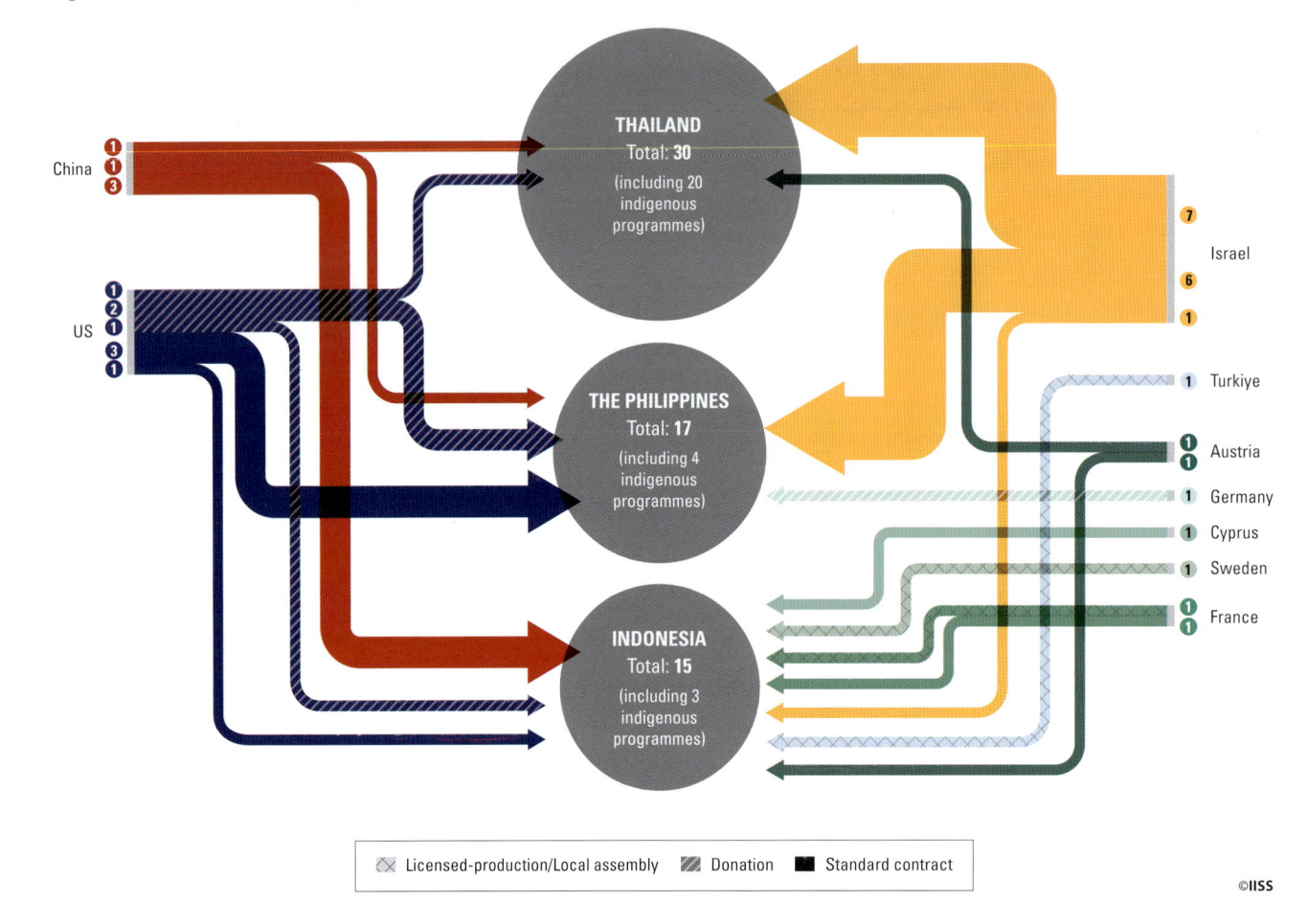

Figure 6.1. **Indonesia, the Philippines and Thailand: major UAV programmes by source country**

Licensed-production/Local assembly   Donation   Standard contract

©IISS

Source: IISS

The RTA, nonetheless, has been able spend significant resources on various projects, with some of their programmes even creating capability redundancies with other armed services (see Figure 6.1). This includes the RTAF, whose UAVs have also been used for border-security and counter-insurgency operations.[84] Indeed, the fixed-wing solar-powered M Solar X series developed by the RTAF Academy had been tested in Thailand's southern provinces.[85] Both the RTA and RTAF have begun developing OWA UAV programmes, perhaps recognising the efficacy of OWA UAVs on the front lines in Ukraine.

The RTA is currently considering integrating the Elbit Systems *SkyStriker* into its D11As (localised versions of the Elbit Systems PULS multiple rocket launcher system). On the other hand, the RTAF has initiated an OWA UAV programme, a requirement outlined in the 2024 Air Force White Paper. These UAVs are designated as the KB series and are designed by the RTAF Academy.[86] Moreover, both the 2020 and 2024 Air Force white papers highlight the opportunities offered – as well as the threat posed – by small, armed, commercial off-the-shelf, electronic-warfare, OWA and FPV UAVs.[87] The 2024 Army White Paper similarly highlights the RTA's need for more armed UAVs.[88]

Meanwhile, the RTAF is tasked with enforcing airspace restrictions against illegal UAV flights, with the necessary legal framework being developed and a dedicated C-UAV unit to be activated.[89] The RTAF began developing C-UAV capabilities in the late 2010s, prior to the conflicts in either Gaza, Myanmar or Ukraine. In 2018, the RTAF procured Israeli IMI

Systems' short-range *Red Sky* 2 C-UAV system to boost its air-base defences.[90] In 2020, the DTI started developing a mobile C-UAV system with the RTA and procured Australian AVT's X-MADIS FS C-UAV systems.[91] C-UAV systems have also been used in counter-narcotics operations as smugglers have started to use UAVs – a recent development that other countries, particularly Indonesia, have had to contend with.[92]

Since the RTAF began developing C-UAV capabilities, its assessment of the threat posed by UAVs has increased dramatically. The 2024 Air Force White Paper describes OWA and FPV UAVs as 'critical threats', its second-highest threat level.[93] Where the 2020 Air Force White Paper made some mention of the threat posed by UAVs, the 2024 Air Force White Paper's heightened threat level stands in stark contrast and could be attributed to the real-world examples of the Middle East, Myanmar and Ukraine.

Myanmar is an especially pressing case for RTAF planners given their neighbour's long-standing history of insurgent armed violence and porous borders. UAVs in this regard can offer resource-constrained forces a cost-effective means to conduct ISR and ground-attack missions. Insurgents in Thailand's southern provinces have, in turn, been paying attention. In June 2024, ISOC Region 4 announced a ban on unauthorised UAVs in four southern provinces after intelligence reports suggested that insurgents were training with small armed UAVs capable of carrying munitions.[94] In light of these developments, legislators have criticised the lack of funding for C-UAV capabilities.[95]

This is not to say the RTAF's operational mandate is limited to C-UAV operations, or that the RTAF has not significantly bolstered its own UAV capabilities. In the past two years, the RTAF has activated an entire UAV wing operating the indigenous fixed-wing RV Connex U1, the *Aerostar* and, most recently, the MALE Israeli Aeronautics Defense Systems' *Dominator* XP.[96]

Whereas the RTA's and RTAF's UAV roles overlap, the Royal Thai Navy (RTN) has sought to carve its own niche by prioritising UAV platforms for shipborne operations. TOP Engineering Corporation's VTOL *Falcon*-V FUVEC is currently in testing, as are the hybrid-VTOL Naval Research & Development Office MARCUS and its larger, longer-range follow-up, the MARCUS-B/C.[97] The MARCUS-B/C was launched from the RTN's carrier, the HTMS *Chakri Naruebet*, a possible indication of the role it could fulfil.[98] These other UAVs in operation with the RTN include the launcher-based Aeronautics Defense Systems *Orbiter* 3B, operated for maritime law-enforcement operations, and the S-100 *Camcopter*.[99] In 2022, the US donated the launcher-based Insitu RQ-21A *Blackjack*.[100] Also in 2022, Elbit Systems announced a contract with the RTN to supply *Hermes* 900s equipped with a maritime-surveillance suite and radar.[101]

NEIGHBOURING LESSONS

In 2008, the Myanmar Armed Forces, or Tatmadaw, enacted a new constitution, setting in motion an era of political reform and liberalisation. Following elections in 2015, a civilian government led by Aung San Suu Kyi and her National League for Democracy entered a power-sharing agreement with the Tatmadaw. Hailed by the international community as a transition towards democracy, the military-led opening brought sanctions relief and rapid economic growth. This granted the Tatmadaw greater access to finances and the international weapons markets, even as it continued to conduct repressive counter-insurgency operations across various parts of the country.

The Tatmadaw began acquiring UAVs in the early 2010s, without an apparent vision for how they could be used or integrated into its wider counter-insurgency doctrine which, despite stated intentions to focus more on external defence, remained the army's principal objective. The Tatmadaw's early use of UAVs was therefore primarily experimental and ad hoc and did not take place as part of a wider rethink about its traditional approach to counter-insurgency.

Aung San Suu Kyi and Tatmadaw chief Senior General Min Aung Hlaing at the presidential palace in Naypyidaw, 30 March 2016

(Ye Aung Thu/AFP via Getty Images)

Illustratively, the Tatmadaw initially deployed ISR UAVs against its opponents in the mid-2010s but only on limited occasions. Its first regular deployment of UAVs began in 2019 with the commencement of the Rakhine war. In addition to ISR roles, the Tatmadaw also deployed UAVs as artillery spotters against the Arakan Army, a non-state armed group based in the western state of Rakhine. Interestingly, these UAV innovations were not observed along other active fronts in northern or southeastern Myanmar, indicating that the Tatmadaw was using Rakhine as a testing ground for new platforms and tactics. Even in Rakhine, however, the Tatmadaw did not appear to seriously consider the offensive-strike potential of UAVs, favouring their use in ISR missions.

On 1 February 2021, the Tatmadaw staged a *coup d'état* against the democratically elected government, instigating a nationwide armed resistance movement. This abruptly changed the conflict landscape and ushered in a new era of UAV warfare. Hundreds of localised resistance cells, which later became known as People's Defence Forces (PDFs), took up homemade weapons to resist the Myanmar Army in the country's heartland. At the same time, multiple pre-existing and better-equipped ethnic-minority forces revived their armed struggles in the borderlands.

Critical to this was the adoption of UAVs. Faced with severe resource constraints, newly formed PDFs acquired UAVs to wage asymmetric attacks against the military regime. Opposition fighters incorporated UAVs into their insurgent strategies using 3D printed models, modified hobby-grade remote-control planes and inexpensive commercial off-the-shelf rotary units to carry out stand-off attacks (from a distance) and ambushes against regime columns, administrative offices, police checkpoints and mobile cell towers.

The role of UAVs further changed in October 2023 when a powerful bloc of ethnic armed organisations (EAOs) known as the Three Brotherhood Alliance (hereafter the Brotherhood) launched a sweeping offensive along the Myanmar–China border, dubbed *Operation 1027*. Unlike the fledgling PDFs, the Brotherhood boasted thousands of well-trained troops under a clear chain of command, significant firepower and decades of combined fighting experience. Equipped with modified commercial and agricultural UAVs purchased in China, the alliance dropped tens of thousands of munitions on remote regime outposts before launching direct ground assaults.

Cut off from reinforcements, the Tatmadaw's forward bases were unable to withstand prolonged bombardment. As the regime's interlocking network of fire-support bases collapsed, the Brotherhood was able to launch assaults on large towns and battalion headquarters across northern Shan State. The alliance achieved a milestone in August 2024 when it overran the regime's Northeastern Regional Military Command and captured the major city of Lashio.

The tactics adopted by Myanmar's opposition forces accentuate the different roles that UAVs can play in asymmetric conflicts and their varying degrees of impact. For the newer, poorly organised and ill-equipped PDFs, UAVs have lowered the barrier to entry for armed struggle and offered new forms of propaganda material like video footage, often shared for fundraising. However, these platforms have not radically altered the strategic dynamics in areas where PDFs operate. Instead, UAVs often served as stand-ins for improvised explosive devices deployed in roadside ambushes, a classic insurgent tactic.

In contrast, UAVs played a more influential role on the battlefield when wielded by better equipped and more established EAOs. For example, the Brotherhood's deployment of UAVs has enabled it to evolve well beyond a traditional insurgent force and achieve greater conventional war-fighting capabilities. This is because UAVs offered a scalable alternative to artillery systems, which are typically difficult for non-state armed groups to acquire in great numbers or transport in the absence of mechanised forces.

Already in possession of adequate small arms, robust command and control and fighting experience, UAVs were the missing link in the Brotherhood's force posture. Once acquired, these systems enabled the Brotherhood to directly assault and dismantle the Tatmadaw's presence in the theatre in just three months. This innovation and the

Map 6.1: **Townships in Myanmar captured by the Brotherhood Alliance, Nov 2023–Dec 2024**

Ta'ang National Liberation Army members at a graduation ceremony near Namhkam, northern Shan State, 9 November 2024

advantage that it has offered to the opposition has radically altered the battlefield balance of power in Myanmar.

Despite a sharp rise in aerial attacks by 2022 (see Figure 6.2), the regime did not appear to fully appreciate the threat posed by UAVs. Instead, it deployed only limited numbers of C-UAV systems such as domestically manufactured jamming packs and handheld C-UAV systems available on the business-to-consumer e-commerce site Alibaba, but only to high-value bases and assets. It did not attempt to deploy countermeasures to its wider network of forward-operating bases in areas with heavy opposition activity, including remote areas across northern Shan, Kachin and Rakhine states. Nor did it prioritise the development of its own UAV tactics or arsenal for offensive purposes.

Instead, it focused on the upkeep and deployment of its air force, which it increasingly relied on in the face of mounting armed opposition. It is not clear why the Tatmadaw did not invest sufficiently in UAV or C-UAV capabilities. The army has historically been slow to adapt, and this dynamic was exacerbated by the widespread corruption and leadership deficit faced in the aftermath of the 2021 coup. After nearly two decades of military dominance, the Tatmadaw may have simply underestimated the threat of new technologies in the hands of highly motivated insurgent forces. It is also possible that the logistical challenges of acquiring, let alone manufacturing and distributing, soft- and hard-kill C-UAV systems at scale is simply beyond the Tatmadaw's ability, given its already strained resources.

Following the devasting losses suffered at the hands of the Brotherhood during *Operation 1027*, the Tatmadaw finally began to prioritise its UAV programme. It suddenly acquired thousands of commercial rotary-wing units, equipped with purpose-built 'drop bombs' manufactured by the regime's Directorate of Defence Industries. These systems are

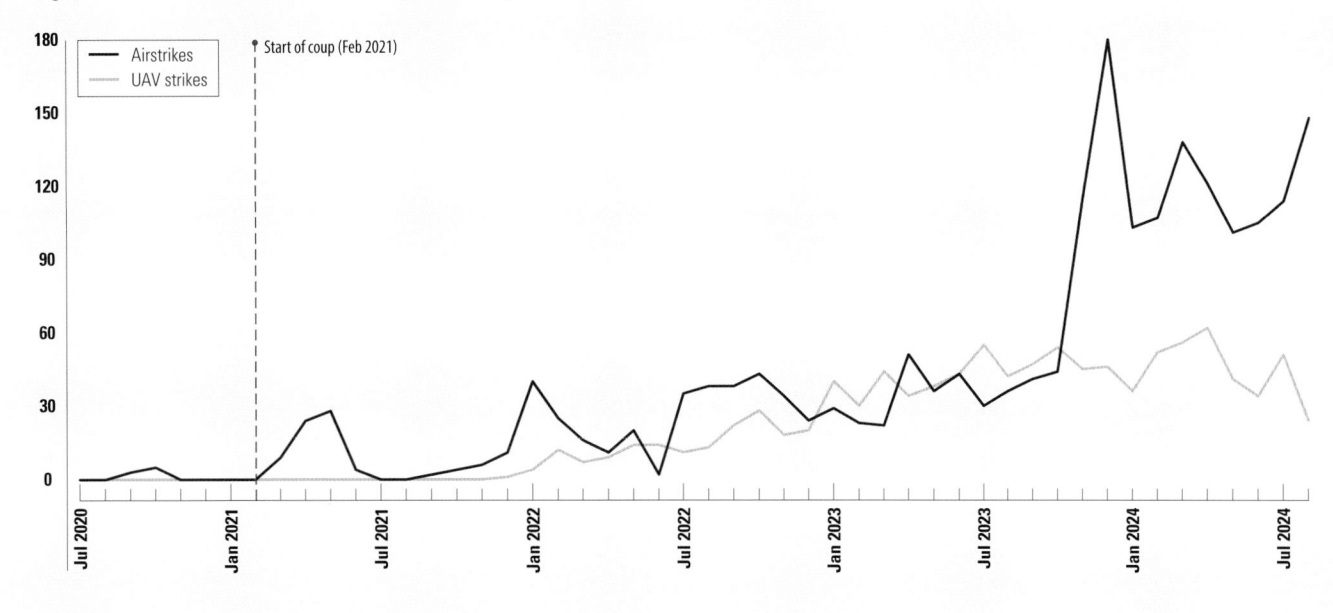

Figure 6.2: **Air and UAV strikes in Myanmar by month, Jul 2020–Aug 2024**

Note: Airstrikes are by the Tatmadaw only; UAV strikes are by both the Tatmadaw and opposition forces.
Source: Armed Conflict Location & Event Data Project (ACLED), www.acleddata.com

©IISS

now provided to front-line infantry units tasked with assaulting enemy positions, as well as remote outposts where they are intended for use in early warning and active defence. The army has now incorporated UAV and C-UAV tactics into its training curriculum, though advances in the latter category are difficult to track.

Moreover, the Tatmadaw has procured UAVs from China and Russia, including armed UAVs such as the CASC CH-3A, as well as ISR UAVs including the Russian Special Technology Centre's *Orlan*-10E and Albatross's *Albatross*-M5.[102] The systems have helped reduce strain on the Tatmadaw's air force, which must provide close air support for units across seven different fronts. UAVs could also fill the role of carrying out intelligence-driven pinpoint strikes on opposition leaders and assets and offer a cost-effective way to maintain pressure on civilian populations with regular harassment and bombardment. In general, UAVs have proven quite effective for the Tatmadaw, given that the opposition forces have almost no anti-air or C-UAV capabilities.

While the Tatmadaw has recognised the utility of UAV platforms and incorporated them into its own arsenal, it does not appear to have fully grasped the implications of UAV warfare for its basic approach to counter-insurgency operations, predicated largely on establishing a forward presence in areas where rebels operate. The advent of UAVs has made it exceedingly difficult for the Tatmadaw to maintain hundreds of isolated outposts as these positions have become vulnerable to a barrage of enemy attacks. Nor can it afford to equip thousands of police stations, checkpoints, bridges, cellular towers, transmission cables, offices and other sites with adequate countermeasures.

Yet the Tatmadaw has insisted on maintaining its forward-defence posture, deploying UAVs to front-line units in hopes of helping to defend increasingly vulnerable and exposed positions. In comments to media, various opposition forces have admitted to the growing challenge that Tatmadaw UAVs are presenting. Although rebel forces pioneered UAV warfare in Myanmar, their initial advantage was largely due to the Tatmadaw's own failure to deploy the capability in a timely manner. Once state forces realised the need to further develop UAV and C-UAV technologies, they quickly filled the gap.

LEARNING ON THE FLY

Over the past decade, prior to and following the commencement of the wars in Myanmar, Ukraine and the Middle East, Southeast Asian countries have built up their UAV capabilities (see Figure 6.1). These capabilities have been predominantly oriented towards counter-insurgency operations, as well as border and maritime surveillance, among others. Indonesia and the Philippines both have long and unresolved internal-security concerns and insurgencies. Both are also archipelagic states increasingly concerned about the South China Sea. Thailand and Myanmar have both focused on border security and internal conflicts for much of their history. All four countries have developed UAV capabilities on the fly and will continue to do so.

The Philippines operated small UAVs during the 2013 siege of Zamboanga City and the 2017 siege of Marawi. These sieges forced the Philippines' military to rapidly improve its small UAV capabilities and fill the gaps of larger fixed-wing and MALE UAVs, now deployed for surveillance missions over the South China Sea. Even while the major insurgencies in the south of the country have simmered down in recent years, concurrently a maritime reorientation is taking place following increased tensions with China.

Indonesia initially prioritised the development and acquisition of small UAVs for operations in border areas though there is arguably an interest in expanding these capabilities. However, unlike in Thailand and Myanmar, Papuan separatists do not possess significant UAV capabilities and thus existing military C-UAV capabilities are mainly oriented towards protecting VIPs and critical infrastructure. In recent years, Indonesia has also prioritised the development and acquisition of MALE UAVs for maritime surveillance around the Natuna Islands and other parts of the country's vast EEZ.

On the other hand, given the possible threat of small commercial off-the-shelf UAV attacks by insurgents in southern Thailand, Bangkok has prioritised the acquisition of C-UAV systems. Larger fixed-wing UAVs are prioritised for monitoring insurgent forces and border regions. Thailand has been incredibly ambitious in its indigenous UAV-development programmes, receiving significant support from Chinese firms and allowing the Thai defence establishment to possibly overcome issues other countries have encountered.

UAVs provide states a practical means to address their respective operational challenges. They allowed the PA to better survey the difficult urban environment in which it found itself when Zamboanga City and Marawi were under siege. They have given Indonesia, the Philippines and Thailand tools to map and traverse the dense jungle environments that insurgents often operate in, allowing for persistent surveillance and situational awareness without the use of costlier platforms or excessive personnel. UAVs have also helped the Philippines and Indonesia to better monitor their vast waters.

In contrast, the development of C-UAV capabilities has been more limited. Some Southeast Asian countries began deploying C-UAV systems towards the late 2010s. This was likely initiated by the proliferation of commercial off-the-shelf UAVs used by civilian hobbyists or individual malign actors, rather than the explicit recognition of the strategic threat that such UAVs could pose when used in coordination. This is evident in how C-UAV systems were primarily deployed to protect high-visibility events attended by VIPs and critical infrastructure. Only a small number of selected military units have access to C-UAV systems, in contrast to their widespread distribution visible in Ukraine and the Middle East.

However, the pace of innovation is arguably far faster than armed forces – whether in Southeast Asia, Ukraine or the Middle East – can keep up with. Prioritising the adoption of specific innovations may come at the expense of other required platforms. Mass production and supply-chain challenges necessitate a certain degree of standardisation. Consequently, strategic context, production capacity and armed forces' posture must be considered stringently when selecting which capabilities to prioritise and develop.

Southeast Asian armed forces have only recently slowly began to enact transformative changes to their posture, doctrine, strategy and operational concepts. Given Southeast Asian armed forces' immediate operational concerns as well as their more limited resources, UAVs and C-UAVs have proliferated unevenly across the region. Where resources do not allow for the development of more conventional capabilities, it may be prudent for these countries to develop more innovative capabilities, taking inspiration from – but also adapting – lessons from other countries to suit their respective circumstances.

DZAKY NARADICHIANTAMA
Resarch Associate (Air) for Defence and Military Analysis, IISS

MORGAN MICHAELS
Research Fellow for Southeast Asian Security and Defence, IISS

NOTES

[1] Raissa Robles, 'Why Philippines' Marcos Jnr Is Openly Showing "Unwavering Support" for Ukraine', *South China Morning Post*, 23 November 2024, https://www.scmp.com/week-asia/politics/article/3287809/why-philippines-marcos-jnr-openly-showing-unwavering-support-ukraine; Royal Thai Air Force, 'Royal Thai Air Force White Paper 2024', 2024, p. 9, https://www.scribd.com/document/762991419/RTAF-White-Paper-2024; and Irene Sarwindaningrum, 'Posisi Indonesia dalam Pembahasan Perdamaian Rusia-Ukraina' [Indonesia's position in the Russia–Ukraine peace talks], *Kompas*, 18 June 2024, https://www.kompas.id/baca/internasional/2024/06/18/posisi-indonesia-dalam-pembahasan-perdamaian-rusia-ukraina.

[2] Joseph Franco, 'Marawi: Winning the War After the Battle', The International Centre for Counter-Terrorism, 29 November 2017, https://icct.nl/publication/marawi-winning-war-after-battle#:~:text=In%20Zamboanga%2C%20500%20disgruntled%20former,and%20165%20security%20forces%20killed; and 'Southern Philippines: Making Peace Stick in the Bangsamoro', International Crisis Group, 1 May 2023, https://www.crisisgroup.org/asia/south-east-asia/philippines/331-southern-philippines-making-peace-stick-bangsamoro.

[3] 'Calming the Long War in the Philippine Countryside', International Crisis Group, 19 April 2024, https://www.crisisgroup.org/asia/south-east-asia/philippines/338-calming-long-war-philippine-countryside.

4   Nurrisha Ismail, 'Locked in Unrest: Southern Thailand's Insurgency 20 Years On', *Diplomat*, 13 November 2024, https://thediplomat.com/2024/11/locked-in-unrest-southern-thailands-insurgency-20-years-on/; and Uday Bakhshi, 'TPNPB Rebels Adopt New Tactics in Indonesia's West Papua Province', Terrorism Monitor, The Jamestown Foundation, 17 November 2023, https://jamestown.org/program/tpnpb-rebels-adopt-new-tactics-in-indonesias-west-papua-province/.

5   Sam Beltran, 'Scarborough Shoal "Completely Surrounded" by Chinese Ships, Filipino Fishers Say', *South China Morning Post*, 30 September 2024, https://www.scmp.com/week-asia/politics/article/3280472/scarborough-shoal-completely-surrounded-chinese-ships-filipino-fishers-say; Department of National Defense, 'Statement of the SND on March 8, 2024', Republic of the Philippines, 8 March 2024, https://www.dnd.gov.ph/Release/2024-03-08/2106/Statement-of-the-SND-on-March-8,-2024/; Priam Nepomuceno, '"Comprehensive Archipelagic Defense" to Help PH Explore EEZ Resources', Philippine News Agency, 24 January 2024, https://www.pna.gov.ph/articles/1217527; and Tessa Wong and Joel Guinto, 'Sabina Shaol: The New Flashpoint Between China and the Philippines', BBC News, 27 August 2024, https://www.bbc.co.uk/news/articles/cp3d4rz922do.

6   See Nirmala Maulana Achmad and Icha Rastika, '2 Skadron Lanud Roesmin Nurjadin Disiapkan untuk Kandang Rafale' [2 Roesmin Nurjadin air force base squadrons prepared to operate Rafale], *Kompas*, 5 February 2024, https://nasional.kompas.com/read/2024/02/05/17443131/2-skadron-lanud-roesmin-nurjadin-disiapkan-untuk-kandang-rafale; and Aristyo Rizka Darmawan, 'Why the New Indonesia–US Maritime Training Centre Is Strategically Important', Fulcrum, 7 July 2021, https://fulcrum.sg/why-the-new-indonesia-us-maritime-training-centre-is-strategically-important/.

7   Elisabeth Gosselin-Malo, 'Are the Once-vaunted Bayraktar Drones Losing Their Shine in Ukraine?', DefenseNews, 31 October 2023, https://www.defensenews.com/global/europe/2023/10/31/are-the-once-vaunted-bayraktar-drones-losing-their-shine-in-ukraine/.

8   For example, field-artillery or brigade-assault UAV units, operating small and FPV UAVs capable of dropping explosives and conducting 'kamikaze' attacks, can be tasked with eliminating targets identified by individual units. See Military Land, '47th Mechanized Brigade', https://militaryland.net/ukraine/armed-forces/47th-mechanized-brigade/; and Mariano Zafra et al., 'How Drone Combat in Ukraine Is Changing Warfare', Reuters, 26 March 2024, https://www.reuters.com/graphics/UKRAINE-CRISIS/DRONES/dwpkeyjwkpm/.

9   'Ukraine's Drone Army Is Transforming War', *The Economist*, YouTube, 16 October 2024, https://www.youtube.com/watch?v=2CpKXr7K6Bc.

10 Giorgi Revishvili, 'Ukraine's Expanding Drone Fleet Is Flying Straight Through Putin's Red Lines', UkraineAlert, Atlantic Council, 21 September 2024, https://www.atlanticcouncil.org/blogs/ukrainealert/ukraines-expanding-drone-fleet-is-flying-straight-through-putins-red-lines/.

11 Adolfo Arranz et al., 'Inside the Tunnels of Gaza', Reuters, 31 December 2023, https://www.reuters.com/graphics/ISRAEL-PALESTINIANS/GAZA-TUNNELS/gkvldmzorvb/; 'Brinc Drones Take on the "Gaza Metro"', Intelligence Online, 10 January 2024, https://www.intelligenceonline.com/surveillance--interception/2024/01/10/brinc-drones-take-on-the--gaza-metro,110136382-art.

12 Marissa Newman, 'Israel's Scrambled GPS Signals Turn Life Upside Down', Bloomberg, 9 April 2024, https://www.bloomberg.com/news/newsletters/2024-04-09/israel-s-scrambled-gps-signals-turn-life-upside-down-in-tel-aviv; and 'GPS War: Israel's Battle to Keep Drones Flying and Enemies Baffled', France24, 23 February 2024, https://www.france24.com/en/live-news/20240223-gps-war-israel-s-battle-to-keep-drones-flying-and-enemies-baffled.

13 Ethan Walton, 'Here's the Counter-drone Platforms Now Deployed in Ukraine', C4ISRNET, 21 November 2023, https://www.c4isrnet.com/opinion/2023/11/21/heres-the-counter-drone-platforms-now-deployed-in-ukraine/.

14 See details of these UAV and C-UAV dynamics between Israel and its various opponents in War Monitor (@WarMonitors), tweet, 8 October 2023, https://x.com/WarMonitors/status/1710998401356071238; Michael Knights, Ameer al-Kaabi and Crispin Smith, 'Tripling of Iraqi Militia Claimed Attacks on Israel in October', The Washington Institute for Near

East Policy, 15 October 2024, https://www.washingtoninstitute.org/policy-analysis/tripling-iraqi-militia-claimed-attacks-israel-october; Seth J. Frantzman, 'After Surprise Tel Aviv Attack, Houthi Drone Arsenal Comes Under Spotlight – Analysis', *Jerusalem Post*, 20 July 2024, https://www.jpost.com/israel-news/defense-news/article-811108; and 'Silent, Deadly Shahed-101 Suicide Drone Used by Hezbollah', *i24NEWS*, 17 July 2024, https://www.i24news.tv/en/news/israel-at-war/artc-silent-deadly-shahed-101-suicide-drone-used-by-hezbollah.

[15] Frances Mangosing, 'PH Army Displays Drones to Public', INQUIRER.net, 19 December 2013, https://newsinfo.inquirer.net/549269/ph-army-displays-drones-to-public.

[16] See Joseph Franco, 'Preventing Other "Marawis" in the Southern Philippines', *Asia & the Pacific Policy Studies*, vol. 5, no. 2, 25 March 2018, https://onlinelibrary.wiley.com/doi/full/10.1002/app5.227; and Thomas Luna, 'DJI Drones Are Getting Shot Down in the Battle of Marawi', WeTalk UAV, 17 July 2017, https://web.archive.org/web/20170930090632/https://www.wetalkuav.com/dji-drones-used-surveillance-battle-marawi/.

[17] See James Lewis, 'The Battle of Marawi: Small Team Lessons Learned for the Close Fight', The Cove, 27 November 2018, https://cove.army.gov.au/article/battle-marawi-small-team-lessons-learned-close-fight; Luna, 'DJI Drones Are Getting Shot Down in the Battle of Marawi'; Raffy Tima, 'Marawi, the Drone War', *GMA News*, 11 November 2017, https://www.gmanetwork.com/news/topstories/specialreports/632793/marawi-the-drone-war/story/; and John Spencer, Jayson Geroux and Liam Collins, 'Urban Warfare Project Case Study Series: Case Study #8 – Marawi', Modern War Institute, 23 May 2024, https://mwi.westpoint.edu/urban-warfare-case-study-8-battle-of-marawi/.

[18] See Froilan Gallardo, 'Drones Prove to Be Game Changer in Fight Against Rebels in Misamis Oriental', Rappler, 26 January 2023, https://www.rappler.com/philippines/mindanao/drones-prove-game-changer-fight-against-rebels-misamis-oriental/; and Prashanth Parameswaran, 'Battle for Marawi Exposes Philippines' Military Intelligence Crisis', *Diplomat*, 16 August 2017, https://thediplomat.com/2017/08/battle-for-marawi-exposes-philippines-military-intelligence-crisis/.

[19] See Eyal Bogulavsky, 'Philippine Air Force Receives Full Delivery of Hermes 900, Hermes 450 UAVs: Report', IsraelDefense, 10 September 2020, https://www.israeldefense.co.il/en/node/45190; Priam Nepomuceno, 'PAF Probes Crash-landing of Hermes 900 Drone', Philippine News Agency, 29 May 2022, https://www.pna.gov.ph/articles/1175364; John Eric Mendoza, 'PAF Reports Crash of Israel-built Hermes 900 Drone', INQUIRER.net, 29 May 2022, https://newsinfo.inquirer.net/1603762/israel-built-hermes-900-drone-of-paf-crashed-in-cagayan-de-oro; and Gallardo, 'Drones Prove to Be Game Changer in Fight Against Rebels in Misamis Oriental'.

[20] 'Unmanned Aerial System (Level 3) (Part 2) Acquisition Project of the Philippine Air Force', Philippine Defense Resource, 31 March 2019, https://www.phdefresource.com/2019/03/unmanned-aerial-system-level-3-part-2.html.

[21] Francisco Tuyay, 'Navy Deploys Drone to Secure Malampaya', *Manila Times*, 21 October 2023, https://www.manilatimes.net/2023/10/21/news/national/navy-deploys-drone-to-secure-malampaya/1915603.

[22] *Ibid.*; US Embassy in the Philippines, 'U.S. Military Delivers Advanced Unmanned Aerial System to Philippine Navy', US Indo-Pacific Command, 30 November 2020, https://www.pacom.mil/Media/News/News-Article-View/Article/2429756/us-military-delivers-advanced-unmanned-aerial-system-to-philippine-navy/; and US Embassy in the Philippines, 'U.S. Military Turns Over New Scan Eagle Unmanned Aerial System to Secretary of National Defense and Philippine Air Force', US Indo-Pacific Command, 14 March 2018, https://www.pacom.mil/Media/News/News-Article-View/Article/1466283/us-military-turns-over-new-scan-eagle-unmanned-aerial-system-to-secretary-of-na/.

[23] Philippine Navy, 'The Drone Potential', https://onsssm.navy.mil.ph/news/The%20Drone%20Potential.pdf.

[24] Philippine Defense Forces Forum, 'Members of reserve units of the Philippine Army, Air Force', Philippine Star, Facebook, 13 September 2024, https://www.facebook.com/philippinesdefense/posts/confirmation-that-the-afp-has-its-own-fpv-drone-program/916308477193191/.

[25] These are designated the Aerial Military Ordinance Carrier and the Military Ordinance Inflictor. PH Defense Community, 'First

Philippine-made armed drone / attack drone made and developed by the Air Force Research and Development Center called the Aerial Military Ordinance Carrier (A.M.O.C)', Facebook, 6 July 2024, https://www.facebook.com/PhDefenseCommunity/photos/first-philippine-made-armed-drone-attack-drone-made-and-developed-by-the-air-for/877850961043680/.

26 Illia Kabachynskyi, 'How Ukraine Transformed a Naval Drone into a Powerful Combat Platform, Now Destroying Russian Ships, Helicopters, and Ground Equipment', United 24, 9 January 2025, https://united24media.com/war-in-ukraine/how-ukraine-transformed-a-naval-drone-into-a-powerful-combat-platform-now-destroying-russian-ships-helicopters-and-ground-equipment-4968.

27 'Ukrainian Naval Drones Hit Seized Gas Platforms', Ukrainian Military Center, 7 December 2024, https://mil.in.ua/en/news/ukrainian-naval-drones-hit-seized-gas-platforms/.

28 Thomas Newdick, 'Ukraine Claims Its Drone Boats Are Now Launching Kamikaze FPV Drones At Russian Shore Targets', The Warzone, 7 January 2025, https://www.twz.com/news-features/ukraine-claims-its-drone-boats-are-now-launching-kamikaze-fpv-drones-at-russian-shore-targets.

29 Philippine Coast Guard, 'LOOK: The Philippine Coast Guard (PCG) has taken a significant step in its modernization journey with the Unmanned Aerial System (UAS) Doctrine Cascading Forum', Facebook, 28 November 2024, https://www.facebook.com/story.php/?story_fbid=1040551871443498&id=100064660843959&_rdr.

30 MaxDefense Philippines, 'In addition to the Philippine Navy's plans to procure and develop Unmanned Surface Vehicles (USVs), here's another new development', Facebook, 8 October 2024, https://www.facebook.com/MaxDefense/posts/in-addition-to-the-philippine-navys-plans-to-procure-and-develop-unmanned-surfac/954749166691939/.

31 Philippine Navy, 'Envisioning Asymmetric Defense Unmanned Aerial Vehicle and Prospects for the Philippine Navy', https://onsssm.navy.mil.ph/news/ENVISIONING_ASYMMETRIC_DEFENSE_UNMANNED_AERIAL_VEHICLE_AND_PROSPECTS_FOR_THE_PHILIPPINE_NAVY.pdf.

32 Aaron Matthew Lariosa, 'U.S. Marine MQ-9A Reapers Now Deployed to the Philippines', USNI News, 3 June 2024, https://news.usni.org/2024/06/03/u-s-marine-mq-9a-reapers-now-deployed-to-the-philippines.

33 Ibid.

34 Martin Sadongdong, 'PH Navy Considering US Drone for Resupply Mission in Ayungin Shoal', Manila Bulletin, 16 July 2024, https://mb.com.ph/2024/7/16/ph-navy-considering-us-drone-for-resupply-mission-in-ayungin-shoal.

35 MaxDefense Philippines, 'The Philippine Marine Corps appears to be developing a VTOL UAV that can be used to deliver supplies and carry loads', Facebook, 9 November 2024, https://www.facebook.com/MaxDefense/posts/the-philippine-marine-corps-appears-to-be-developing-a-vtol-uav-that-can-be-used/978674077632781/.

36 Spencer, Geroux and Collins, 'Urban Warfare Project Case Study Series: Case Study #8 – Marawi'.

37 Ibid.

38 Tima, 'Marawi, The Drone War'.

39 See Emmanuel Tupas, 'Police to Shoot Down Drones During SONA', Philippines Star, 20 July 2024, https://www.philstar.com/headlines/2024/07/20/2371596/police-shoot-down-drones-during-sona; and DroneShield, 'DroneShield Successfully Protects 30th SEA Games', 9 December 2019, https://www.droneshield.com/media/press-releases/droneshield-successfully-protects-30th-sea-games-bpnns-y8eb7.

40 See Department of National Defense, 'DND Bids and Awards Committee 2', 2020, https://www.dnd.gov.ph/Procurements?t=DND%20Bids%20and%20Awards%20Committee%202; and 'Unmanned Aerial Systems (Level) 3 Lot 2 – Electronic Warfare System for Hermes 900 Acquisition Project of the Philippine Air Force', Philippine Defense Resource, 22 January 2023, https://www.phdefresource.com/2023/03/unmanned-aerial-systems-level-3-lot-2.html.

41 RJ Rosalado, 'PH Navy Eyes Anti-drone Technology', ABS-CBN, 3 October 2019, https://www.abs-cbn.com/news/10/03/19/ph-navy-eyes-anti-drone-technology.

42 Riski Ardandhitya Dwi Krisnanda and Michael Augustinus, 'Foto: Uji Coba Anti-Drone Kemhan RI dan PT Pertamina' [Photos: Ministry of Defense and Pertamina Trial Anti-Drone Systems], Kumparan News, 30 September

2019, https://kumparan.com/kumparannews/foto-uji-coba-anti-drone-kemhan-ri-dan-pt-pertamina-1rxjbfg0Aqi/full.

43 Ministry of Defense, 'Kebijakan Penyelenggaraan Pertahanan Negara Tahun 2020-2024' [Policy for the implementation of national defence 2020–2024], 2021, https://www.kemhan.go.id/wp-content/uploads/2022/08/LAMP-JAKGARA-HANNEG-17-Mei-Final.pdf.

44 See TNI Angkatan Darat, 'Doktrin TNI AD Kartika Eka Paksi' [Indonesian Army doctrine *kartika eka paksi*], 2020, https://manajemenhan.akmil.ac.id/wp-content/uploads/2021/12/Doktrin-TNI-AD-KEP.pdf; and 'Pesawat Nirawak Awasi Wilayah Perbatasan' [Uninhabited aerial vehicles monitor border regions], Kompas, 15 April 2015, https://nasional.kompas.com/read/2015/04/15/15000041/Pesawat.Nirawak.Awasi.Wilayah.Perbatasan.

45 See Malvyandie Haryadi, 'Prajurit TNI AD di Perbatasan Berlatih Operasikan Drone' [Indonesian Army soldiers in the border regions train to operate drones], TribunNews, 16 August 2016, https://www.tribunnews.com/tribunners/2016/08/16/prajurit-tni-ad-di-perbatasan-berlatih-operasikan-drone.

46 Other intended small-UAV programmes include the American Teledyne FLIR's *Black Hornet*s, procured in 2021. These were deployed in a 2022 TNI-AD combined armed-forces exercise. See 'Digunakan Yonhub TNI AD, Inilah Kecanggihan Drone Intai "Nano" Black Hornet PD-100'[Used by the TNI AD Yonhub, this is the sophistication of the "Nano" Black Hornet PD-100 reconnaissance drone], IndoMiliter, 12 September 2022, https://www.indomiliter.com/digunakan-yonhub-tni-ad-inilah-kecanggihan-drone-intai-nano-black-hornet-pd-100/.

47 Tom Allard and Stanley Widianto, 'Insight: Mystery Surrounds How Munitions Imported for Indonesia's Civilian Spies Were Used in Attacks on Villages', Reuters, 3 June 2022, https://www.reuters.com/world/asia-pacific/mystery-surrounds-how-munitions-imported-indonesias-civilian-spies-were-used-2022-06-03/; Osprey514 (@gara_nam), tweet, 26 October 2023, https://x.com/gara_nam/status/1717339339963920430; and Defenceview (@defenceview_id), 'Indonesian Paramilitary Police force (BRIMOB) using Chinese-made Blowfish A3 UAV', tweet, 29 May 2022, https://x.com/defenceview_id/status/1530910535708856320.

48 'Defense Minister Introduces Indonesian Drone Rajawali 720', Tempo, 27 July 2017, https://en.tempo.co/read/895026/defense-minister-introduces-indonesian-drone-rajawali-720.

49 'Local Manufacturers Supply Drones for Indonesian Defense', Bhinneka Dwi Persada, 16 September 2019, https://bhinnekadwipersada.co.id/blog/2019/09/16/162/; and Gilang Perdana, 'Elang Laut 25: Telah Resmi Dioperasikan Direktorat Topografi TNI AD' [Elang Laut 25: officially operated by the Indonesian Army topography directorate], IndoMiliter, 13 August 2017, https://web.archive.org/web/20170816045351/https://www.indomiliter.com/elang-laut-25-telah-resmi-dioperasikan-direktorat-topografi-tni-ad/.

50 See TNI-AD, 'Danpussenarmed Kodiklatad Kunjungi Industri Drone Kesisteman Armed Berbasis Field Artillery Observer (FAO)' [Commander of the field artillery weapons centre of the Indonesian Army education training and doctrine command visits drone industry manufacturing field artillery observer (FAO) platforms], 11 July 2022, https://tniad.mil.id/danpussenarmed-kodiklatad-kunjungi-in-dustri-drone-kesisteman-armed-berbasis/; and Penpussenarmed, 'Danpussenarmed tinjau uji coba perangkat UAV baru dari Benua Eropa yaitu ALPHA A900 Unmaned Systems di Lapangan Terbang Lanud Husein Sastranegara Bandung' [The commander of the armament and aviation center reviews the trial of a new UAV device from Europe, the ALPHA A900 unmanned systems, at Husein Sastranegara airbase in Bandung], https://pussenarmed-tniad.mil.id/?fbclid=PAZXhobgNhZWoCM-TEAAabAnIie18_AxsxPgXPuMCJ50JZ_099cIWn-pGv0eg6CveTnRE1O7EEmtQU_aem_IorTrQl8AQndTHrZ2gmhKA.

51 Indonesian Aerospace, 'UAV (Unmanned Aerial Vehicle) WULUNG', https://indonesian-aerospace.com/techdev/index/set/uav.

52 See Rangga Baswara Sawiyya, 'Mengamati PUNA Wulung di PTDI, Sang Elang Pengawas dari Langit' [Observing the Wulung at Dirgantara Indonesia, the eagle keeping watch from the skies], Airspace Review, 24 July 2018, https://www.airspace-review.com/2018/07/24/mengamati-puna-wulung-di-ptdi-sang-elang-pengawas-dari-langit/; and Feby Dwi Sutianto, 'Wulung, Drone Pertama di ASEAN yang Berstandar Industri Pesawat'

[Wulung, the first ASEAN drone of aerospace industry standard], *DetikNews*, 25 January 2016, https://finance.detik.com/industri/d-3126063/wulung-drone-pertama-di-asean-yang-berstandar-industri-pesawat?f9911023=.

53 The flight-control systems were procured from Spanish company Magline Composites y Sistemas while the engine was procured from Austrian company Rotax Aircraft Engines. See Gordon Arthur, 'Indonesia Suspends Black Eagle MALE UAV Programme', Shephard Media, 19 September 2022, https://www.shephardmedia.com/news/air-warfare/indonesia-suspends-black-eagle-male-uav-programme/; and 'Jelang Uji Terbang Perdana, Prototipe Drone Elang Hitam Disebut Gunakan Mesin Piston Rotax 915 IS' [Awaiting its maiden flight, the Elang Hitam drone prototype is said to have the Rotax 915 IS piston engine], IndoMiliter, 6 January 2022, https://web.archive.org/web/20220106140626/https://www.indomiliter.com/jelang-uji-terbang-perdana-prototipe-drone-elang-hitam-disebut-gunakan-mesin-piston-rotax-915-is/.

54 Images of the *Elang Hitam* with a new livery were released in 2023 and in 2024. A DI executive unexpectedly stated in an interview that the programme was, in fact, ongoing. See Ridzwan Rahmat, 'Indonesia Pulls Plug on Strike-capable Military UAV Programme', Janes, 15 September 2022, https://www.janes.com/osint-insights/defence-news/air/indonesia-pulls-plug-on-strike-capable-military-uav-programme; JATOSINT (@Jatosint), tweet, 13 August 2023, https://x.com/Jatosint/status/1690544826025132032; and Ahmad Fikri, 'PTDI Bicara Kabar Drone Tempur Elang Hitam, Sembut Pengembangan Masih Berlanjut' [Dirgantara Indonesia speaks on the state of the Elang Hitam armed drone, says development is ongoing], Tempo, 28 September 2024, https://tekno.tempo.co/read/1922032/ptdi-bicara-kabar-drone-tempur-elang-hitam-sebut-pengembangan-masih-berlanjut.

55 See Ahmad Faisal Adnan, Sandi Arizona and Risbeyhi, 'Debut pesawat nirawak di HUT TNI' [Debut of uninhabited aerial vehicle at Indonesian Armed Forces anniversary], Antara News, 5 October 2019, https://pon.antaranews.com/video/1098300/debut-pesawat-nirawak-di-hut-tni; Raden Sadjad, 'Skadron Udara 52 Lanud Raden Sadjad Natuna Raih Terbaik I di Askomlek Kasau Awards 2024' [52 Squadron Raden Sadjad air base in Natuna achieves number one rank in 2024 Chief of the Air Force's Assistant for Communications and Electronics awards], TNI Angkatan Udara, 9 October 2024, https://tni-au.mil.id/berita/detail/skadron-udara-52-lanud-raden-sadjad-natuna-raih-terbaik-i-di-askomlek-kasau-awards-2024; 'Aerostar TUAV: Drone Intai Andalan Skadron Udara 51 TNI AU' [Aerostar TUAV: the reliable reconnaissance drone of the Indonesian Air Force's 51 Squadron], IndoMiliter, 5 October 2015, https://web.archive.org/web/20160319065435/https://www.indomiliter.com/aerostar-tuav-drone-intai-andalan-skadron-udara-51-tni-au/; and TNI Angkatan Udara, 'Skadron Udara 51 (Lanud Supadio)' [51 Squadron (Supadio air base)], https://imap.tni-au.mil.id/tentang-kami/profilsatuan-detail/skadron-udara-51-lanud-supadio/1452.

56 See Indonesian Aerospace, 'ANKA Drone Kelas Dunia Pengubah Permainan Segera Dibuat Bersama PTDI, Utusan Presiden Indonesia Sudah Temui CEO TUSAS di Turki' [Game-changing world-class ANKA drone will soon be co-manufactured by Dirgantara Indonesia, Indonesian president's representative has met with the CEO of TUSAS in Turkey], 19 August 2024, https://indonesian-aerospace.com/news/detail/1311_anka+drone+kelas+dunia+pengubah+permainan+segera+dibuat+bersama+ptdi%2C+utusan+presiden+indonesia+sudah+temui+ceo+tusas+di+turki; and Indonesian Aerospace, 'Inovasi & Penguasaan Teknologi PTDI: Dorong Kemandirian Melalui Produk Pesawat N219 dan UAV MALE di InaRI Expo 2024' [Innovation and technological mastery by Dirgantara Indonesia: driving self-reliance through the production of the N219 and MALE UAV at InaRI Expo 2024], 8 August 2024, https://indonesian-aerospace.com/siaranpers/detail/284_inovasi+%26amp%3B+penguasaan+teknologi+ptdi%3A+dorong+kemandirian+melalui+produk+pesawat+n219+dan+uav+male+di+inari+expo+2024.

57 Chen Chuanren, 'Indonesian Air Force to Acquire Bayraktar TB2 UAS', Aviation Week, 2 August 2024, https://aviationweek.com/defense/aircraft-propulsion/indonesian-air-force-acquire-bayraktar-tb2-uas.

58 See Garett Reim, 'Jordan Military Tries to Sell Off "Knock-off" Chinese Drones', FlightGlobal,

4 June 2019, https://www.flightglobal.com/helicopters/jordan-military-tries-to-sell-off-knock-off-chinese-drones/132985.article; Joseph Tervithick, 'Only One of Iraq's Chinese CH-4B Drones Is Mission Capable as Other Buyers Give Up on Them', The War Zone, 13 August 2019, https://www.twz.com/29324/only-one-of-iraqs-chinese-ch-4b-drones-is-mission-capable-as-other-buyers-give-up-on-them; and International Crisis Group, 'Turkiye's Growing Drone Exports', 20 December 2023, https://www.crisisgroup.org/europe-central-asia/western-europemediterranean/turkiye/turkiyes-growing-drone-exports.

59 Republikorp, 'Indonesia and Turkey Strengthen Stategic Partnership in the UAV Industry through Joint Venture Agreement', 13 February 2025, https://republikorp.com/blog-details/Indonesia-and-Turkey-Strengthen-Strategic-Partnership-in-the-UAV-Industry-through-Joint-Venture-Agreement/72.

60 Joe Saballa, 'Indonesia Eyes Squadron of Domestically-Built Drones', The Defense Post, 30 October 2023, https://thedefensepost.com/2023/10/30/indonesia-squadron-domestic-drones/.

61 TNI-AU, 'Kasau Aktifkan Kembali Skadron Pendidikan 103 Wingdik 100 Terbang' [Chief of the Air Force reactivates 103 Training Squadron 100 Flying Training Wing], 22 August 2023, https://portal.tni-au.mil.id/berita/detail/kasau-aktifkan-kembali-skadron-pendidikan-103-wingdik-100.

62 Swarmly Aero, 'Indonesia Acquires Poseidon-type UAVs – VIDEO', *DEFENCE ReDEFINED*, 10 August 2023, https://defenceredefined.com.cy/swarmly-aero-indonesia-acquires-poseidon-type-uavs-video/.

63 'Pesawat UAV Lapan Ikut Latgab TNI' [National Institute of Aeronautics and Space UAV participates in Indonesian Armed Forces Joint Tri-Service Exercise], Majalah Sains Indonesia, 30 May 2013, https://web.archive.org/web/20140423120956/https://www.sainsindonesia.co.id/index.php?option=com_content&view=article&id=601:pesawat-uav-lapan-ikut-latgab-tni&catid=40&Itemid=145.

64 TNI-AL, 'Drone ScanEagle TNI AL KRI Abdul Halim Perdanakusuma-355 Sukses Jelajah Angkasa di Perairan Selat Madura' [Indonesian Navy ScanEagle drone from KRI Abdul Halim Perdanakusuma-355 successfully traverses the skies over the waters of the Madura Strait], 17 June 2022, https://koarmada2.tnial.mil.id/2022/06/17/drone-scaneagle-tni-al-kri-abdul-halim-perdanakusuma-355-sukses-jelajah-angkasa-di-perairan-selat-madura/; and ECA Group, 'STERNA Flies for Indonesian Navy – the first Magnetic Measurement Mission by UAV', 25 September 2018, https://www.ecagroup.com/en/business/sternatm-flies-for-indonesian-navy-the-first-magnetic-measurement-mission-by-uav#:~:text=The%20UAV%20based%20solution%20STERNA,Indonesian%20Navy%20in%20July%202018.&text=STERNATM%20is%20based%20on,a%20magnetometer%20and%20its%20digitizer.

65 Swarmly Aero, 'Indonesia Acquires Poseidon-type UAVs – VIDEO'; and Kemhan RI (@Kemhan_RI), tweet, 24 June 2024, https://x.com/Kemhan_RI/status/1805027655160561689?ref_src=twsrc%5Etfw%7Ctwcamp%5Etweetembed%7Ctwterm%5E1805027655160561689%7Ctwgr%5E2e06d9eacec5ef08b0d79f-35507c8fe431d8334f%7Ctwcon%5Es1_c10&ref_url=https%3A%2F%2Fwww.turkiyetoday.com%2Fturkiye%2Findonesia-to-enhance-naval-capabilities-with-uav-acquisitions-from-turkiye-23986%.

66 See TNI Angkatan Darat, 'Kadislitbangad Serahkan Sertifikat Hasil Uji Coba Sertifikasi Prototipe Sistem Senjata Anti Drone Berbasis Gelombang Elektromaknetik hasil Litbanghan Pussenarhanud' [Head of the Indonesian Army research and development department hands over test certificate certifying prototype of electromagnetic spectrum-based anti-drone system developed by the Anti-Air Artillery Weapons Centre's Research and Development Agency], 20 June 2024, https://dislitbang-tniad.mil.id/read/kadislitbangadserahkansertifikathasilujicoba-sertifikasiprototipesistemsenjataantidroneber-basisgelombangelektromaknetikhasillitbang-hanpussenarhanud; and TNI Angkatan Darat, 'Alsus Anti Drone mobil dan perlengkapanya' [Mobile anti-drone systems and their equipment], 17 April 2024, https://lpse.tniad.org/eproc4/lelang/27376638/pengumumanlelang.

67 Sekretariat Presiden, 'LIVE: Upacara Peringatan HUT ke-79 Tentara Nasional Indonesia Tahun 2024, Jakarta, 5 Oktober 2024' [LIVE: 79th Indonesian Armed Forces Anniversary

Ceremony 2024, Jakarta, 5 October 2024], 5 October 2024, https://www.youtube.com/live/ldzqInOnyC0?feature=shared&t=6944.

68 See PT Pindad, 'HUT Ke-79 RI, PINDAD Perkenalkan Senjata Anti Drone SPS-1 & Maung MV3 Mobile Jammer di IKN' [79th Indonesian Armed Forces Anniversary Ceremony, PINDAD unveils anti-drone system SPS-1 and Maung MV3 Mobile Jammer in Nusantara Capital City], 2024, https://pindad.com/hut-ke79-ri-pindad-perkenalkan-senjata-anti-drone-sps1-maung-mv3-mobile-jammer-di-ikn.

69 See TNI Angkatan Udara, 'Mulai Rudal Chiron Hingga Senjata Anti Drone Milik Kopasgat Siaga Amankan KTT ASEAN Labuan Bajo' [From the Chiron missile to the anti-drone systems of Kopasgat on standby to secure the ASEAN summit in Labuan Bajo], 9 May 2023, https://kopasgat.tni-au.mil.id/id/berita/mulai-rudal-chiron-hingga-senjata-anti-drone-milik-kopasgat-siaga-amankan-ktt-asean-labuan-bajo#; and Audrey Santoso, 'Begini Cara Kerja Alat Antidrone Milik TNI AU' [This is how the anti-drone system operated by the Indonesian Air Force functions], DetikNews, 12 April 2021, https://news.detik.com/berita/d-5529707/begini-cara-kerja-alat-antidrone-milik-tni-au.

70 Ekapol Nakphum, 'Norinco จีนเป็นผู้ชนะโครงการจัดหาอากาศยานไร้คนขับขึ้นลงทางดิ่ง VTOL UAV ของกองทัพบกไทย' [China's Norinco wins Royal Thai Army's VTOL UAV procurement project], AAG_th บันทึกประจำวัน, 13 September 2023, https://aagth1.blogspot.com/2023/09/norinco-vtol-uav.html.

71 Sompong Nondhasa, 'Thai Army Is Flying Hermes 450', Shephard Media, 20 June 2018, https://www.shephardmedia.com/news/uv-online/thai-army-flying-hermes-450/.

72 DTI, 'นวัตกรรมใหม่ UAV รุ่น D-eyes 01 ซึ่งเป็นระบบอากาศยานไร้คนขับขนาดเล็ก (Multi-Rotor) แบบขึ้นลงทางดิ่ง มีคุณสมบัติอย่างไรบ้าง ไปรับชมได้จากคลิป' [What are the features of the new innovation of the D-eyes 01 UAV, a small vertical take-off and landing multi-rotor unmanned aerial vehicle system? Let's watch the clip], Facebook, 10 July 2021, https://www.facebook.com/dti.utc/videos/%E0%B8%99%E0%B8%A7%E0%B8%B1%E0%B8%95%E0%B8%81%E0%B8%A3%E0%B8%A3%E0%B8%A1%E0%B9%83%E0%B8%AB%E0%B8%A1%E0%B9%88-uav-%E0%B8%A3%E0%B8%B8%E0%B9%88%E0%B8%99-d-eyes-01-%E0%B8%8B%E0%B8%B6%E0%B9%88%E0%B8%87%E0%B9%80%E0%B8%9B%E0%B9%87%E0%B8%99%E0%B8%A3%E0%B8%B0%E0%B8%9A%E0%B8%9A%E0%B8%AD%E0%B8%B2%E0%B8%81%E0%B8%B2%E0%B8%A8%E0%B8%A2%E0%B8%B2%E0%B8%99%E0%B9%84%E0%B8%A3%E0%B9%89%E0%B8%84%E0%B8%99%E0%B8%82%E0%B8%B1%E0%B8%9A%E0%B8%82%E0%B8%99%E0%B8%B2%E0%B8%94%E0%B9%80%E0%B8%A5%E0%B9%87%E0%B8%81-multi-rotor/183014590459969/.

73 Defence Technology Institute, 'Mini UAV: อากาศยานไร้คนขับแบบส่งขึ้นด้วยมือ (Hand-Launched)' [Mini UAV: hand-launched unmanned aerial vehicle], *Defence Technology Journal*, vol. 9, no. 33, January–March 2019, p. 18, https://www.dti.or.th/pdfimage/index.php?cid=97&cno=5928#page-22-23.

74 From the series of tests conducted, issues highlighted include the limited operational time, poor communication links and the lack of autonomous tracking and identification systems. Defence Technology Institute, 'การสาธิตการใช้งานอากาศยานไร้นักบิน Siam UAV ในพื้นที่จังหวัดชายแดนภาคใต้' [Demonstration of the Use of SIAM UAV Unmanned Aerial Vehicles in the Southern Border Provinces], *Defence Technology Journal*, vol. 7, no. 26, April–June 2017, p. 28, https://www.dti.or.th/pdfimage/index.php?cid=97&cno=5456#page-29-29; and Defence Technology Institute, 'Mini UAV: อากาศยานไร้คนขับแบบส่งขึ้นด้วยมือ(Hand-Launched)' [Mini UAV: Hand-Launched Unmanned Aerial Vehicle].

75 See Defence Technology Institute, 'ครั้งแรกของไทย!!! การทดสอบทิ้งระเบิดแบบนำวิถีด้วยแสงเลเซอร์ ไม่ติดหัวรบ (War Head) จากอากาศยานไร้คนขับ DP16 UAV' [The first time in Thailand!!! Testing of a laser-guided bomb without a warhead from a DP16 UAV], Facebook, 13 July 2023, https://www.facebook.com/dtithailand/posts/pfbid036v-9JNbFxKnjNVPpBPqE68UKh8DJarAHeSHeq-vdmXqXC59TwDWDtr183yTKrtyjKJl?__cft__[0]=AZWuPkgcDSORambbnkn9A_hhPzcw8_gyRAioQbjbJmTq3t_oFS84qdFU12cVm_Bf_16e1C2WF8NGmkokAsv3tSiz7HVLIW6KY8HM0QF0X0Ql-coNfuVL-w3XhkNDx2WC9akSCTmbXRRcDyl2JF1aBGTPheS47fsCRPCzkuOxgLnIeg&__tn__=%2CO%2CP-R; Ekapol Nakphum, 'Defense & Security 2023: ATIL ไทยเปิดตัวอากาศยานรบไร้คนขับ DP18A UCAV' [Defense & Security 2023: ATIL Thailand unveils DP18A

75 UCAV unmanned combat aircraft], AAG_th บันทึกประจำวัน, 15 November 2023, https://aagth1.blogspot.com/2023/11/defense-security-2023-atil-dp18a-ucav.html; Royal Thai Army, 'การวิจัยและพัฒนาระบบอากาศยานไร้คนขับขนาดกลางของกองทัพบก' [Research and development of the army's medium-sized UAV system], *Royal Thai Army News*, 3 November 2021, https://drive.google.com/file/d/1Wrow8DOXgpGK1b-M3JUvd-iBOU3CWXAAy/view?pli=1; and Amit Kalra, 'Defense & Security 2022: ATIL Unveils DP-20/A MALE UAS', Janes, 30 August 2022, https://www.janes.com/osint-insights/defence-news/air/defense-security-2022-atil-unveils-dp-20a-male-uas.

76 'DS2022: ATIL เปิดตัวอากาศยานไร้คนขับ 3 รุ่น พร้อมสนับสนุนกองทัพไทยและให้ไทยเป็นฐานการผลิตเพื่อส่งออก' [DS2022: ATIL unveils three UAV models to support the Royal Thai Army and make Thailand a production base for export], Thai Armed Force, 29 August 2022, https://thaiarmedforce.com/2022/08/29/ds2022-atil-unveil-the-uav-portfolio/.

77 JATOSINT, (@Jatosint), tweet, 22 September 2024, https://x.com/Jatosint/status/1837818471301730390.

78 See Ekapol Nakphum, 'DTI ไทยมีความคืบหน้าการวิจัยพัฒนาอากาศยานไร้คนขับ DP20 UAS สำหรับกองทัพบกไทย' [DTI Thailand has made progress in research and development of the DP20 UAS unmanned aerial vehicle for the Royal Thai Army], AAG_th บันทึกประจำวัน, 3 March 2023, https://aagth1.blogspot.com/2023/03/dti-dp20-uas.html; and Royal Thai Army, 'การวิจัยและพัฒนาระบบอากาศยานไร้คนขับขนาดกลางของกองทัพบก' [Research and development of the army's medium-sized UAV system].

79 Thanarith Satrusayang, 'Thailand Seeks to Develop Military Production Facilities with China', Reuters, 21 December 2016, https://www.reuters.com/article/world/thailand-seeks-to-develop-military-production-facilities-with-china-idUSKBN14A0G3/.

80 Paul Chambers, 'Thai–US Relations: Amity with Some Caveats', Fulcrum, 28 May 2024, https://fulcrum.sg/thai-us-relations-amity-with-some-caveats/.

81 Kosuke Inoue, 'Thai Investment Applications Hit 5-year High, Led by Chinese Money', Nikkei Asia, 9 February 2024, https://asia.nikkei.com/Economy/Thai-investment-applications-hit-5-year-high-led-by-Chinese-money.

82 Chambers, 'Thai–US Relations: Amity with Some Caveats'.

83 Zaheena Rasheed, 'How China Became the World's Leading Exporter of Combat Drones', Al-Jazeera, 24 January 2023, https://www.aljazeera.com/news/2023/1/24/how-china-became-the-worlds-leading-exporter-of-combat-drones; and Agnes Helou, 'Chinese and Saudi Firms Create Joint Venture to Make Military Drones in the Kingdom', DefenseNews, 9 March 2022, https://www.defensenews.com/unmanned/2022/03/09/chinese-and-saudi-firms-create-joint-venture-to-make-military-drones-in-the-kingdom/.

84 See Ekapol Nakphum, 'กองทัพอากาศไทยทำพิธีบรรจุประจำการอากาศยานไร้คนขับตรวจการณ์ บร.ต.๓ Dominator XP UAV' [Royal Thai Air Force holds ceremony to induct Dominator XP UAV surveillance drone], AAG_th บันทึกประจำวัน, 3 September 2023, https://aagth1.blogspot.com/2023/09/dominator-xp-uav.html; 'Thailand Uses Air Force UAVs in Fight Against Illegal Migration, Covid-19', Global Business Press, 12 January 2021, https://gbp.com.sg/stories/thailand-uses-air-force-uavs-in-fight-against-illegal-migration-covid-19/; 'Air Force Drones Used for Border Covid Surveillance', *Bangkok Post*, 7 December 2020, https://www.bangkokpost.com/thailand/general/2031423/air-force-drones-used-for-border-covid-surveillance; and Ekapol Nakphum, 'กองทัพอากาศไทยเปิดตัวอากาศยานไร้คนขับพลีชีพตระกูล KB UAV ที่พัฒนาในประเทศ' [Royal Thai Air Force unveils domestically developed KB UAV family of suicide drones], AAG_th บันทึกประจำวัน, 2 December 2024, https://aagth1.blogspot.com/2024/12/kb-uav.html.

85 *Ibid.*

86 Jon Grevatt, 'Thailand Considers SkyStriker for D11A Rocket Launcher', Janes, 14 November 2023, https://www.janes.com/osint-insights/defence-news/industry/thailand-considers-skystriker-for-d11a-rocket-launcher; and Ekapol Nakphum, 'กองทัพอากาศไทยเปิดตัวอากาศยานไร้คนขับพลีชีพตระกูล KB UAV ที่พัฒนาในประเทศ' [Royal Thai Air Force unveils domestically developed KB UAV family of suicide drones]; see also Royal Thai Air Force, 'Royal Thai Air Force White Paper 2024'.

87 See Royal Thai Air Force, 'Royal Thai Air Force White Paper 2024'.

88 Wassana Nanuam, 'Thai Army Says it Needs Armed Drones, Attack Helicopters', 28 July

2024, https://www.bangkokpost.com/thailand/general/2837246/army-says-it-needs-armed-drones-attack-helicopters.

89 Defence Technology Institute, '"โดรน" กำกับดูแลเพื่อความปลอดภัย และความมั่นคงของชาติ' ["Drones" are regulated for national safety and security], *Defence Technology Journal*, vol. 9, no. 33, January–March 2019, p. 103, https://www.dti.or.th/pdfimage/index.php?cid=97&cno=5928#page-22-23; and Defence Technology Institute, 'อนาคตของเทคโนโลยีการต่อต้านอากาศยานไร้คนขับ' [The future of counter-UAV technology], *Defence Technology Journal*, vol. 12, no. 43, 2022, p. 46, https://www.dti.or.th/pdfimage/index.php?cid=97&cno=6615#page-64-65.

90 'First Operational Use of IMI Systems' Red Sky 2 Drone Defender System in Thailand', IsraelDefense, 28 January 2018, https://web.archive.org/web/20180201172628/https://www.israeldefense.co.il/en/node/32820.

91 See Royal Thai Air Force, 'Royal Thai Air Force White Paper 2020', 2020, https://mzv.gov.cz/file/3896487/Thailand_RTAF_White_Paper_2020_ENG_complete_text.pdf; Defence Technology Institute, 'อนาคตของเทคโนโลยีการต่อต้านอากาศยานไร้คนขับ' [The future of counter-UAV technology], *Defence Technology Journal*, vol. 10, no. 40, October–December 2020, p. 64, https://www.dti.or.th/pdfimage/index.php?cid=97&cno=6479#page-70-71; and Mike Ball, 'AVT Supplies Counter-UAS Systems to Thai Defense Agency', Unmanned Systems Technology, 5 June 2020, https://www.unmannedsystemstechnology.com/2020/06/avt-supplies-counter-uas-systems-to-thai-defense-agency/.

92 Government Public Relations Department, 'Thai PM Emphasizes Enhanced Measures Against Drug Trafficking', 19 July 2024, https://thailand.prd.go.th/en/content/category/detail/id/52/iid/308101.

93 See Royal Thai Air Force, 'Royal Thai Air Force White Paper 2024'.

94 Wassana Nanuam, 'Flying of Drones Banned in Far South', *Bangkok Post*, 19 June 2024, https://www.bangkokpost.com/thailand/general/2813954/flying-of-drones-banned-in-far-south#:~:text=Security%20authorities%20have%20banned%20the,military%20outposts%20in%20the%20region.

95 Aekarach Sattaburuth, 'MFP Slams Military Budget, Questions Anti-drone Funding', *Bangkok Post*, 22 June 2024, https://www.bangkokpost.com/thailand/politics/2815430/mfp-slams-military-budget-questions-anti-drone-funding.

96 Analayo Korsakul, 'Achieving Superiority: Modernising the Royal Thai Air Force', Key.Aero, 18 January 2022, https://www.key.aero/article/achieving-superiority-modernising-royal-thai-air-force.

97 Defence Technology Institute, 'โครงการวิจัยและพัฒนาเทคโนโลยีอากาศยานไร้คนขับ สทป' [Unmanned Aircraft Technology Research and Development Project], *Defence Technology Journal*, vol. 9, no. 33, January–March 2019, p. 12, https://www.dti.or.th/pdfimage/index.php?cid=97&cno=5928#page-14-15; see also Defence Technology Institute, 'การจัดหาและพัฒนาอากาศยานไร้นักบินในเอเชีย: ภูมิภาคแห่งโอกาสและการแข่งขัน' [Acquisition and Development of Unmanned Aircraft in Asia: A Region of Opportunity and Competition], 2020, http://dspace.dti.or.th/jspui/bitstream/123456789/1293/1/%E0%B8%81%E0%B8%B2%E0%B8%A3%E0%B8%88%E0%B8%B1%E0%B8%94%E0%B8%AB%E0%B8%B2%E0%B9%81%E0%B8%A5%E0%B8%B0%E0%B8%9E%E0%B8%B1%E0%B8%92%E0%B8%99%E0%B8%B2%E0%B8%AD%E0%B8%B2%E0%B8%81%E0%B8%B2%E0%B8%A8%E0%B8%A2%E0%B8%B2%E0%B8%99%E0%B9%84%E0%B8%A3%E0%B9%89%E0%B8%99%E0%B8%B1%E0%B8%81%E0%B8%9A%E0%B8%B4%E0%B8%99%E0%B9%83%E0%B8%99%E0%B9%80%E0%B8%AD%E0%B9%80%E0%B8%8A%E0%B8%B5%E0%B8%A2.pdf; and Ekapol Nakphum, 'กองทัพเรือไทยสาธิตอากาศยานไร้คนขับขึ้นลงทางดิ่ง MARCUS-B และเปิดตัว RQ-21 Blackjack UAV สหรัฐฯ' [Royal Thai Navy demonstrates MARCUS-B VTOL UAV and unveils US RQ-21 Blackjack UAV], AAG_th บันทึกประจำวัน, 7 March 2022, https://aagth1.blogspot.com/2022/03/marcus-b-rq-21-blackjack-uav.html.

98 SDT Composites, 'MARCUS-B Technical Specification', Facebook, 3 October 2022, https://www.facebook.com/siamdrytech/videos/marcus-

b-technical-specificationtypefixed-wing-with-vertical-take-off-and-landin/498242155495794/; and Combat Zones, 'ภาพและวิดีโอของอากาศยานไร้นักบิน MARCUS-B (2024) สาธิตการขึ้นลงบน รล.จักรีนฤเบศร เพื่อให้ผู้บัญชาการทหารเรือและผู้บังคับบัญชาระดับสูงรับชม เมื่อวันที่ 19 กันยายน 2567' [Images and video of the MARCUS-B (2024) UAV demonstrating take-off and landing on HTMS Chakri Naruebet for the Royal Thai Navy Commander and senior commanders to view on 19 September 2024], Facebook, https://www.facebook.com/permalink.php/?story_fbid=908091841354085&id=100064598325695.

99 Sompong Nondhasa, 'Thai Navy Deploys Orbiter 3Bs Over Water', Shephard Media, 15 March 2021, https://www.shephardmedia.com/news/uv-online/premium-thai-navy-deploys-orbiter-3bs-over-water/; and Schiebel, 'Schiebel Wins Prestigious Follow-on Contract with Royal Thai Navy', 15 April 2022, https://schiebel.net/wp-content/uploads/2022/05/2022-04-15-SCHIEBEL-WINS-PRESTIGIOUS-FOLLOW-ON-CONTRACT-WITH-ROYAL-THAI-NAVY.pdf.

100 US Embassy and Consulate in Thailand, 'U.S. Navy Formally Hands Over Unmanned Aircraft System to the Royal Thai Navy', 24 May 2022, https://th.usembassy.gov/u-s-navy-formally-hands-over-unmanned-aircraft-system-to-the-royal-thai-navy/.

101 Elbit Systems, 'Elbit Systems Awarded a $120 Millon Contract to Supply Hermes 900 UAS to the Royal Thai Navy', 28 September 2022, https://elbitsystems.com/pr-new/elbit-systems-awarded-a-120-million-contract-to-supply-hermes-900-uas-to-the-royal-thai-navy/.

102 Rebecca Tan, Caleb Quinley and Yan Naing, 'Myanmar Military Unleashes Drones to Counter Rebel Advances', *Washington Post*, 12 October 2024, https://www.washingtonpost.com/world/2024/10/12/myanmar-civil-war-drones/.

INDEX

A

ACES 28, *29*, 31

Airbus 23, 24, *25*

Armed Forces of the Philippines (AFP) 113, 117, 117, *126*, *132*, *136*

Assad, Bashar al- 55

Association of Southeast Asian Nations (ASEAN) 48, *50*, 51, 114
   China Free Trade Area (ACFTA) 51
   ICT Masterplan 2020 98
   Regional Comprehensive Economic Partnership (RCEP) 51

AUKUS agreement 77, 87, 91–92

Australia *19*, *53*, 56–57, 77, 92, *93*

B

Bangladesh *93*, 94

Biden administration 51, 52, 57

Boustead Heavy Industries Corporation (BHIC) 27

Boustead Naval Shipyard (BNS) 27

BrahMos missile programme 18, 31–35, *32–33*, *34*

C

Canada *19*, *53*, 92

China *19*, 50, 51, *51*, 52, 56, 64, 65, 67, 68, 71, 74, *93*, *109*, *133*
   economic engagement with Japan 65–66
   military modernisation 35, 58
   perception of Japan's defence strategy 64–65
   relations with India 56, 57
   relations with Japan 64–66, *65*, 70
   relations with North Korea 67, 69–70, 71, *71*, 72
   relations with Russia 35, 67–69, *67*, *68*, 70, 74, *74–75*
   stance on Russia–Ukraine war 71
   strategic competition with United States 57–59, 64, 65, 66
   submarine capabilities 87–89, *93*
   uninhabited aerial vehicles (UAVs) 128, 132, 133, *133*, 134, 135, 139, 141, 142

China Coast Guard (CCG) 66, 68, 69

China Electronics Technology Group Corporation (CETC) 28, *29*, 31

China–North Korea–Russia triangular relationship 10, 70–73
   competing interests 70, 71, 72, 78
   strategic challenge for Japan 64, 66, 70, 72, 73, 74, 75, 76
   strategic challenge for United States 70

China–Russia military exercises 66, *67*, 68–69, *68*, 74, *74–75*

Comprehensive and Progressive Agreement for Trans-Pacific Partnership (CPTPP) 52

counter-UAV (C-UAV) systems 126, 128, 130, 131, 134, 136, 137, 140, 141, 142, 143

critical underwater infrastructure (CUI) *see* submarine cables

currency-exchange rates 50–51

cyber forces, civilian 110, 114–115

cyber forces, military 10–11, 108, *109*, 110, *111*, 116, 118–119
   capability maturity 110, *111*, 116–118
   Indonesia *109*, 112, 113, 115, *117*
   institutional maturity 110, *111*, 114–116, 118
   Philippines *109*, 113, 117, *117*, 118
   recruitment 116–117
   Singapore *109*, 112, *117*
   strategic maturity 110, 111–113, *111*, 118
   Thailand *109*, 113, *117*
   United States 117, *116–117*, 118

cyber intelligence-gathering 108, 119

cyber operations 108
   against Indonesia 112, 116
   against Singapore 112

cyber threats 108, 119

D

defence-industrial partnerships 8–9, *17*, 25, 26, 29
   China *29*
   drivers of 16, 18, 27–28
   India *29*
   Indonesia 23–24, *25*, 26, *26*, *29*, 30
   offset programmes 17, *17*, 22, 38
   potential benefits and challenges 17, 18–21, 38, 39
   Saudi Arabia 28, *29*, 30–31
   Singapore *29*
   South Korea *29*
   United Arab Emirates (UAE) 27–28, *29*, 30–31

Defense Acquisition Program Administration (DAPA) 28, *29*, 30

Dirgantara Indonesia (DI) *18*, 23–24, *132*

DRB-HICOM Defence Technologies (DEFTECH) 24, 26

E

EDGE 27–28, *29*, 30

F

FNSS 24, *25*, 26, *26*

France 19–20, *19*, 36, 37, *93*

Free and Open Indo-Pacific 56

G

Germany 19–20, *19*, 36, 37

Global Combat Aircraft Programme (GCAP) 18, 35–37, *36*, *37*, 38

grey-zone operations, maritime 9, 95–96, 98, 99

H

Hamas 55

Hanwha Corporation 28, *29*

Hindustan Aeronautics (HAL) 27, *29*, 30

Hizbullah 55

Houthis (Ansarullah) 55

I

India *19*, 28, 34, 51, 56–57, 93, *109*, 113, *116*, 117
  BrahMos missile programme 18, 31–32, 34–35, *34*
  relations with China 56, 57
  relations with Russia 31, 35, 57
  relations with the United States 57
  submarine capabilities 93, 94
Indian Navy 93, 94, *97*
Indonesia *19*, 22, *25*, 26, 28, 48, *93*, *109*, 116, *132*, 136
  cyber operations against 109, 112, 116
  defence-industrial partnerships 22, 23–24, *25*, 26, *26*, 30
  defence spending 21, *22*
  military cyber forces *109*, 112, 113, 115, *116*, 117, *117*
  non-state armed groups (NSAGs) 126, 142
  offset programme 22
  relations with the United States 59
  submarine capabilities *93*, 94
  uninhabited aerial vehicles (UAVs) 126, 127, 130, 131, *132*, 133, *136*, 142
Indonesian National Armed Forces (TNI) *10*, 23, 24, 26, *93*, *97*, 112, 115, *115*, *117*, *132*, 136
Indo-Pacific Economic Framework (IPEF) 52, 66
insurgencies *see* non-state armed groups (NSAGs)
International Golden Group (IGG) *29*, 30
Iran *19*, 54, 55–56, *55*
Israel *19*, 127, 128, 134
Israel–Hamas war 55–56, 126, 127, 128, 129, 133
Italy 19–20, *19* 35, 36, 37, *37*, 38

J

Japan *19*, 35, 36, 37, 51, 52, *53*, 56–57, 64, 65, 76, *93*, 109, 116
  cyber programme 74, *109*, *116–117*
  defence spending 21
  defence strategy *10*, 31, *37*, 64, 65, 76–77
  economic engagement with China 65–66
  Global Combat Aircraft Programme (GCAP) 35, 37
  relations with Australia 77
  relations with China 64–66, *65*, 70
  relations with Europe 77
  relations with Philippines 76–77
  relations with South Korea 76
  relations with Taiwan 65
  relations with United States 49, 58, 65, 75–76, *76*
  space programme 74
  submarine capabilities 92, *93*
Japan Maritime Self-Defense Force (JMSDF) 92, *93*, 94, *97*
Japan–Philippines–United States relationship 76, *77*
Japan Self-Defense Forces *37*, 66, 73, 74, 75, *76*, 115, *116–117*
Japan–South Korea–United States relationship 76

M

Malabar exercise 57
Malaysia *19*, 21, *21*, 22, *22*, 24, *25*, 26–27, 48, *93*, *109*, 117
Marcos Jr, Ferdinand 59
Middle East, uninhabited aerial vehicles (UAVs) 126, 127, 128, 143
mine warfare 97
Modi, Narendra 57
Myanmar *93*, 139, 140, 141
  non-state armed groups (NSAGs) 137, 138, 139, *139*, 140, *140*, 141, 142
  submarine capabilities *93*, 94
  uninhabited aerial vehicles (UAVs) 126, 127, 138, 139, 140, 141, *141*

N

NATO 49, 53, 54, *54*
Naval Group *21*, *25*, 26, 27
non-state armed groups (NSAGs) 126, 128, 129, 130, 131, 138, 139, 140, 141, 142
  uninhabited aerial vehicles (UAVs) 127, 141
NORINCO 27, *28*, *29*, 30
North Korea 67, 71, 93, 97
  relations with China 69–70
  relations with Russia 66, 71–72
  relations with South Korea 70
  submarine capabilities 93, 94
nuclear deterrence, maritime 86, 88, 90, 94

P

Pakistan *19*, *93*, 94
People's Liberation Army Navy (PLAN) *33*, 87–89, *93*, 94, 96, 97, *98*
People's Liberation Army (PLA) *33*, 68

Philippines 22, *33*, *109*, 116–117, *132*, *136*
   BrahMos missile purchase 18, 33, 34, 35
   defence spending 21, 22
   military cyber forces 109, 113, 116, 117, 118
   non-state armed groups (NSAGs) 126, 142
   relations with Japan 76–77
   relations with the United States 33, 59
   Self-Reliant Defense Posture (SRDP) Revitalization Act 22
   submarine programme 94
   uninhabited aerial vehicles (UAVs) 126, 127, 128, 129, 130, 132, 136, 142

Pindad 26, 29

Prabowo Subianto 59, 115

Putin, Vladimir 32, 53, 54, 57, *67*

Q

Quadrilateral Security Dialogue (Quad) 48, 56–57, 114

R

Royal Australian Navy (RAN) 87, 91, *93*, 94, 97

Royal Malaysian Navy (RMN) *21*, 26–27

Royal Thai Armed Forces *97*, 113, 116, *132*, 135, 136

Rubio, Marco 56, *57*

Russia *19*, 20, 35, 67, 68, 71, 74, 88, *93*
   BrahMos missile programme 31–32, 34–35
   relations with China 35, 67–69, 70, 74
   relations with India 31, 57
   relations with North Korea 66, 67, 71, 72
   submarine capabilities 93, 94

Russian Armed Forces 68, 93

Russian Coast Guard 69

Russia–Ukraine war 11, 35, 48, 53, 70, 72, 128
   2025 peace negotiations 48, 53–54
   China's stance on 54, 71
   rare-earth minerals deal 48, 54
   Russian war aims 54
   uninhabited aerial vehicles (UAVs) 126, 127, 128, 129, 133, 136, 143

S

Saudi Arabia 17, 27, 28, *29*, 30–31

Saudi Arabian Military Industries (SAMI) 28, *29*, 30

Scopa Defense 30

seabed warfare *see* grey-zone operations, maritime

security policy, drivers of 6–8, 9, 10, 11

Senkaku/Diaoyu islands 65, 66, 67

Shigeru, Ishiba 57

Singapore *19*, *22*, 23, 25, *93*, 94, 109, 116
   cyber operations against 112
   'Cyber Specialist' scheme 117
   defence spending 21, 22, 23
   military cyber forces *109*, 112, 116
   submarine capabilities *93*, 94

Singapore Armed Forces (SAF) *93*, 94, 97, 112, 117

South China Sea 126, 127, 129, 131, 142

South Korea *19*, 28, 50, 51, *53*, 70, *93*, *96*, *97*, *116*, 118
   relations with Japan 76
   relations with the United States 49, 58, 118
   submarine capabilities 92, 93

ST Engineering 28, *29*, 30

submarine cables 9, 97–99, *100*

submarines *21*, 86, 87, 89, 91–94, 102
   anti-submarine warfare (ASW) forces 94, 95
   KSS-III 92
   Los Angeles-class 89, 90
   Ohio-class 90
   Taigei-class 92
   Type-094 88
   Type-095 88
   Virginia-class 89, 90, 91

subsea intelligence 86, 89, 95, 96

Syria 55

T

Taiwan *19*, 51, *53*, 58, 69, 74, *93*, 99, *109*
   relations with Japan 65
   submarine capabilities 92, 93

Tawazun Council 30

Thailand *22*, *25*, *109*, 116, *132*, 136
   cyber-defence academy 117
   defence spending 21, 22
   military cyber forces *109*, 113, 117
   non-state armed groups (NSAGs) 126, 134, 136, 137, 142
   submarine programme 94
   uninhabited aerial vehicles (UAVs) 126, 127, *132*, 134, 136

Tonga 99

Trump administration 11, 48, 49
  foreign policy 49, 50
  Gaza plan 56
  ideological background 48–49
  international security guarantees 49, 54, 58
  obstacles to legislative programme 49
  tariffs 50–51, 57, 58

Turkish defence exports *see* FNSS

Turkiye *19*, *53*, 133

U

uninhabited aerial vehicles (UAVs) 9–10, 126, 127, 128, 129, 132, 133, 141
  Aerostar 133, 137
  Albatross-M5 141
  Anka-S 133
  Bayraktar Akinci 134
  Bayraktar TB2 127, 133
  Blowfish A3 131
  border-security operations 131, 134, 136, 142
  CH-3A 141
  CH-4 *133*
  CH-4B 132
  D-Eyes 02 *132*
  D-Eyes 03 *132*
  Dominator XP 137
  DP 16 *132*
  DP 18A *132*
  DP 20 *132*
  DP 20-A *132*
  Elang Hitam 131, *132*
  Elang Laut 25 131, *132*
  Falcon-V FUVEC *132*
  first-person view (FPV) 127, 129, 136, 137
  fixed-wing 127, 128, 129, 134, 142
  Hermes 450 128, 134
  Hermes 900 128, 137
  intelligence, surveillance and reconnaissance (ISR) 127, 128, 134, 135, 137, 138, 141
  KB-5E *132*
  KB-10G *132*
  Knight Falcon 128, *132*
  LSU-02 *132*
  MARCUS *132*
  MARCUS-B/C *132*
  maritime operations 128, 129, 130, 131, 133, 134, 137, 142
  Maung MV3 134
  medium altitude long endurance (MALE) 133, 142
  MQ-9A *Reaper* 130
  one-way attack (OWA) 127, 128, 130, 134, 136, 137
  Orbiter 3B 137
  Orlan-10E 141
  Poseidon H6 133
  PTTA *132*
  Rajata *132*
  Rajawali 131
  Raptor 128, *132*
  Red Sky 2 137
  RQ-21A *Blackjack* 137
  S-100 *Camcopter* 133, 137
  ScanEagle 2 129, 133
  Searcher 134
  Siam UAV *132*
  Skylark 128
  SPS-1 134
  STERNA IT180 133
  THOR 128
  TRV-150C 130
  U1 *132*, 137
  vertical take-off and landing (VTOL) 128, 130, 133
  Wulung 131, *132*

uninhabited maritime vehicles (UMVs) 95

uninhabited underwater vehicles (UUVs) 86, 95, 96–97, 98

United Arab Emirates (UAE) 17, *19*, 27–28, *29*, 30–31

United Kingdom *19*, 35, 36, 37, 38, *53*, 93

United States *19*, 20, *33*, 36, 37, 51, *53*, 76, *93*, *116*, 118
  defence strategy 75–76
  Indo-Pacific Strategy (2017) 57
  military cyber forces 116, 117, 118
  relations with India 57
  relations with Japan 65, 75–76
  relations with Philippines 33
  relations with South Korea 76, 118
  strategic competition with China 57–59, 64
  submarine capabilities 89–91, 93

United States-led regional order, opposition to 64, 65, 67

United States Navy *33*, *73*, 88, 89–91, *93*, 94, 97

US–China trade war (2018) 51

USSR *see* Soviet Union

V

Vance, J.D. 53

Vietnam 21, *22*, 23, *25*, *93*, *109*

W

Waltz, Mike 52

X

Xi Jinping 58, *58*, *65*, 66, 67, 69

Z

Zelenskyy, Volodymyr *11*, *52*, 53

Asia-Pacific Regional Security Assessment 2025 (Print ISBN 978-1-041-10439-1, Online ISBN 978-1-003-65504-6) is published annually for a total of one issue per year by Taylor & Francis Group, 4 Park Square, Milton Park, Abingdon, Oxon, OX14 4RN, UK.

Send address changes to Taylor & Francis Customer Services, Informa UK Ltd., Sheepen Place, Colchester, Essex CO3 3LP, UK.

Subscription records are maintained at Taylor & Francis Group, 4 Park Square, Milton Park, Abingdon, OX14 4RN, UK.

Subscription information: For more information and subscription rates, please see tandfonline.com/pricing/journal/TSTD. Taylor & Francis journals are available in a range of different packages, designed to suit every library's needs and budget. This journal is available for institutional subscriptions with online only or print & online options. This journal may also be available as part of our libraries, subject collections, or archives. For more information on our sales packages, please visit: librarianresources.taylorandfrancis.com.

For support with any institutional subscription, please visit help.tandfonline.com or email our dedicated team at subscriptions@tandf.co.uk.

Subscriptions purchased at the personal rate are strictly for personal, non-commercial use only. The reselling of personal subscriptions is prohibited. Personal subscriptions must be purchased with a personal check, credit card, or BAC/wire transfer. Proof of personal status may be requested.

Back issues: Please visit https://taylorandfrancis.com/journals/customer-services/ for more information on how to purchase back issues.

Ordering information: To subscribe to the Journal, please contact: T&F Customer Services, Informa UK Ltd, Sheepen Place, Colchester, Essex, CO3 3LP, United Kingdom. Tel: +44 (0) 20 8052 2030; email: subscriptions@tandf.co.uk.

Taylor & Francis journals are priced in USD, GBP and EUR (as well as AUD and CAD for a limited number of journals). All subscriptions are charged depending on where the end customer is based. If you are unsure which rate applies to you, please contact Customer Services. All subscriptions are payable in advance and all rates include postage. We are required to charge applicable VAT/GST on all print and online combination subscriptions, in addition to our online only journals. Subscriptions are entered on an annual basis, i.e., January to December. Payment may be made by sterling cheque, dollar cheque, euro cheque, international money order, National Giro or credit card (Amex, Visa and Mastercard).

Permissions: See help.tandfonline.com/Librarian/s/article/Permissions.

Disclaimer: The International Institute for Strategic Studies and our publisher Taylor & Francis make every effort to ensure the accuracy of all the information (the 'Content') contained in our publications. However, The International Institute for Strategic Studies and our publisher Taylor & Francis, our agents (including the editor, any member of the editorial team or editorial board, and any guest editors), and our licensors make no representations or warranties whatsoever as to the accuracy, completeness, or suitability for any purpose of the Content. Any opinions and views expressed in this publication are the opinions and views of the authors, and are not the views of or endorsed by The International Institute for Strategic Studies and our publisher Taylor & Francis. The accuracy of the Content should not be relied upon and should be independently verified with primary sources of information. The International Institute for Strategic Studies and our publisher Taylor & Francis shall not be liable for any losses, actions, claims, proceedings, demands, costs, expenses, damages, and other liabilities whatsoever or howsoever caused arising directly or indirectly in connection with, in relation to, or arising out of the use of the Content. Terms & Conditions of access and use can be found at http://www.tandfonline.com/page/terms-and-conditions.

All Taylor & Francis Group journals are printed on paper from renewable sources by accredited partners.